# TRANSGRESSIVE UTOPIANISM

# Ralahine Utopian Studies

**Series editors:**
Raffaella Baccolini (University of Bologna at Forlì)
Antonis Balasopoulos (University of Cyprus)
Joachim Fischer (University of Limerick)
Michael J. Griffin (University of Limerick)
Naomi Jacobs (University of Maine)
Michael G. Kelly (University of Limerick)
Tom Moylan (University of Limerick)
Phillip E. Wegner (University of Florida)

Volume 22

PETER LANG
Oxford • Bern • Berlin • Bruxelles • New York • Wien

Edited by Raffaella Baccolini and
Lyman Tower Sargent

# TRANSGRESSIVE
# UTOPIANISM

ESSAYS IN HONOR OF LUCY SARGISSON

PETER LANG

Oxford • Bern • Berlin • Bruxelles • New York • Wien

Bibliographic information published by Die Deutsche Nationalbibliothek
Die Deutsche Nationalbibliothek lists this publication in the Deutsche
Nationalbibliografie; detailed bibliographic data is available on the
Internet at http://dnb.d-nb.de.

A catalogue record for this book is available from the British Library.

Library of Congress Cataloging-in-Publication Data

Names: Baccolini, Raffaella, editor. | Sargent, Lyman Tower, 1940- editor.
  | Sargisson, Lucy, 1964- honouree.
Title: Transgressive utopianism : essays in honor of Lucy Sargisson /
  [edited by] Raffaella Baccolini, Lyman Tower Sargent.
Description: Oxford ; New York : Peter Lang, [2021] | Series: Ralahine
  utopian studies, 1661-5875 ; vol 22 | Includes bibliographical
  references and index.
Identifiers: LCCN 2020033684 (print) | LCCN 2020033685 (ebook) | ISBN
  9781789978803 (paperback) | ISBN 9781789978810 (ebook) | ISBN
  9781789978827 (epub) | ISBN 9781789978834 (mobi)
Subjects: LCSH: Utopias. | Utopias in literature.
Classification: LCC HX806 .T76 2021  (print) | LCC HX806  (ebook) | DDC
  355/.02–dc23
LC record available at https://lccn.loc.gov/2020033684
LC ebook record available at https://lccn.loc.gov/2020033685

Cover image: Bench in Central Park, NY (Photo: Raffaella Baccolini, August 2016).

ISSN 1661-5875
ISBN 978-1-78997-880-3 (print) • isbn 978-1-78997-881-0 (ePDF)
ISBN 978-1-78997-882-7 (eBook) • isbn 978-1-78997-883-4 (mobi)

© Peter Lang Group AG 2021

Published by Peter Lang Ltd, International Academic Publishers,
52 St Giles, Oxford, OX1 3LU, United Kingdom
oxford@peterlang.com, www.peterlang.com

This publication has been peer reviewed.

# Contents

RUTH LEVITAS

# Foreword

Lucy: warmth sheds light
on different paths towards
a better future.

It is a pleasure to be invited to write a foreword to this Festschrift for Lucy Sargisson which has been compiled to mark her early retirement from her post as Professor of Utopian Studies at the University of Nottingham. She is, I think, the first, and possibly the only, person to be awarded that title, and it is well-earned. Although her academic career has been shorter than some, she leaves an impressive legacy and has played a key part in the development of utopianism as a field of study. One part of this, the most public and most obvious, is a body of writing. Her first book, *Contemporary Feminist Utopianism* (1996), was based on her PhD thesis and quickly became a key source for feminist work in the field. This early work combined political and social theory, and the explication of complex texts, with literary analysis. That vision was broadened further over the years, bringing sometimes marginal themes of feminism, ecology, interpersonal relations as well as questions of property relations into the mainstream of utopian analysis. Her last major book, *Fool's Gold?* (2012), widened her scope further. In looking at expressions of utopianism in the twenty-first century she encompassed architecture, robotics, computer gaming, sexual identity, and intentional communities as well as utopian and dystopian literature.

Most utopian scholars have focused on one of three areas of utopian expression – political thought, literature, or intentional communities. The increasing influence of Ernst Bloch on anglophone utopists following the translation of his book *The Principle of Hope* in 1986 encouraged a broader field of study. Sargisson's work, however, was distinctive because she did not simply extend the application of a theoretical lens to new arenas. Rather, the intervening years between these two major interventions had included extensive direct fieldwork on intentional communities both in Britain and in New Zealand. This fed into two other books, *Utopian Bodies and the Politics of Transgression* (1999) and *Living in Utopia* (2004, with Lyman Tower Sargent), as well as a series of articles. Her interviewing and observational skills, as well as her analytical approach, proved to be formidable. That kind of fieldwork, especially when undertaken alone, is extraordinarily demanding. It requires from the outset a capacity to secure trust and establish rapport very quickly – both to get access to communities at all and to find out anything worthwhile. It necessitates the ability to sustain that rapport and convey acceptance of the other, while at the same time maintaining a critical distance. Such fieldwork skills (or soft skills, or social skills) can only be taught to a limited degree because they depend fundamentally on the underlying disposition of the person. Sargisson's habitual mode of inhabiting what Martin Buber termed the "I-Thou" relationship underpinned the sheer quality of her fieldwork, as well as infusing all her work with a kind of dispassionate critical sympathy.

There are two other aspects of Sargisson's legacy which also rest in no small part on these personal qualities: her role in the institutional development of utopian studies and her work as a teacher. The Utopian Studies Society was set up in 1988 at a conference in New Lanark. Although there already was a Society for Utopian Studies with an annual conference based in North America, transatlantic travel was very expensive and travel funds especially in UK universities almost non-existent. There was a need for an additional network for European scholars. That initiative was swiftly followed by the fall of the Berlin Wall and a political and intellectual climate quite antipathetic to utopianism. For some years, the society limped along with occasional newsletters and one-day meetings, and without widespread access to email. By the late 1990s, communications were easier, and the approaching millennium produced a more sympathetic political and intellectual climate. The Society was relaunched in 1999 with a residential conference at the University of East Anglia in Norwich. At this critical juncture, Sargisson organized two conferences at Nottingham, in

2000 and 2002, and Utopian Studies Society conferences have been held annually throughout Europe ever since. She also, in this period, served for some years as Secretary of the Society. The depth of her contribution went beyond the sheer hard work of undertaking these tasks at a key point in the development of the Society. The manner in which she did so was marked by wisdom, warmth, openness, and inclusivity, and did much to establish the culture of Utopian Studies conferences in the following years. And, like others who were part of building the field over the last twenty-five years and more, I came to value those qualities in her as a friend as well as a colleague.

The legacy of all academics lies in large part in their influence on students – an influence that is often slow-burning and not obvious even to the students themselves. But teachers with Sargisson's combination of humane warmth and clear perception are rare, and she has always had an evident concern both for their personal welfare and their intellectual development. And I have had the privilege of meeting and hearing some of her graduate students give their own conference presentations and make their own ongoing contributions to utopian studies. That several of her students have chosen to honor Sargisson by contributing to these chapters speaks for itself.

RAFFAELLA BACCOLINI AND LYMAN TOWER SARGENT

# Introduction

In 2014, when Lucy Sargisson was promoted to Professor in the School of Politics and International Relations, at the University of Nottingham, she became the first and, so far, only Professor of Utopian Studies. This choice symbolized the centrality of utopianism to her life, thought, and educational practice. In three books, each in their own way ground-breaking, a fourth book co-authored by one of us, and in important art-icles, her work falls into four primary areas, political theory, feminism, environmentalism, and intentional communities, with much of her work intersecting two, three, or even all four. And in all her work, she brings the lens of utopianism to bear on the subject and, in doing so, illuminates both utopianism and the subject at hand.

## Political Theory

Sargisson was trained as a political theorist, earning her doctorate at Keele University in 1996, and a concern with issues of both political theory and politics can be found throughout her work. In her first book, *Contemporary Feminist Utopianism*, she introduces the idea of a "trans-gressive utopianism" within political theory, and this concept perme-ates the rest of her work. In her last book she characterizes transgressive utopianism as stepping "over boundaries that order and separate," thus "renders the boundaries meaningless and/or emphasizes their porosity," and by "crossing boundaries and showing them to be porous [it] creates a space where previously there was none. In this space, new and different ways of relating to the world can be practised" (Sargisson, *Fool's* 21).

But she is well aware that utopianism is not accepted by many polit-ical theorists; and in one of her earliest articles, "Contemporary Feminist

Utopianism," she said that "Utopias and utopianism add creativity to political thought and activity – as well as being critical of the status quo, they express desires for something different and better. They explore alternatives" (Sargisson, "Contemporary" 272). Also, in an abstract for an article from 2013, referring to the study of politics, she wrote,

> This article offers a controversial argument, namely that a utopian approach adds something valuable to the study of politics. I develop this position by showing how utopian fiction and experimentation can contribute to a recent debate in environmental politics: the call for a democracy that "includes nature." I argue that a utopian approach has limits – for example it cannot provide all the answers or offer blueprints for a perfect world – but that it can create spaces in which to imagine a different and better political relationship. Simply put, a utopian approach can shift the parameters of what is conceivable. (Sargisson, "A Democracy" 124)

In this statement she makes a point that she and other scholars regularly make, that utopianism should not be equated with perfection. Sargisson stresses this most strongly in her essay, "Religious Fundamentalism and Utopianism in the 21st Century," in which she notes that religious fundamentalism's "attachment to perfection [...] permits a malign form of utopianism to propel religious actors into a politics of 'divinely sanctioned' violence" (269).

And in her "Why Utopias Matter," she says that utopias "always gesture toward a better way of life, and a better way of being. As such, utopias provide points of inspiration, aspiration and debate. They permit us to imagine how our world can be better and this is the first step towards changing" (53). And the last phrase makes another point about her work, and her educational practice; she was always concerned with betterment, with changing the conditions.

## Feminism

Probably her best-known work is her first, *Contemporary Feminist Utopianism*, and her concept of "transgressive utopianism" is widely cited by others, including many of the authors of the chapters in this volume. Her other works concerning feminism applied her understanding of utopianism to issues within feminism. In "Why Feminism Needs Utopianism," she said that "Reading feminist science fiction and utopian novels can [...] help us pick our way through the mess academic feminists have gotten into, and to think more clearly about some difficult issues that face women today." And she went on to say, "Utopias also help us think seriously about difficult things. Often, they contain complex theoretical models and debates, that most of us might not ordinarily think about on a day to day basis," concluding that "utopias are inspirational. [... T]hey inspire and facilitate a change in the way we think about the world" (53, 54, 55). Also, in "What's Wrong with Ecofeminism?" she argues that "what's really wrong with ecofeminism is that it denies its full potential. Ecofeminism is utopian in all senses of that term and it fails to acknowledge and exploit this" (52).

## Intentional Communities

Sargisson's second book, *Utopian Bodies and the Politics of Transgression*, focused on environmentalism, in large part through research on and in intentional communities in the UK. And from the time that book was published to her last two articles, "Lived Utopianism: Everyday Life and Intentional Communities" and "Swimming Against the Tide: Collaborative Housing and Practices of Sharing," she regularly published articles on intentional communities, always based on empirical research.[1] And these last two articles reflect two of Sargisson's interests within intentional communities, how people within such communities organize their lives and housing.

Her third, co-authored, book, *Living in Utopia: New Zealand's Intentional Communities*, combined archival research by Sargent with Sargisson's research based on visiting intentional communities throughout New Zealand and interviewing the people living in them. In addition to the

---

1    "Lived Utopianism" was co-authored with Lyman Tower Sargent, but while the idea was his, most of the research and writing was hers.

material present in the book, Sargisson used her research to illuminate specific questions regarding intentional communities in "Justice Inside Utopia? The Case of Intentional Communities in New Zealand" and "Surviving Conflict: New Zealand's Intentional Communities." In the first, she explores the use of consensual decision-making in egalitarian communities, and in the second she analyzes how the unusually long-lived intentional communities in New Zealand have managed internal conflicts that have torn other communities apart.

Her "Strange Places: Estrangement, Utopianism, and Intentional Communities" is an important study that scholars of both utopias and intentional communities need to incorporate in their work. In it she applies estrangement as used by Darko Suvin in defining utopia to intentional communities. She argues that estrangement "performs similar functions inside intentional communities as it does with utopia by facilitating critical distance and group coherence." At the same time, she notes, "estranged relationships are complex and difficult" and pose serious problems for the people living in community (393). "Friends Have All Things in Common: Utopian Property Relations" might be thought of as a case study of the issues raised by estrangement. In it she compares two communities in New Zealand, Centrepoint and Riverside, with the former an example of everything that can go wrong in a community and the latter an example of a community founded in 1941 that is still going strong.

In 2012 Sargisson published an important article on cohousing, "Second Wave Cohousing: A Modern Utopia?" Within the cohousing movement, there is a deep divide between those who identify cohousing with intentional communities and utopianism and those who vehemently deny any connection. Sargisson explores the divide among those living in cohousing communities in North America and concludes that it accurately reflects the reality in that the people are "comfortable with the values of mainstream culture but seeking a better way of life for their members" (51). And in her last article she argued that collaborative housing or cohousing "offers a viable alternative housing model based on ideas about sharing" ("Swimming" 145).

## Environmentalism

As noted above, *Utopian Bodies and the Politics of Transgression* is concerned with environmentalism through the study of intentional communities, but particularly Findhorn in Scotland, that are trying to create a sustainable lifestyle. In "Sustainability and the Intentional Community: Green Intentional Communities," Sargisson gives an overview of specifically green communities discussing how they have been both overrated and underrated politically and in academic debates. She argues, though, for their importance as examples of what people can do who are willing to experiment with their own lives. Here and in "Imperfect Utopias: Green Intentional Communities," she makes the point that all such communities fall short of their own goals. In "Politicising the Quotidian," she focuses on such failures by examining six UK communities that are doing just that while also trying to act as exemplars of a more sustainable life.

In examining cohousing, she was also concerned with its environmental advantages, as in her "Utopianism in the Architecture of New Urbanism and Cohousing." There she says that New Urbanism is "classically utopian" and then looks at two New Urbanist communities, Seaside in Florida and Poundbury in Dorset, both of which tried to create green communities. At the same time, she notes that both communities reflect a "paternalist utopianism" in which "the vision of one person [...] is imposed on a physical space and realized" (Sargisson 227, 232). It is worth noting that the residents of both communities have pushed back against the paternalism and demanded more local input.

She contrasts the New Urbanism model with cohousing, which is participatory and non-hierarchical with the residents responsible for the day-to-day management of the community. In radical contrast with the New Urban communities, the first-generation members of cohousing communities "codesign the community with the architects" so that the communities directly reflect the values of the founders, which can lead to a lengthy founding period (Sargisson, "Utopianism" 237).

## Fool's Gold

In her response to this volume, Sargisson notes that *Fool's Gold? Utopia in the Twenty-First Century* is her favorite among her books, and it is very different from the others in being both more wide-ranging and more accessible to the non-academic reader. After introducing the varieties of utopianism, *Fool's Gold* has chapters on religious fundamentalism; feminism and gender; sex and sexual identity; climate change and catastrophe fiction; human attitudes to nature; green intentional communities; fantastic architecture and the case of Dubai; domestic architecture: new urbanism and cohousing; computer gaming; and cloning, cyborgs, and robots. So, the book reflects both themes that she discussed throughout her career and adds new subjects, including what appears to be one of the first examination within utopianism of computer games. The book concludes with a wide-ranging discussion of what the various subjects discussed reveal about the variety of utopianisms (she identifies seven) and the strengths and dangers of utopianism. And at the end she reminds the reader of the title of the book and stresses that "the search for perfection [...] is a fool's errand" but that the search for utopia is essential (Sargisson 242).

***

As this brief overview of her publications shows, Sargisson's work represents an important legacy for the utopian studies community, one that this volume in her honor attests to. Many colleagues and friends, in fact, seized the opportunity to testify to Sargisson's legacy by contributing with their chapters. Their contributions are divided into four sections, preceded by a "Foreword" by Ruth Levitas and the editors' "Introduction." The four sections are: "Utopian Literature," "Intentional Communities," "Film and Television," and "Teaching." A "Responses" section includes an "Afterword" by Davina Cooper and a response by Sargisson herself concludes the volume.

The volume opens with Ruth Levitas's "Foreword," which traces Sargisson's impressive legacy and recognizes the key role she has played in the development of utopianism as a field of study not only through her body of works but also with her role in the institutions and her work as a teacher. As Levitas notes, most utopian scholars have focused on one of three areas of utopian expression – political thought, literature, or intentional communities. Not only is this volume a testament to the thriving variety of the field that Sargisson helped to establish; it also testifies to the importance of her work beyond the confines of her discipline.

The first part of the volume, dedicated to "Utopian Literature" – as a matter of fact – contains the most chapters, proof that Sargisson's work has been fundamental not only in the fields directly related to her research (politics, feminism, and intentional communities), but also to the field of utopian literature. With a personal chapter entitled "Lucy Sargisson: Becoming (a) Utopian," Tom Moylan traces Sargisson's life and career as that of a scholar, teacher, "and indeed a person, [who], literally and figuratively, embodies a utopian way of being." For Moylan, in fact, throughout her career, Sargisson has been part of "the process of breaking the boundaries of the dominant social order and becoming utopian in all aspects of her life." Stemming always from discontent with the now and working toward a better life, utopia finds itself at the core of her work, because it "lives within politics and utopias are political" (Sargisson, "Curious" 31). Moylan, like many other authors in this volume, stresses one of Sargisson's main contributions to the field of utopian studies in her theorization of a "transgressive utopianism," which is "internally subversive," "flexible and resistant to permanence and order," and "intentionally and deliberately utopian" (*Utopian Bodies* 2).

For Sarah Lohmann as well, Sargisson's notion of transgressive feminist utopianism informs her reading of utopian literature. In " 'What isn't living dies': Utopia as Living Organism in Joanna Russ's *The Female Man* and Marge Piercy's *Woman on the Edge of Time*," the author contends that the two novels she examines "place themselves at the oscillating boundaries of the real, the imagined and the achievable." In doing so, they generate a new utopian materiality and can be read as living organisms that produce unique models of sustainable utopianism by creating an atmosphere of constant renewal. In these places, communities not only shape their environments but, Lohmann argues, are also shaped by the structure of their utopian societies. In this way, "utopia sustains itself as both inherently generative of change and in itself formed by its emerging expressions." The utopian impulse is therefore generated by the anger and the frustration of the disenfranchised, such as women and people of color. But while change is achieved in Russ's novel through critical awareness and in Piercy's through personal, direct action, both strategies are nonetheless necessary "to the open-ended utopian striving [...] that may escape closure on Sargisson's terms."

Maria Varsam's chapter, "A Quantum of Hope? J.M. Coetzee's (Post) Colonial Dystopia *Life & Times of Michael K*," investigates the difficulty of imagining and, therefore, narrating a better future for postcolonial societies. However, she identifies in Coetzee's novel an outstanding dystopia both for its formal innovations in the genre's conventions and for its engagement with the specific topos of South Africa. Its character, moreover, can be seen as a model of resistance: unlike conventional dystopian characters, he remains a utopian hero. Following Sargisson's notion that "realization or realizability" are not necessarily part of the conventions of the utopian genre but rather belong to what she calls "the myth of utopia," which assumes utopia to be a blueprint, Varsam applies Sargisson's "utopian transgression" to some literary tropes, modes, and conventions "to disentangle and illuminate a hereto neglected perspective on Coetzee's poetics, ethics, and aesthetics." Reading the novel from the viewpoint of utopian thought and its relationship to postcolonial fiction is a way to bring to light, for Varsam, "aspects of the dystopia and the postcolonial which are mutually elucidating."

Dystopia is also at the center of Almudena Machado-Jiménez's chapter, "Bleak Bodies: Genetically Engineered Women in Louise O'Neill's (Anti-) Utopian Patriarchal Satire *Only Ever Yours*." Moving from Sargisson's list of possible utopianisms in *Fool's Gold*, Machado-Jiménez adds the patriarchal utopia – "any manifestation of utopian thought, fictional or real, that presents dominance over women, regardless of other possible sets of relations among their inhabitants." In line with Sargisson's statement that "utopianism is everywhere but not everything is utopian," she reads Louise O'Neill's novel, *Only Ever Yours*, as an example of a patriarchal utopia (*Fool's* 6). One characteristic of the patriarchal utopia is its lifelong process of perfection-seeking that is imposed upon women. This makes the patriarchal utopia an example of what Sargisson calls "sham utopianism." Feeling pressure to become a utopian product, female bodies and desires are commodified and women become passive producers and consumers. While many works by feminist authors escape the patriarchal utopia in different ways, others – and O'Neill's novel is one of them – are less clearly positioned, blurring the boundaries between what is utopian and what is anti-utopian.

Investigating the potentialities of diffracting Lucy Sargisson's notion of "contemporary transgressive utopianism" with recent critical perceptions that destabilize a persistent binary logic, Dunja M. Mohr's contribution, "Entangled Utopianism in the Anthropocene," explores the critical potential of these approaches that offer (postanthropocentric) ways of going beyond binary thinking and follow a transgressive utopian path located in the past, the present, and the future. By looking at Margaret Atwood's *MaddAddam* trilogy, Larissa Lai's *Salt Fish Girl*, and Jeff VanderMeer's *Southern Reach* trilogy, Mohr interrogates how these texts narrate such "entangled utopianism, the agency of matter, a vital materiality, sympoetic systems, cognitive assemblage, and oddkin," and finds that utopian transgressions and connectedness emerge. These novels invite us to question separateness, rigid categorizations, and fixed solutions. Reading about enmeshed inter-acting, fused existences, and widened kinship increases the readers' awareness about the rich abundances of entanglements and collisions of the present temporality. Transgressive entangled utopianism in the Anthropocene gives readers critical hope to cope with the complexities of dystopian realities and turn them into livable future utopian ones.

The "Utopian Literature" part closes with José Eduardo Reis's chapter, "Literary Utopianism and Ecological Literacy," an exploration of some of the canonic literary contributions that the utopian tradition has made to contemporary environmentalist thought. Focusing primarily on the key concept of sustainability, Reis examines first the literary sources of "ecological utopianism" – that is, such fundamental texts as the *Genesis*, the *Epic of Gilgamesh*, and Homer's *Odyssey*. He then moves to more strictly utopian, canonical texts, such as Thomas More's *Utopia*, Francis Bacon's *New Atlantis*, William Morris's *News from Nowhere*, and Aldous Huxley's *Island*. By tracing a course through the history of literary utopianism, Reis shows the different ways in which nature has been represented idealistically – from elemental foundation to ally, from a model of virtue and a manifestation of divine intelligence to the element that compensates the imbalances caused by the impact of human technology, up to a pedagogic, redemptive force.

Two chapters form the part "Intentional Communities." The first, "On Being Studied: A Utopian Remembers," by Chris Coates, is an insider's view on the world of communitarianism and its relationship with academia. Turning the lens toward those who usually do the research, the chapter offers the view on utopian academics from the perspective of those that they study. Coates draws on firsthand experience of being studied by a number of academics – including Andrew Rigby, Bill Metcalf, David Pepper, and Lucy Sargisson – during his forty years as a member/participant in UK intentional communities. If in the early years of academic interest on the communities, research was rarely shared with those who were the subject of the studies, things changed with the publication of *Diggers & Dreamers: The Guide to Communal Living*, and with academics like Lucy Sargisson, who is credited for having framed "intentional communities within a theoretical political context" and having recognized "their personal and political significance to those [...] who live in them."

In a similar vein, Suryamayi Clarence-Smith's chapter, "Auroville: An Experiment in Spiritually Prefigurative Utopian Practice," looks at the experience of Auroville from the inside – the author being a second-generation member. Clarence-Smith offers an insight into the role of spirituality in Auroville, an experimental township founded in 1968 by The Mother, based on the philosophy and practice of Integral Yoga, whose premise is the spiritualization of all aspects not only of self, but of society. An in-depth autoethnographic account of how a culture of "transgressive utopianism" comes to be articulated, developed, sustained, and socially reproduced, the chapter contributes insights into how communal utopian practice is enabled that could be relevant for fostering and spreading such a culture beyond the boundaries of intentional community contexts. Such an endeavor can be, for Clarence-Smith, a positive development for an increasingly interconnected global society that aspires to radical collective change in the face of environmental, political, and socio-economic crises.

The part "Film and Television" comprises two chapters. In Simon Spiegel's "The Utopia of the Holy Land: The Zionist Propaganda Film

*Land of Promise* as Utopian Text," the author contends that utopian studies have almost exclusively looked at dystopian films, since utopia lacks the elements that are needed to make a film successful. However, such an argument overlooks other filmic forms beside fiction movies, for example, documentary and propaganda films. Following a discussion of the relationship between Zionism and utopianism, the chapter examines Juda Leman's *Land of Promise* (1935), a propaganda film that opposes old and new Palestine, a utopia of place rather than time. The film presents utopia as already existing: the better future is already here – just somewhere else. In a curious temporal and spatial compression, Palestine serves as both – as the negative past that has to be overcome and as the future utopia that is being established. Spiegel advances the idea that such a rhetorical structure may be quite common for a certain type of propaganda: in order to mobilize its audience, the promised better times must not be out of reach; they must be presented as almost palpable.

The second contribution to "Film and Television," Laura Winter's " 'Trial and Error' – Mediating Estrangement in the Quest for Utopia in *The Walking Dead* (2010–Present)," focuses on the popular figure of the zombie in one of the most successful television series. In a brutish post-apocalyptic landscape, survival is the crucial drive for the formation of groups. Over the course of eight seasons, the main group has evolved into a strong community, eutopic in intent, struggling to create "a good life." Responding to Sargisson's claim that estrangement is fundamental to utopianism, Winter explores the ambivalence of estrangement in the "safe place" of a fictional post-apocalyptic landscape. By both maintaining and mediating estrangement, the community seems finally able to create a safe haven to explore sustainable utopian practices. However, more than a story about zombies, *The Walking Dead* is a story about the extent of social cohesion and the evolvement of communities in a perpetually estranged space. The wide resonance of the TV series promises its relevance as a fictional microcosm not only for the study of the contemporary dominant mood in society but also for gaining insights into utopian discourse in the twenty-first century.

The last part, "Teaching," is composed of a conversation among three of Lucy Sargisson's current PhD students, Ibtisam Ahmed, Elena Colombo, and Robyn Muir, and one former PhD student, David M. Bell. A response from Rhiannon Firth, another of Sargisson's erstwhile students, completes the section. The voices of Ahmed, Bell, Colombo, and Muir interweave and alternate in their contribution, "Utopia, Pedagogy, and Care: A Conversation," a reflection on how deeply Sargisson's utopian thought and generosity has informed their own work in and beyond utopian studies. Each contributor comments on different aspects of Sargisson's work to show how it has been woven into projects that have diverse applications, from the critique and deconstruction of colonial and anti-colonial attempts at utopia to the analysis of contemporary critical dystopias, from the feminist examination of popular culture to a fertile dialogue on utopian place. Particular attention is given to Sargisson's "ethics of care" that comes across in her utopianism. The format of the chapter attests to the collaborative spirit and the drive for innovation that Sargisson has nurtured.

"Gratitude for a Utopian Friendship," by Rhiannon Firth, concludes the part. It is a personal recollection of Firth's interactions with Sargisson, which allows her to reflect and to express gratitude for the ways in which Sargisson's mentorship, encouragement, and guidance have impacted on her life. Observing that one of Sargisson's political projects has been about breaking down the boundaries between the public and the private, Firth recognizes that Sargisson's advice to express one's own vulnerabilities openly and honestly is a powerful act of rebellion in a hostile and competitive academic environment.

The volume ends with an "Afterword" by Davina Cooper, followed by Lucy Sargisson's own response. Responding to some of the themes explored in this collection, Cooper's "Afterword" focuses in particular on the relationship between utopian studies and other radical political literatures; on the contribution utopian thinking makes to place and home; and on care, attachment, and movement. Cooper sees in utopia's unique relationship to an oppressive counterpart that gives way to a relationship of "co-constitution, anticipation and entanglement, as hope and warning mingle" one of the features distinguishing utopia from other radical approaches. For instance, while utopia channels the longing for something better, prefiguration calls for its active, animating presence. It seeks to enact the better future, even if such attempts may fail. Cooper also notices that, in the volume, relations of care and cultivation appear as important practices. Care and tending – not only of self and others, but also of places – generally have a positive valence. But too much management can lead to an overly disciplined, stifling world. Care and responsibility, then, can benefit from discussion, experience, and even conflict. Finally, looking at the contribution that utopia can bring to the issue of change and travel through time and space, Cooper concludes that the volume not only speaks to the need to reclaim utopia's value by re-centering its thinking and practice within wider political projects, but also attests to the need to focus on its conditions of creation.

With the witty title, "The Strangest Place: Thoughts on Being a Guest at Your Own Funeral, or 'Regrets, I Have a Few,' " Sargisson expresses the strange and yet pleasant, at times overwhelming feelings she has experienced after reading the collection. Her response, however, is not just an expression of gratitude, but it becomes what she, playfully, calls an "auto-ethnographic auto-critique," the occasion to reflect about Moylan's idea of "becoming (a) utopian." Such a concept, for Sargisson, breaks down into being someone who studies utopianism; being someone who has a utopian sensibility; and finally, the ways in which someone might have been a better utopian. The touching contribution ends on the important recognition that the thread underlining her account is "the importance of other people, connection, community, collaboration, support, challenge, critical friendship, critical mass (or indeed any mass)." Being (a) utopian requires a collective; it requires collaboration; and, in order to have agency, it requires organization and choice.

In honoring Lucy Sargisson's contribution to the field of utopian studies, this collection explores its relationship to other disciplines and approaches, among which are history, literary criticism, social theory, politics, postcolonialism, film studies, environmental, and women's and gender studies. Throughout her career, Sargisson has produced scholarship in the three areas that constitute the field of utopian studies and, to judge from the contributions to this volume, scholars, colleagues, students, and friends have all benefited from her inspiring work.

# Bibliography

Sargisson, Lucy. *Contemporary Feminist Utopianism*. London: Routledge, 1996.
——. "Contemporary Feminist Utopianism: Practising Utopia on Utopia." *Literature and the Political Imagination*. Ed. John Horton and Andrea T. Baumeister. London and New York: Routledge, 1996. 238–255.
——. "Contemporary Feminist Utopianism: The Equality/Difference Dilemma." *Contemporary Political Studies* – Political Studies Association of the United Kingdom 1 (1997): 272–282.
——. "The Curious Relationship Between Politics and Utopia." *Utopia Method Vision: The Use Value of Social Dreaming*. Ed. Tom Moylan and Raffaella Baccolini. Oxford: Peter Lang, 2007. 25–46.
——. *Fool's Gold? Utopianism in the Twenty-First Century*. London: Palgrave Macmillan, 2012.
——. "Friends Have All Things in Common: Utopian Property Relations." *British Journal of Politics and International Relations* 12.1 (2010): 22–36.
——. "Imperfect Utopias: Green Intentional Communities." *Advances in Ecopolitics* 1.1 (2007): 1–24.
——. "Justice Inside Utopia? The Case of Intentional Communities in New Zealand." *Contemporary Justice Review* 7.3 (2004): 321–333.
——. "Politicising the Quotidian." *Environmental Politics* 10.2 (2001): 68–89.
——. "Religious Fundamentalism and Utopianism in the 21st Century." *Journal of Political Ideologies* 12.3 (2007): 269–287.
——. "Second-Wave Cohousing: A Modern Utopia?" *Utopian Studies* 23.1 (2012): 28–56.
——. "Strange Places: Estrangement, Utopianism, and Intentional Communities." *Utopian Studies* 18.3 (2007): 393–424.
——. "Surviving Conflict: New Zealand's Intentional Communities." *New Zealand Sociology* 18.2 (2003): 225–250.
——. "Sustainability and the Intentional Community: Green Intentional Communities." *The Transition to Sustainable Living and Practice*. Ed. Liam Leonard and John Barry. Bingley: Emerald, 2009. 171–192.
——. "Swimming Against the Tide: Collaborative Housing and Practices of Sharing." *Sharing Economies in Times of Crisis*. Ed. Anthony Ince and Sarah Marie Hall. London: Routledge, 2018. 145–159.
——. *Utopian Bodies and the Politics of Transgression*. London and New York: Routledge, 2000.

——. "Utopianism in the Architecture of New Urbanism and Cohousing." *Green Utopianism: Perspectives, Politics and Micro-Practices*. Ed. Karin Bradley and Johan Hedrén. London: Routledge, 2014. 226–242.

——. "What's Wrong with Ecofeminism?" *Environmental Politics* 10.1 (2001): 52–64.

——. "Why Feminism Needs Utopianism." *Diggers & Dreamers 2000–2001*. Ed. Sarah Bunker, Chris Coates, David Hodgson, and Jonathan How. London: Diggers and Dreamers Publications, 1999. 51–57.

——. "Why Utopia Matters." *Utopia Matters: Politics and Theory. Politics, Literature and the Arts*. Ed. Fátima Vieira and Marinella Freitas. Oporto: Editora da Universidade do Porto, 2005. 51–53.

Sargisson, Lucy and Lyman Tower Sargent. "Lived Utopianism: Everyday Life and Intentional Communities." *Communal Societies* 37.1 (2017): 1–23.

——. *Living in Utopia: New Zealand's Intentional Communities*. Aldershot: Ashgate, 2004.

Utopian Literature

TOM MOYLAN

# Lucy Sargisson, Becoming (a) Utopian

Quite simply, politics needs Utopia and Utopia needs politics.
Lucy Sargisson, "The Curious Relationship Between Politics and Utopia" (44)

In 2007, Lyman Tower Sargent, writing in *Utopia Method Vision* of his own journey into the realm of utopia and utopian studies, eloquently conveyed the conviction that many of us who share in the utopian persuasion deeply believe: "Thus, we must choose Utopia. We must choose the belief that the world can be radically improved; we must dream socially; and we must allow our social dreams to affect our lives. The choice for Utopia is a choice that the world can be radically improved" ("Choosing" 306).

If ever there was a person who has clearly chosen utopia, it is Lucy Sargisson. As a scholar, teacher, and indeed a person, she, literally and figuratively, embodies a utopian way of being, as she has been involved through the years in the process of breaking the boundaries of the dominant social order and becoming utopian in all aspects of her life. As she put it in her own contribution to the *Utopia Method Vision* collection, her engagement with utopianism has emerged in a series of expressions which "stem always from discontent with the now and gesture always toward a better life" ("Curious" 26). Working from a scholarly base within the discipline of politics, and drawing on feminist and poststructuralist paradigms and methods, she has from the beginning of her professional work positioned herself within the terms of the "symbiotic relationship" between politics and utopia ("Curious" 25). However, for Sargisson this chosen standpoint has not been just a matter of intellect and profession, but also one of affect and personal and political existence. Thus, she has always worked within the realm of political scholarship as a utopian, and she has always worked within the realm of utopianism as an intellectual and citizen imbued with the importance of political engagement, in all its manifestations.

For Sargisson, drawing on Sargent and Ruth Levitas, utopianism is best understood as "social dreaming" (Sargent, "Three Faces" 3) based in "the desire for a better way of being" (Levitas 7). In her own particular deployment of political theory and practice, utopia is core to her work: as she puts it, utopia "lives within politics and utopias are political" ("Curious" 31). In this reflection, she does not consider politics as a normative practice of discussion and debate but rather as a "process or activity that subverts and changes our world" ("Curious" 32). Thus, she is continually attuned to the way that utopianism (as form or practice) does not simply critique the present social order but also explores ways successfully to transform it, doing so most fundamentally by provoking and developing "paradigm shifts in consciousness, permitting us to glimpse new conceptual spaces from which to approach the world anew" ("Curious" 37–38). However, drawing on the sensibility of critical utopianism, Sargisson is keen to assert that the effective utopianism with which she is affiliated, and which she has extensively studied and taught, is not a matter of realized, certainly not closed, social arrangements but rather a radical and open process which reaches *toward* such realizations, doing so by creating "new space for the exploration of alternatives" and "rupturing boundaries – whether it be through inter- or cross-disciplinary study, or by contesting oppositional concepts such as mind and body, or public and private" in order to generate opportunities "to look at things fresh, from a new estranged perspective" ("Curious" 38).

Thus, in her account of her own journey through utopianism, Sargisson eloquently argues the following: "Politics without Utopia would be bleak indeed. Utopias (in the sense of visions of a better way of living) give politics a sense of where it wants to be. In this sense, Utopia lies at the heart of politics" ("Curious" 42). Significantly, this utopian desire and drive within political realities addresses what she describes as "the most difficult and often unanswered problem within utopian studies – that of *agency*" ("Curious" 43, my emphasis). Understanding utopia in terms of "transgression and transformation" therefore helps to describe the nature of the radical personal agency required to challenge and change an oppressive social order by enabling previously compliant subjects to become utopian, to be active and engaged citizens in the most revolutionary of ways.

As a working intellectual, all through her career Sargisson has produced scholarship within what Sargent has identified as the "three faces of utopianism" (namely, utopian literature, communitarianism, and utopian social theory); and scholars and students of utopia have benefited from her meticulous and engaged work across this triad.

Sargisson's first book, *Contemporary Feminist Utopianism* (1996), grew out of her PhD research, and initially took the form of two Keele University research papers. Based in the discourse of political thought, this monograph regards feminist utopianism in a broad socio-political scope that includes both literary and theoretical expressions. Herein, she draws on her feminist and poststructuralist framework to consider utopian productions in terms of Levitas's categories of form, content, and function (4); drawing on my work on critical utopianism and on feminist political theory, she argues strongly for a utopian function that is more dynamic than the abstract projection of blueprints and therefore productive of concrete and self-critical socio-political change (cf. Levitas, Moylan). To me, this book has always been a strong expression of the best of progressive feminist utopianism, even as it came at a time when such arguments were diminishing, not very least within utopian studies. It is a work that established the productive foundation for all of her future projects, and one that anyone involved in utopian studies and radical utopian change should revisit on a regular basis.

Sargisson continued her exploration of a transgressive utopianism in *Utopian Bodies and the Politics of Transgression* (1999), but this time she focused on the additionally pressing need for a radical green politics. Writing with strength and clarity, she argues for a "transgressive utopianism" and sums up its qualities in the following way:

> It is internally subversive, which is to say that it challenges from within the aims and assumptions of the ground whence it comes (political theory, utopian philosophy, academic study, etc.).

> It is flexible and resistant to permanence and order and even while it constructs an account (of, e.g., "politics") it accepts its own imminent dissolution. Nothing lasts forever in a changing environment.

It is intentionally and deliberately utopian. The book asserts, contra popular assumptions, that a certain utopianism is essential to process and dynamism. (*Utopian
Bodies* 2)

With this framework, as a timely expression of radical millennial
thought, she develops the concept of *bodies* in her theoretical discussion
as well as her case studies: particularly focusing on a critical utopian engagement with bodies of thought and with the praxis of actually existing
communities/bodies of people. What clearly comes across in this work is
Sargisson's growing emphasis on effective utopian action, that which is
both pragmatic and visionary, rather than detached theoretical abstrac-
tion. Shaping this emphasis is her insistence on the necessity for holistic
thought and intervention, both in the existing knowledge bases (bodies of
thought) in utopian studies and political theory and in the socio-political
realities (physical and communal bodies by which we act and with which
we interact, as especially seen in ecologically based intentional communities in Britain).

Importantly in this book, as Sargisson argues for an oppositional utopianism, she takes care to emphasize that it should not be unilateral, not
dominated by a singular leadership. Rather, she calls for a "multiple conception of opposition in which many voices are directed at an issue" – in
other words, a politics of coalition rather than singularities (*Utopian Bodies*
4). This was a crucial intervention in its historical moment, especially as
the surge of identity and various modes of micro-politics of the 1990s was
progressively unfolding into a larger alliance politics growing out of such
formations as the anti- or counter-globalization movements, or the World
Social Forum. However, Sargisson takes care to step back from the global
dimension of such developments and stress her call for a concomitant im-
mersion in local politics, albeit a local politics that is interconnected (or
intersectional, as we might term it today). From this base, she breaks open
the binary of public and private so as to render all human behaviors and
actions as socio-politically imbricated, even as she also addresses the importance of the private, of affect, in everyday life and public praxis. More
specifically, she examines this interrelationship in terms of the category and
practices of property (especially addressing questions of privileged ownership), the relation between work and value, the role of money, and the

significance of self-worth and esteem. She therefore argues that much can be learned from the lived experience in "utopic spaces of the communities" as people work through and out of the cage of contemporary capitalist relations into a new utopian horizon (*Utopian Bodies* 5). In her closing chapter, she focuses on the relation of Self and Other, again reading against a singular binary and arguing for an interconnected, holistic, comprehension of the totality of individuals and community, indeed of species. This, she argues, is the "core theme of the book" (*Utopian Bodies* 5).

Overall in this study, Sargisson's theoretical and political framework allows her to address these issues by way of not only contemporary feminist and utopian thought but also deconstruction, psychoanalysis, social psychology, and deep ecology. Further, and presaging her future work, she especially draws on her ethnographic work with the New Age community of Findhorn. No one can describe the strengths of this book better than the author herself, wherein she argues that this work is "at once flexible, fallible, modest, ambitious, pragmatic and principled": thus, *Utopian Bodies* "is, quite simply, an attempt at a new approach to thinking about theory" (5). I couldn't agree more, and I would argue that this is a work that is too often under-referenced and neglected by too many of us.

Carried out in collaboration with Lyman Tower Sargent, Sargisson's next project focused on actually existing utopianism. As an extension of, and progression from, *Utopian Bodies, Living in Utopia: New Zealand's Intentional Communities* (2004) examined the utopian qualities of a range of intentional communities, historically and in the present, throughout the nation's two islands. Dividing their labor by way of archival work by Sargent and fieldwork by Sargisson, and influenced by feminist methodology and utopian hermeneutics, the authors sought to engage with the New Zealand communities on their own terms, thereby adducing the qualities exhibited by the very groups from an engagement with and reading of their own self-understanding and daily practice. Continuing Sargisson's argument for a primary emphasis on utopian process, the authors emphasized the experience of living in community over the apparent "lessons" of previously valued abstract approaches to communal studies (such as Rosabeth Moss Kanter's emphasis on communal longevity). The study therefore comes alive in its detailed accounts of the individual communities, which range from religious, to cooperative, to environmental – and which exhibit alternative visions from Buddhism, to feminism, pacifism, and anarchism. Overall, the study made a significant contribution to the existing body of work on communal studies, as well as furthering the theoretical and methodological emphasis on process and on the importance of practices of everyday life in utopian analysis (an emphasis that is shaping a new collaborative project by Sargisson and Sargent).

Valuable as this book is in its own terms, what I have always found particularly significant is the creative change of methodological gears taken by Sargisson herself in pursuing this project. Stepping fully into ethnographic fieldwork, she drew on her sense of feminist and utopian practice not only to focus on this particular object of study but also on the terms and conditions of her own methodology. As a result, she carried out a considered and careful participant observation of a variety of communities over several months that to my mind (as one who is not an anthropologist, much less an ethnographer) sensitively brought the everyday life of each community to the reader with a degree of immediacy, indeed intimacy. In my estimation, Sargisson herself, as a scholar and a person, was further changed in a utopian manner by her self-reflective and self-critical practice as she brought her sensibility as a utopian into her practice as a social scientist, thereby furthering her own utopian becoming.

Then, in *Fool's Gold: Utopianism in the Twenty-First Century* (2012), Sargisson produced a work that eloquently pulls together her wide range of scholarship and intervention throughout the years. Again, as in the method of Birmingham cultural studies, she lets the "object speak" as she takes up an intriguing collection of studies of contemporary phenomena and conducts an interpretive reading of each to adduce their utopian potential or surplus (in the tradition of Ernst Bloch's hermeneutics, though again deeply informed by a feminist problematic). Thus, she plunges into the phenomena of twenty-first society and considers a series of nodal points in order to present the ways in which humanity's "fears, dreams and desires" interact to generate a complex utopianism for our time (*Fool's* 1). She therefore moves from religious fundamentalism; to feminism and gender; sex and sexual identity; climate change and catastrophic fiction; human attitudes toward nature; green intentional communities; fantastic architecture and the case of Dubai; domestic architecture and new urbanism and cohousing; computer gaming; and cloning, cyborgs, and robots in a socio-cultural anatomy of contemporary culture. Immersed in the specificities of these multiple objects of study, Sargisson applies utopian interpretive methodology to her interactions with each of them and, importantly, allows each of them to offer up their own utopian qualities, their own specific utopian surplus. Yet, she then shifts into a larger register as she traces a richly renovated and expanded sense of the qualities of utopian production and utopian theory and method in this new century. Here then, in a rich accumulation of the sensibilities and concerns running through her previous work, she brings each of her methodological skills to this project: her capacity for political and utopian theorizing, her capacity for textual interpretation and her capacity for ethnographic engagement – even as all this work is embedded in her deep personal commitment to the lived utopian project of transgressive and transformative change.

*Fool's Gold* therefore is a treasure trove of utopian case studies but more so of a meta treatment of utopian theory and practice, one that especially speaks to each and every one of us, in all our diversity, in these dark times. For me, pedagogically, it has been a key source in the fifth year architecture seminar that I teach on "Utopia, Imagination, Method, Social Design": the students benefit, first, from its powerful theoretical and pedagogical first chapter, as Sargisson moves deftly through crucially important definitions, her constant challenge to anti-utopian thought and practice (as found in each of her books), and then to her profound articulation of the important standpoint for our time: anti-anti-utopianism; the students then learn from the specific studies (especially those on architecture and intentional communities) that enable them (especially newer students of utopianism) to immerse themselves and better grasp the nuances of the utopian project.

However, the deeper theoretical, political, and especially existential power of this book lies within Sargisson's meta-images of the *fool* and of *fool's gold*. As she beautifully tells it in her introduction, the figure of the "utopian fool" runs through the book in "a number of guises": "Sometimes she is the wise fool who tweaks our noses and tells us truths that we don't want to hear. Sometimes she is simply foolish and dumb, rushing in where angels fear to tread, returning to her follies (like the dog to its vomit) and generally making a fool of herself. Sometimes she is playful; fooling around, having fun" (*Fool's* 5).

Then, Sargisson invokes the figure of *gold*, both authentic and fake. As she puts it: "Gold also streaks the pages of this book. It serves a cautionary purpose; for all that glisters is not gold. It also stands for the nuggets of valuable stuff (sometimes buried in the dross)" (*Fool's* 5). Here then, she pointedly engages the image of pyrite: the term for the false substance (and thus promise or expectation) so often sought by adventurers (dominant or desperate); and she, self-reflexively, notes that the book "relentlessly pursues fool's gold," as each of her case studies teases out the authentic utopian seed or surplus, the true wealth, from the empty hypoglycemic offerings of contemporary global capitalism and its attendant cultural productions, the abstractions of a false utopian emptiness (*Fool's* 5).

Combining both figures in the overall title of the book, Sargisson tells readers that this is a study pursuing authentic value even as it sorts through the detritus of all too quickly evaporated everyday promises. For me, the figure of the *fool* bespeaks not only the general utopian agent but also, profoundly and humbly, the specific agency of the author herself; and that of *fool's gold* enhances that promising subject position with the sobering warning always to look critically, always to take a second look, to take a holistic view of what is and what could be and never to settle for a provincial sense of reality. Therefore, the holistic image conveyed in the book's title points back to Sargisson's key concern for utopian agency. That is, it evokes, names or interpellates, a utopian person who speaks from the hopeful horizon of a better way and is undaunted by the given world, a person who is able and willing to bring all she knows and is to her studies of that world in order to make it better, a person who is unafraid of being foolish in the acts of doing so, but also a person who remembers that we should not "take ourselves too seriously – and to be careful what we wish for" (*Fool's* 5). In short, the book hails a person who is always already becoming utopian.

Sargisson concludes her powerful text by reminding readers that the utopian project is dangerous, "full of pitfalls, traps and diversions" (*Fool's* 243). She declares that the project requires humanity to look beyond what is immediately available, to be willing to "give up today's comforts for an uncertain tomorrow," to no longer be "locked into economic and political structures that are inappropriate to long-term global planning and action," and to no longer be "locked into mutually destructive ways of thinking about nature" (*Fool's* 243). In answer to the long-standing radical question of "what is to be done," she suggests the following: "Think. And think hard and carefully about the world around us. Act. And act boldly. Try. And try together. Fail. And try again" (*Fool's* 243). She then closes quite appropriately, with a reference that I myself have been using more and more in these dark times: "In the words of Samuel Beckett: 'Ever tried. Ever failed. No matter. Try again. Fail again. Fail better'" (Beckett qtd. in Sargisson, *Fool's* 243).

As one who has been "becoming utopian" throughout her life, and who has encouraged students, readers, and colleagues to also become utopian, Sargisson exemplifies the "choice" of which Sargent wrote. In doing so she has exercised the dynamic "utopian energy" (another formulation by Sargent) that has challenged many in this bad old world to be better (Sargent, "Choosing" 309). As Sargent explains his use of the term, he makes clear that such energy, like the utopian impulse itself, is always available but can be misplaced or misused:

> The general idea of utopian energies is that the will/willingness/ability to create new forms can be channeled in a number of different directions, that there may be only a limited amount of such energy at any given time, and that if it is going elsewhere, it will not be going into actual utopias for intentional communities [...] Specifically, utopian energy is often displaced into other projects that have a tinge of utopianism but are not normally considered utopian, like nation building, reform, and social movements advancing the status of a subgroup in society. All of these are, I want to argue, projects into which utopian energies can be displaced. However, these very projects can then give rise to a new cycle of utopian thinking. ("Choosing" 309–310)

While Sargent is speaking primarily at the level of the social, I believe that we can further understand how utopian energy is also available to each person, in their own unfolding, in their own process of becoming utopian. Therefore, I employ it here, in both senses, to testify that Sargisson has consistently tapped that energy and directed it in clear utopian channels.

As a utopian, in all aspects of that word, Lucy Sargisson has indeed made a significant contribution to making the world a better place. She has engaged in what Sara Ahmed describes as hopeful "acts of refusal and rebellion" while carrying on the "quiet ways we might have of not holding onto things that diminish us" (1); and in doing so she has lived a life of what Ann Cvetkovich describes as a "utopia of ordinary habit" rooted in personal experience yet blossoming through the years into the wider socio-political process of total transformation (189).


## Bibliography

Ahmed, Sara. *Living a Feminist Life*. Durham, NC and London: Duke University Press, 2017.

Beckett, Samuel. "Worstward Ho!" *Company Ill Seen Ill Said Westward Ho Stirrings Still*. Ed. Dirk van Hulle. London: Faber and Faber. 79–105.

Cvetkovich, Ann. *Depression: A Public Feeling*. Durham, NC and London: Duke University Press, 2012.

Levitas, Ruth. *The Concept of Utopia*. Syracuse, NY: Syracuse University Press, 1990.

Moylan, Tom. *Demand the Impossible: Science Fiction and the Utopian Imagination*. New York and London: Methuen, 1986.

Sargent, Lyman Tower. "Choosing Utopia: Utopianism as an Essential Element in Political Thought and Action." *Utopia Method Vision: The Use Value of Social Dreaming*. Ed. Tom Moylan and Raffaella Baccolini. Oxford and Bern: Peter Lang, 2007. 301–319.

——. "The Three Faces of Utopianism Revisited." *Utopian Studies* 5.1 (1994): 1–37.

Sargisson, Lucy. *Contemporary Feminist Utopianism*. London and New York: Routledge, 1996.

——. "The Curious Relationship Between Politics and Utopia." *Utopia Method Vision: The Use Value of Social Dreaming*. Ed. Tom Moylan and Raffaella Baccolini. Oxford and Bern: Peter Lang, 2007. 25–47.

——. *Fool's Gold: Utopianism in the Twenty-First Century*. London: Palgrave Macmillan, 2012.

——. *Utopian Bodies and the Politics of Transgression*. London and New York: Routledge, 2000.

Sargisson, Lucy and Lyman Tower Sargent. *Living in Utopia: New Zealand's Intentional Communities*. Aldershot: Ashgate, 2004.

SARAH LOHMANN

# "What isn't living dies": Utopia as Living Organism in Joanna Russ's *The Female Man* and Marge Piercy's *Woman on the Edge of Time*

## Introduction: Dream and Reality

In *Contemporary Feminist Utopianism*, Lucy Sargisson suggests that feminist utopianism is "transgressive of the standard view of utopias as perfection because of a desire to escape closure" (4); her proposed model of utopian thought resists such closure by going beyond binary systems regarding the construction of meaning. Applied to utopian literature, Tom Moylan appears to identify a similar sense of innate openness or dynamism within a group of primarily feminist utopian novels that he terms "critical utopias" (cf. *Demand*). These novels, which include Joanna Russ's *The Female Man* (1975), Marge Piercy's *Woman on the Edge of Time* (1976), Ursula K. Le Guin's *The Dispossessed* (1974), and Samuel R. Delany's *Triton* (1976), are distinguished by the fact that what Bülent Somay calls the fictive "utopian locus" is shifted from individual to community, thus conceiving of a better world for those who need it most: the marginalized and systemically oppressed, such as women and people of color (25). According to Moylan, this in turn allows these narratives to "dwell on the conflict between the originary world and the utopian society opposed to it so the process of social change is more directly articulated"; this, he claims, renders them "more recognizable and dynamic alternatives" to the "systematizing boredom of the traditional utopia" while "negat[ing] the negation of utopia by the forces of twentieth century history" (10). Moreover, the fact that these authors all have their literary origins in science fiction appears to contribute to this dynamism: the genre's creation of fictionally extrapolated futures lends it a "uniquely privileged symbolic response to the conditions of existence in this century" (41), Moylan suggests, while Darko Suvin terms science fiction "a creative approach towards a dynamic transformation rather than [...] a static mirroring of the author's environment" (9).

Curiously, however, despite this dynamic articulation of social change between utopia and what Suvin calls the "'zero world' of empirically verifiable properties around the author,"[1] Moylan and other scholars of the critical utopia nevertheless describe the utopian worlds explored in these novels as no more than dreams or fantastic imaginings, akin to William Morris's "Nowhere." Moylan, for instance, writes that "a central concern in the critical utopia is the awareness of the limitations of the utopian tradition, so that these texts reject utopia as blueprint while preserving it as a dream," and he describes utopian Whileaway in *The Female Man* as "not the answer but the vision that provokes change" (10, 54). Frances Bartkowski, meanwhile, declares that "the status of utopia as waking dream is clear in Piercy's novel," citing the protagonist Connie's "need and desire for fantasy" (52). Science fiction is not fantasy, however, and there is a sense in which the identification of these vibrant worlds as visions, dreams, or fantasies within their storyworlds (and by extension ours) – necessary and stimulating as these vehicles of desire undoubtedly can be – does not quite do justice to their unique functionality as powerful critical instruments. In fact, what creates the particular open-ended dynamism of these novels and distinguishes them from their predecessors, I would argue, is precisely the *reality* of both the connections between utopia and zero world in these utopias, as well as the reality of utopia itself – particularly in *The Female Man* and *Woman on the Edge of Time*, both of which incorporate utopia within a complex multiplicity of dynamically interconnecting spatiotemporalities. In doing so, these texts go beyond the historical divide between spatially or temporally remote though "complete" and thus perhaps more realistic utopias – or "ideal-society models," as J. C. Davis terms them – and less true-to-life constructs even further removed in space, time, and probability,

---

1    Suvin clarifies that "zero" here is to be understood "in the sense of a central reference point in a coordinate system, or of the control group of an experiment" (23).

such as the Cockaigne and the millennium, which scholars such as Lyman Tower Sargent ascribe utopian dimensions to despite their lack of realism (9). Instead, they place themselves at the oscillating boundaries of the real, the imagined, and the achievable; accordingly, I would suggest that rather than succeeding or failing as more or less representational, these novels create a new utopian materiality through these very oscillations – it is the substantiality of their liminal junctures and linkages themselves that I would like to draw attention to. Indeed, I will make the case that both utopias can be thought of as *living systems* or organisms, creating unprecedented models of sustainable utopianism by embedding their utopian (im)pulse in the self-regulating, life-giving rhythms of sustainable feedback systems. Moreover, I will show how this sustained vitality is both intimately connected with and enabled by the social egalitarianism that sets the critical utopias apart, thereby making these novels compelling examples of Sargisson's transgressive feminist utopianism.[2]

## Critical Connections

To begin with, zero world and utopia are interwoven in an unprecedented manner in these narratives, which gives the zero world itself an unusually strong presence in these novels – and as its role is to generate utopia, this paradoxically also gives concreteness to the idea of the utopia

---

2    My analysis will be restricted to *The Female Man* and *Woman on the Edge of Time* in this essay because these novels share a distinct dynamism related to the kinetics of their spatiotemporal storyworlds. Of the other two novels identified by Moylan as critical utopias, Le Guin's *The Dispossessed* could also be shown to display a similar organic, self-regulating criticality, but on a different scale and for fairly different reasons, which is why it is not included here. Delany's *Triton*, moreover, is excluded due to its perhaps somewhat less radically feminist perspective, as described by Russ in her essay "Recent Feminist Utopias," which in turn makes it less suitable for my later analysis in terms of "crux times" and the explosive energy resulting from systemic sexist (and racist) oppression (146).

in question itself. Both utopian Mattapoisett in *Woman on the Edge of Time* and Whileaway in *The Female Man* are only *possible* futures that may or may not come about, and we witness the contacts established between utopia and zero world (or another timeline) in order to make the future existence of utopia more likely.[3] In Piercy's novel, this contact takes place between utopian citizen Luciente and Connie, a 37-year-old impoverished Chicana woman in present-day (1975) New York, who might be a past version of Luciente; Luciente solicits Connie's help in the present to aid in the fight for the existence of utopian Mattapoisett, a village in New England in 2137. In Russ's novel, the connection forms between utopian citizen Janet and three other women who can be seen as her possible selves in alternate realities: Joanna, the author's avatar in the New York of the present (1969); Jeannine, from a present version of New York in which the Second World War has not ended; and Jael, a part-cyborg feminist avenger fighting on the side of "Womanland" against "Manland" in an extended battle of the sexes in near-future Earth.[4] Here, though, it is not utopian Janet who initiates the connection, but martial Jael, who

3    Mattapoisett is only one village in a utopian network that spans at least a dozen or
     so communities, and possibly far more than that; however, I have chosen to refer
     to this utopian network as a whole as "Mattapoisett" since we are not given a col-
     lective term for these communities, and it makes no difference to my analysis.
4    Whileaway is also the setting of "When It Changed," a 1972 short story by Joanna
     Russ which predates *The Female Man* and which features some additional brief de-
     scriptions of the structure of Whileawayan society that could provide support for
     my analysis of Whileaway as a dynamic organism. However, I have not included it
     here because its spatiotemporal setting is different, featuring not multiple strands of
     probability of which Whileaway is one, but a simplified or even "collapsed" reality
     in which current Whileawayan society is uncontestably the result of a plague which
     killed the male half of the population, and in which visitors from Earth appear
     to present a real threat to the current utopian system with their planned reintro-
     duction of men. As such, it is both less amenable to my interpretation below of
     Whileaway as an open-ended, self-organizing system in its spatiotemporal develop-
     ment, as well as less open-ended in terms of its own ultimate realizability or sustain-
     ability as a single-sex utopia – in contrast to the ambiguity at the end of *The Female
     Man*, which is key to my understanding of the text. As such, I have decided to treat
     the novel as presenting a complete and authoritative description of Whileaway,
     rather than a time-slice of its existence before the events of the short story.

aims to recruit the others to her cause by convincing them to offer their worlds as weaponry bases. In both narratives, significant textual space is dedicated to all possible timelines (including a brief possible dystopia in Piercy's novel), which gives these worlds equal metaphysical weight in the reader's mind. In fact, a strong telepathic connection between Luciente and Connie allows the two women to visit each other's reality at will, while the four J's representing our world and others are so intimately linked by their ontological kinship that Bartkowski describes them as "more than themselves and *parts* of each other; women at a number of edges of time, they form multiple, collective protagonists" (59).

Within the cadence of both narrative structures, this also facilitates a textual dynamism that is unusual for the utopian genre, in that these intimate and intersecting connections result in frequent and energetic transitions between worlds: Connie and Luciente pull each other's consciousnesses back and forth between present-day New York and Mattapoisett, sometimes abruptly losing their connection; the story of the four J's, meanwhile, is told in jumps between text fragments, including brief descriptions of Whileaway, outbursts condemning present sexism, and cross-temporal tales of the J's adventures. Bartkowski describes the latter as "emphasizing a structure that is disruptive to the reader and reminds us that utopian fiction with its otherworldly setting is deliberately estranging," thus allowing the science-fictional dynamic transformation that Suvin mentions (59). However, once again, it seems insufficient to relegate this transformation to the realm of dream or fantasy, as is once more implied by the term "otherworldly." Instead, it appears to be the embodied nature of these transformative connections themselves that gives this process its estranging power, and the shared textual space between worlds as well as their energetic connection helps to create this tangibility; "otherworldly" could then be seen in a direct sense as indicating actually *other* worlds, rather than imaginary or spiritual ones.

Accordingly, the utopian worlds of Mattapoisett and Whileaway are in themselves also presented as no less actual than the zero worlds and other timelines – in fact, to dismiss them as less substantive than the others would, I suggest, detract from the disruptive and regenerative potential at the heart of the multi-temporal conceits in these novels. There is also no

indication that the reader should do so. For instance, when Janet first successfully visits Earth, her fellow experimenters in teleportation are reduced
to violent laughter, "for it was not a dream," and she also later breaks the
arm of her host at a party in present-day New York for infantilizing her (5).
Likewise, Luciente's presence is given similar sensory substance in Connie's
world when Connie's niece, Dolly, overhears the two women speaking on
Luciente's first visit ("I thought I heard voices," 4), and when both present-
day women note Luciente's body heat in the chair she has left behind, as
plainly present as Connie's meagre dinner: "Dolly had said the chair was
warm: she had been sitting in the other chair, in front of the plate from her
supper of eggs and beans" (4). In another unorthodox move for utopian
literature,[5] Russ and Piercy's utopias (or at least their representatives) thus
dare to step *back* in time, to literally touch our world(s) directly. In doing
so, they are then able to pull us, via the embodied interplay of protagonists, into direct contact with an improved reality that is not only born out
of the most pressing issues of our own, but also explicitly engaging with
its own past in its bid to exist.


## Living Utopia


Moreover, the reified dynamism of this powerful connection between
zero world and utopia is also evident in the structure of Russ and Piercy's
utopian societies themselves: I suggest that this vital energy of transformative interconnectivity also comes about in Mattapoisett and Whileaway

5   The "sleeper wakes" trope within utopian literature, which takes its name from
    H. G. Wells's *The Sleeper Awakes* (1910, originally published as *When the Sleeper
    Wakes* in 1899) and, for example, includes Edward Bellamy's *Looking Backward*
    (1988) and its numerous successors, establishes a direct connection between zero
    world and utopian future, but there is to my knowledge no back-and-forth move-
    ment on the same level of reality (i.e., apart from dream states and the like), and
    no explicit presence of utopia or its representatives in the zero world of the same
    materiality as Luciente's physical visits to Connie, for example.

through the distinctive rhythms and cadenced connections that act as life-giving pulses for these communities. For example, their engagement with the natural environment tends to follow a strong seasonal rhythm, as evident in the regularity and cyclicality of the festivals that play a large part of everyday life in both worlds: on Whileaway, the celebration of solstices, equinoxes, the flowering of trees, and so forth form a big part of communal life (101–103), and in Mattapoisett, the "domes-ticking of corn and wheat," "the turning of the sun north and south," and so on are considered "important events" that form the basis of "tens and tens of holidays" (126). In fact, both societies could be said to exist "neither here nor now," but "in the time of the festival with its 'arcadian anarchy,'" as Bartkowski says of Whileaway (76). However, though they can both be described as anarcho-communist, this assessment does not quite do justice to the fact that the cadenced relationship of human and non-human in these worlds also indicates a holistic, four-dimensional cosmology: on Whileaway, "there is no pebble, no tile, no excrement, that is not Tao" (99–100), and Luciente tells Connie that in Mattapoisett, "we're part of the web of nature. [...] We have a hundred ceremonies to heal us to the world we live in with so many others" (303). Rather than being outside of time, then, and outside of responsibility and care, it appears that these communities see themselves as fundamentally integrated with the non-human environment across spacetime – in the same rhythmic, corporeal way, in fact, in which they engage with their fellow utopian citizens. On Whileaway, human connections such as "jokes," "longing," and happy and "unhappy copulation" also form the basis of festivities (102), for example, while Mattapoisett celebrates utopian history and "famous liberators" alongside natural events (126).

Indeed, such rhythms of interpersonal engagement characterize everyday life in these communities, forming patterns of interaction by which people relate to one another: on her first visit to Mattapoisett, for instance, Connie is taken aback by the "strong energy level" in the "fooder," or communal dining hall, where "people were arguing heatedly, laughing and telling jokes, and a child was singing loudly at the table nearest the door" (76); she notes that "the pulse of the room was positive but a little overwhelming" (77). Here, connections take place through body language and physical touch as well as through conversation, with people "touching and caressing, hugging and [...] hand[ling] each other constantly" (78). On Whileaway, a similar pattern of interpersonal connection can be observed, though it seems to be less in the service of the embrace of shared communal experience and more about interacting in a way that enables both together-ness and the "characteristic independence" (52) of Whileawayans: though they are not afraid to solve disputes through duels rather than conversa-tion, Whileawayans also recognize that "the cure for [aggression] is dis-tance" (48), and their movements consciously reflect the ebb and flow of mutual affinity. In particular, this is enabled directly through a complex system of greetings, with "Hello-yes?," "Hello-no," and so forth indicating everything from friendliness to "Get away or I'll do that to you which you don't like" (142).

These interpersonal oscillations, I suggest, give life to their commu-nities not just through the energy of frequent contact, but through the resulting self-regulation that Jane Jacobs and Henri Lefebvre, for example, see as fundamental to the creation and maintenance of living, dynamic spaces. Although both Jacobs and Lefebvre are referring to cities, the same findings seem to hold for Mattapoisett's village life and Whileaway's global network. Jacobs, for instance, praised the "complex order" that emerges from the "intricate ballet" of contacts on the sidewalks of busy city streets (50), and which is embodied perfectly in Whileaway's greeting system, while Lefebvre saw dynamic urban interactive spaces of the sort that would in-clude Luciente's fooder as "the greatest hope for a vital, liberatory everyday life" (McLeod 24). Indeed, Lefebvre studied these cadences in detail in his work on "rhythmanalysis" and identified them as "multiple tensions that will generate an unpredictable transformation" within the society in question, a "concrete reality open to the future" (McLeod 16). As such, one might see these rhythmic connections in Whileaway and Mattapoisett as *feedback* relations that bring about the emergence of something greater than themselves: the sustainability of communal utopian life through self-directed flow.

Such self-regulation can also be observed at other levels within these worlds in the service of sustainable co-existence – for example, there is a regulatory, communally agreed-upon rhythm to individual lifespans that allows for both individual space and communal exchange while maximizing resources and skill-sharing. On underpopulated Whileaway, for instance, large chosen families offer a "geographical home base" to young Whileawayans after a traditional period of wandering, but their size caps at a certain point, so "approximately every fourth girl must begin a new or join a nearly-new family" (52). In Mattapoisett, young people also go soul-searching for a while ("we set our children free," 123) before choosing their new companions, but adults live independently and only come together in small (usually non-romantic) groups to parent children. These children, moreover, will have gestated in "brooders," which safeguards the population constancy while ensuring that parenthood is chosen freely and prudently. Likewise, there are distinctive, regular patterns of self-regulation within the socio-economic systems of both worlds: on Whileaway, for instance, a broad early education enables young women to "do any job on the planet" and they are set to work "where they're needed, not where they wish" (51–52), while Mattapoisett allows more freedom regarding job choice but prescribes sabbaticals for individual development every seven years. Similarly regular, impartial arrangements inform governmental decision-making in both societies: Whileawayans must exert their civic duty after joining families by entering the "Geographical Parliament [... or] the Professional Parliament" (51), while volunteers chosen by lot on a yearly basis make all political decisions in Mattapoisett, including at the highest level of "Grandcil," which mostly attempts to "divide scarce resources justly" (162).

Besides facilitating continued co-existence, these nested self-regulatory movements can in fact be seen as facilitating life on a quasi-biological level: the individuals and social groupings in question work together to keep the communal organism alive in a similar way to the feedback relations that Walter Cannon deemed necessary to living systems in his 1932 book, *The Wisdom of the Body*. In attempting to prove the physiologist Charles Richet's assertation that "the living being is stable" in that it is "capable of modifying itself according to external stimuli and adjusting its response to the stimulation" (Cannon 21), Cannon credited this stability to the communal efforts of several "coöperating factors" in the body that may act simultaneously or successively (300): for instance, the feedback systems governing temperature regulation, oxygen supply to tissues (295), and the regulation of fat and protein by the thyroid gland (295). He even coined a new term, "homeostasis," to describe the process, which he deemed "not accidental, but [...] a result of organized self-government" (300). Likewise, one might identify the people, institutions and networks that make up and facilitate the cadence of individual and communal life on Whileaway, such as working citizens, councils, and the brooder, as "coöperating factors" that keep the utopian communal body alive through their self-regulation beyond individual lives and lifespans.

Again, the concept of feedback is key here, as the continued life of the total organism depends on the internal communication and self-management of its components: in the field of cybernetics that Cannon's work went on to contribute significantly to, feedback based on "*actual* performance rather than [...] *expected* performance" was deemed fundamental to the functioning of various organic and inorganic systems (Wiener 24). This internal network of communication and adjustment is accordingly central to the continued rhythms of Mattapoisett and Whileaway: the "Hello-yes?"/"Hello-no"-system of greetings on Whileaway, for example, functions with direct input and immediately modified output in much the same way that the "governor" of a steam engine does, which helped give cybernetics its name. Likewise, conflict resolution in Mattapoisett occurs through "wormings" in which grievances are aired and responded to over and over until organic solutions are arrived at, while developments such as the genetic "shaping" technology are subject to seemingly interminable council debates.[6]

---

6    Indeed, this feedback-based self-management has in itself been described as con-
     stitutive of life, most notably by Humberto Maturana and Francisco Varela, who
     invented the term "autopoiesis" (or "self-making") to characterize the process of
     self-regulation as defining living systems, claiming that "the notion of *autopoiesis is
     necessary and sufficient to characterize the organization of living systems*" (Maturana
     and Varela 82). Moreover, they directly drew on Cannon's work by stating that "an
     autopoietic machine is an [sic] homeostatic (or rather a relations-static) system
     which has its own organization (defining network of relations) as the fundamental
     variable which it maintains constant" (79).

## Open Utopia

However, it does not seem correct to see these life-giving feedback relations as merely ensuring homeostasis, though the concept may well
apply to the system's internal workings in both worlds. After all, these
utopian societies seen as a *whole* represent a desire to escape closure and
bring about social change, which in turn implies growth and development rather than maintenance or the stasis their literary predecessors
suffered from – indeed, this brought us to seek their identification with
living systems or organisms in the first place. As such, one might instead,
while remaining within the realm of systems theory, read these utopias as
*open* systems that self-regulate internally while remaining open to their
environment. In such structures, growth and change are not only possible
but inherently significant: open systems are described as functioning at a
point "far from equilibrium" which Fritjof Capra describes as a "'steady
state' characterized by continual flow and change" (48).[7] Such a reading,
then, gives us an even better idea of these communities as displaying a
four-dimensional, *sustainable* life force of the sort that appears particularly appropriate for a stasis-threatened utopia, as well as utopian in
itself: as Luciente tells Connie, "We're always changing things around.
As they say, what isn't living dies" (71). In fact, this inherent adaptability
to change is also key to the utopian developments that are under current
debate in these worlds, particularly the induction principle according to
which Whileawayan industry is being reorganized (56) and the aforementioned shaping technology of Mattapoisett, which could have an equally
radical effect on the "shape" of lived experience in this community.

Crucially, both of these technologies are concerned with literal *growth*
and the effects it may have on society as a whole, which seems symptomatic

7   This idea of a state of being "far from equilibrium" – alternatively described by
    Paul Cilliers as the "point of criticality" (97) and by Roger Lewin as "the edge
    of chaos" – is what the biologist Ludwig von Bertalanffy also used earlier on, in
    Vienna in the 1920s, to describe the phenomenon of life as an example of dynamic
    balance or *Fliessgleichgewicht* (flowing balance) in recognition of the limits of clas-
    sical thermodynamics in describing self-regulation in living systems.

of a general drive on behalf of these communities to nurture the constant maturation of their own lived environment, the evolving organism of which they form a crucial part. In doing so, they are able to "generate an unpredictable transformation" in Lefebvre's terms, and create an atmosphere of constant renewal in which, as Connie observes of Mattapoisett, "growth seem[s] to swarm over the land" (127). Indeed, this calls to mind Lefebvre's comparison of a dynamic city, like his hometown of Navarrenx, to a seashell that is shaped by its inhabitants over the years: "A seashell is the product of a living creature that's slowly 'secreted a structure,'" Andy Merrifield writes, and "Navarrenx's shell, Lefebvre says, embodies the forms and actions of a thousand-year-old community, 'shaping its shell, building and rebuilding it, modifying it again and again and again according to its needs'" (63–64). The only significant difference between Navarrenx's seashell-shaping and that of Whileaway and Mattapoisett, one might say, is that the latter communities not only shape their environment, but are in themselves "shaped" by the structure of their utopian societies in the feedback-based patterns we have observed above; in this way, utopia sustains itself as both inherently generative of change and in itself formed by its emerging expressions.

As such, the living, open systems of Whileaway and Mattapoisett are not only self-regulating, but self-*organizing*, in that they incorporate change by maintaining an openness to their environment – as evidenced, for example, by their identification with a holistic ecosphere – and toward the continued cross-temporal existence of utopia, as evidenced both by future-focused developments and by a strong sense of the historical contingency of utopia in its emergence from the zero world. As Alvin Toffler notes, self-organization in open systems allows "order and organisation [to] arise 'spontaneously' out of disorder and chaos," which is particularly fitting for a utopia that develops through unpredictable feedback relations (xv). Accordingly, as Toffler adds, systems in far-from-equilibrium conditions are characterized by non-linear relationships, in that they "become inordinately sensitive to external influences" and "small inputs yield huge, startling effects," which means that "the entire system may reorganise itself in ways that strike us as bizarre" (xvi). This nonlinearity can be seen both in the unpredictability of the utopian innovations in these societies that emerge from unplanned feedback relations, as well as on a smaller scale in such processes as Mattapoisett's aforementioned wormings, which are conducted in part to avert the disproportionate communal harm that may arise from small interpersonal conflicts: "to get revenge against someone an individual thinks wronged [them], individuals have offered up nations to conquest," Luciente explains (225).

In fact, the same nonlinearity and disproportion is evident in the very emergence, or birth, of these utopias as living systems in the first place: both Whileaway and Mattapoisett are the result of self-organization of unprecedented scale and quality following major periods of rupture that could well be described as "far from equilibrium," though their specific nature is not always agreed upon. Janet claims that her society has emerged from a major plague that left (the male) half of the population dead, while Jael insists that her war was the upheaval in question: "that 'plague' you talk of is a lie. [...] I, I, I, I am the plague, Janet Evason. I and the war I fought built your world for you [...] and the Whileawayan flowers nourish themselves on the bones of the men we have slain" (211).

Mattapoisett, meanwhile, is the possible eventual outcome of a war that began at a critical "crux time," which is the imbalanced present of Connie's (and by extension our) zero world: "at certain cruxes of history ... forces are in conflict. [...] Too few have too much power. Alternate futures are equally or almost equally probable ... and that affects the ... shape of time" (212). Indeed, Whileaway likewise exists on a strand of potentiality that may or may not come about: "every choice begets at least two worlds of possibility [...] or very likely many more [...]. It's possible, too, that there is no such thing as one clear line or strand of possibility, and that we live on a sort of twisted braid, blurring from one to the other without knowing it" (6–7). It is these "crux times" within the respective "twisted braid[s]" of both texts, then, that allow for clusters of zero-world feedback to come together on a larger scale and facilitate the existence of utopia itself as a *possibility* in these worlds and ours: as Luciente explains, "Much I don't comprend that led to us [...] But *not inevitably*, grasp? [...] All things interlock. We are only one possible future" (191). The dynamically intersecting timelines forming what Bartkowski terms a "knotting together of spatial and temporal frames," however, are not "knotted" at all, I suggest – as this implies stasis – but engaged in a high-frequency dynamic exchange of information that has the potential to catalyze a living utopia through its feedback mechanisms.

Here, then, is Lefebvre's unpredictable transformation once again, directly in service of a "concrete reality open to the future": the crux times are themselves "brooders" that mix not genetic information but the seeds of possible futures, ready to germinate given the right conditions; these possibilities shift and spark against each other like the "sparks and bumps" of the wormings in order to form points of criticality replete with the possibility of utopian life (Piercy 224). In fact, the explosive energy of the crux times, ready to give birth to the living utopia of Whileaway or Mattapoisett, can in itself be said to be powered by *frustrated* life force in both cases: the impetus for a better future comes here from those who have been denied it thus far, such as women and people of color. As Connie is told, "the powerful don't make revolutions" (213), and it is accordingly the raised consciousness of the disenfranchised that allows these novels to "give new life to the utopian impulse" (Moylan 31): "the anger of the weak never goes away," Connie agrees, "it just gets a little moldy. It molds like a beautiful blue cheese in the dark, growing stronger and more interesting" (50). This anger, then, channeled through "revived, active subject[s]" like Connie and the J's, has the potential to ultimately bring about the existence of the utopian worlds of Mattapoisett and Whileaway, in which complete equality has replaced deeply embedded sexist and racist power structures (Somay 28). Indeed, it is there transformed into *joie de vivre* – as evident in the festivals above, in the joyful energy of Luciente's fooder, and in the "incredible explosive energy" and "gaiety of high intelligence" that we are told balance out the Whileawayans' solitary nature (54).[8] Moreover, through the future-generating clashes of the crux times, the life-giving moving patterns that I previously located in these utopian societies are also present in their larger spatiotemporal frameworks; here, though, it is the possibility of utopia itself rather than everyday utopian existence

8   Whileawayans are said to possess, "under it all, the incredible explosive energy, the gaiety of high intelligence, the obliquities of wit [...] that makes industrial areas into gardens and ha-has, that strews across a planet sceneries, [...] culs-de sac, comic nude statuary [...] and the best graffiti in this or any other world" (54).

that is given life, as vital energy marks the very process of its overdue yet uncertain nascency.

## Generating Equality

In addition, I suggest that this crux-creating force of equality, historically suppressed through sexist and racist, ageist, and classist institutions and customs in the zero world, in turn further facilitates the complex, self-regulatory rhythms of utopia:[9] in the non-hierarchical utopias born of these systemic oppressions, the "flatness" of the social structure allows its elements to easily take on different roles as required by the system. In turn, this flexibility perpetuates equality, since all communal decisions in a leaderless system must benefit all, long as it may take: as Luciente says, "there's no final authority [...] We argue till we close to agree. [...] Oh, it's disgusting sometimes" (164). The result is a world in which equal treatment and individual safety are embedded in the structure of society, and in which gendered violence, for example, is basically non-existent: rape is unheard of in Mattapoisett (226), and on Whileaway, adults and children roam the globe freely, as "you cannot fall out of the kinship web and become sexual prey for strangers, for there is no prey and there are no strangers" (82). As Pamela Annas notes of Mattapoisett, "the possibilities of human freedom are located not so much within the individual characters as within the social structure and the relations between the individual and that social structure" (154).

The central technologies allowing these utopian organisms to thrive are likewise both the product and partial cause of non-hierarchical equality – while fittingly being mostly generative of life themselves, given their association with the traditionally gendered fields of childbirth and child-care. For instance, Mattapoisett's gene-mixing brooders allow both the erasure

9    Ageism and classism particularly also come into play regarding Connie's zero-world experience, as described below.

of racial discrimination and the sharing of burdens associated with mother-hood: Luciente explains that "it was part of women's long revolution. [...] Cause as long as we were biologically enchained, we'd never be equal. [...] So we all became mothers" (110). As Somay notes, this can be seen as the "socialization of childbirth that feminists like Shulamith Firestone called for as part of 'negating the social character of male/female opposition'" (28). This negation is less evident on single-sex Whileaway, but the genetic technique of ova-merging may count as socialized and socialist, as can the "induction helmet" that cuts down on domestic labor: Lisa Yaszek points out that "technologically enabled reproduction in Russ's single-sex utopia liberates women to engage in everything from romance to duelling" (392), to the extent that motherhood is seen as a relaxing "slowing-down of life" (49). As such, the creation of these egalitarian utopian structures seems to be about enabling free, equal, and fulfilling existence on an individual level as much as on that of a living and sustainable collective utopian body; and it is the open-ended self-regulation of the utopian system that facilitates both of these realities.

## Birthing Consciousness

Returning to the overall narrative structures of which these utopian soci-eties form only a part, however, one notes that the two texts engage with their utopias "struggling to be born" in quite different ways (Somay 28). Indeed, Janet herself appears to be so representative of the Whileawayans' "characteristic independence" that she ultimately feels no personal re-sponsibility to help activate her utopian temporal strand in the pre-sent – after all, she believes the crux in question was not Jael's war but a plague, and when Jael tries to convince her otherwise, she straightfor-wardly refuses to accept it, saying "No, [...] I don't believe" (212). In a paradoxical extension of the living reality of utopian Whileaway I have demonstrated thus far, Janet thereby ends up denying any reality that is not hers, despite having experienced the other J's worlds; she even terms the others not "fully human" (68). And yet, it is Janet's own bodily presence throughout the text, bursting onto the scene in Jeannine's New York and then physically asserting her vibrant existence at various points (breaking noses, following strangers, making love to young Laura of Anytown), that not only personifies Whileaway's dynamic energy in the narrative, but also shakes up the lives of the other J's by giving them a vital source of hope: the living possibility of a better world to live for, fight for – and yes, dream about. Janet, too, rather than Jael, awakens this rebellious spirit in Joanna, who represents both author and reader, and who announces her own small embodied crux geared toward utopia near the end: "I committed my first revolutionary act yesterday. I shut the door on a man's thumb" (203). She says she did it "for no reason at all," but it is her first physical assertion against the patriarchy, allowing her pent-up anger to impact her reality – perhaps in anticipation of more utopia-generating disruption to come.

It is not the guaranteed actualization of Janet's specific living utopia that also gives life to the utopian text of *The Female Man* itself: instead, in keeping with contemporary feminism, it is the germination and birth of *consciousness* that comes about through the cruxes and clashes of the J's lived experience, including Whileaway – the awareness that a better existence is possible, even if only beyond our lifetimes, and that it must be egalitarian at heart. Ultimately, this message finds its own physical expression in the utopian text within the reader's lived reality: "Go, little book," Russ writes on the final pages,

> trot through Texas and Vermont and Alaska [...] and England and France; bob a curtsey at the shrines of Friedan, Millet,[10] Greer, Firestone, and all the rest [...]. Live merrily, little daughter-book, even if I can't and we can't [...]. Do not get glum when you are no longer understood, little book. [...]
>
> Rejoice, little book!
>
> For on that day, we will be free. (213–214).

---

10    This appears to be a misspelling by Russ of "Millett" in reference to Kate Millett, the American feminist writer and author of *Sexual Politics* (1970).

## Birthing Agency

In *Woman on the Edge of Time*, on the other hand, written a few years
later at a slightly different point in second-wave feminism,[11] the utopian
message is less textual and even more embodied, particularly by Connie's
own personification of intersectional suffering as a middle-aged, impoverished, Hispanic, and thus multiply oppressed woman of color: "through
her personal struggle the political is laid bare," Bartkowski writes (53).
When Luciente first contacts Connie, she finds her trapped in cycles of
poverty and state violence that stand in stark contrast to the dynamic
living cycles and rhythms of Mattapoisett; indeed, Connie's own lived
reality has been systematically denied her: "from an early age she had
been told that what she felt was unreal and didn't matter" (308). Connie
has also been symbolically barred from her own future by losing custody
of her only child, Angelina, after injuring her in a fit of frustration. In
the course of the story, then, Connie even loses direct control of her own
present experience, as she is unjustly imprisoned in a mental asylum and
forcibly implanted with an emotion-regulating "dialytrode," which robs
her of selfhood and agency in a way that borders on death or zombification: "Connie was an object. [...] She felt distanced from her own life,
as if it had ended with the implantation of the dialytrode. She could not
resume her life, therefore Connie was no more. Yet she lived on" (329).
In fact, Connie's description of the device as "something that would rule
her feelings like a thermostat" (308) invokes a central example employed
by Cannon and the cyberneticists for closed feedback systems, perhaps
underlining the inadequacy of such systems for sustained life in contrast
with the open structure of the alternate utopia. Mattapoisett's life-giving
feedback networks, on the other hand, directly oppose this forced control and dehumanization: "we want to root that forebrain back into a net
of connecting," Luciente says (148). Curiously, Somay actually critiques

11   *Woman on the Edge of Time* was published in May of 1976, and although *The
      Female Man* was first published only a year earlier, in February of 1975, it was ori-
      ginally written in 1970.

the narrative depiction of Connie's neuro-surgical intervention, standing "between humanity and utopia," as a "barrier which lacks social, cultural and economic dimensions" (31). But as Luciente explicitly identifies the biotechnological arms race as central to the crux time that might bring about her utopia, its significance seems clear: "It's that race between technology, in the service of those who control, and insurgency – those who want to change the society in our direction. [...] But the crux, we think, is in the biological sciences. Control of genetics. Technology of brain control" (242).

While Connie's friends in Mattapoisett help her to self-regulate her own neurological patterns in a way that eventually leads to the removal of the dialytrode, the biotechnological and societal fight for control is ongoing both on the larger four-dimensional scale of the story and beyond it, as Piercy points out in her 2016 introduction to the novel. And yet, Mattapoisett serves as a living example of how one might re-balance this control: through a system whose impartial self-regulation, partially enabled by technology, facilitates full lives and meaningful connections between equals. Significantly, enmeshed as she is in the body politics of her zero world, Connie in fact shows no interest in Mattapoisett's genetic shaping and is initially horrified by the brooder, despite Luciente's explanation of its significance for "women's long revolution" – she sees motherhood as women's remaining sacred domain. However, Connie eventually embraces Mattapoisett's utopian reality – having nearly lost her own – through this very connection, the one she finds most meaningful: fixated on motherhood to the point that Luciente tells her off ("Birth! Birth! Birth! That's all you can dream about!" 274), she begins to envisage herself as a (co)mother in Mattapoisett (272–274) and sees her own child in Luciente's daughter, Dawn (206). Ultimately, then, Connie reaches her own moment of utopian interconnectivity when she mentally agrees to let Angelina symbolically live in utopia without her – thus allowing her the freedom and fullness of life that Connie has never had: "Suddenly she assented with all her soul to Angelina in Mattapoisett, to Angelina hidden forever one hundred fifty years into the future, even if she would never see her again. [...] Yes, you can have my child, you can keep my child. [...] People of the rainbow with its end fixed in earth, I give her to you!" (150). Like the author in *The*

*Female Man*'s final missive, Connie realizes that she may never be part of utopia herself, nor probably through her biological offspring, but that this better world must nevertheless be given the chance to exist – and that it is her duty on behalf of those oppressed across time to assist in its generation. This realization, then, allows her to finally reclaim her agency and self-control to the extent that she endangers her own life for the cause, poisoning her doctors in an effort to directly alter the "shape of history" and bring about Mattapoisett. "We can imagine all we like," Connie tells a friend in the asylum, "but we got to do something real" (373). In doing so, Connie is thus paradoxically "reborn" herself, as an active agent of change: as Josephine Carubia Glorie writes of Piercy's story in relation to Hannah Arendt's concept of "natality,"[12] "action, according to Arendt, is like a deliberate second birth: it is the free insertion of oneself into the political world through word and deed" (150).

## Conclusion: Utopia Reborn

To conclude, whereas *The Female Man* animates our collective consciousness regarding the possible living, breathing reality of a better future like Whileaway, *Woman on the Edge of Time* emphasizes that such a world as Mattapoisett may only come about if we as embodied agents within the zero world take responsibility in fighting for utopia on behalf of both ourselves and future generations. One urges critical awareness while the other advocates personal, direct action within the resulting struggle for collective freedom; however, both approaches are represented as ultimately vital to the open-ended utopian striving, in itself reminiscent of life itself, that may escape closure on Sargisson's terms. Moreover, both rely on the fundamental continued *reality* of utopia as a living organic system: it

---

12    Glorie describes "natality" here as "the quality of initiative, of beginning once again anew that characterizes the human condition due to the fact of individual, unique human birth" (150).

must be both sustainably self-regulating and a realizable, interlinked possibility within the realm of spacetime in order to inspire change – be it in the J's, Connie, or the reader. Finally, both novels hereby present their utopias as fundamentally enabled by, and generative of, social equality, which is arguably where their true power lies: they provide a promising new approach to dynamic feminist utopianism by demonstrating that a sustainable better world must constantly be re-birthing itself at a point far from equilibrium, thus remaining open to growth and change; this point, in turn, may only be reached as long as all elements of the system are able to participate freely in its genesis. In making this case, Russ's and Piercy's utopias can thus be said to have played a large part in keeping the utopian spirit alive in all its transformative potential, as well as undeniably contributing to a brief but powerful rebirth of the utopian genre itself.

# Bibliography

Annas, Pamela. "New Worlds, New Words: Androgyny in Feminist Science Fiction." *Science-Fiction Studies* 5.2 (July 1978): 143–156.

Bartkowski, Frances. *Feminist Utopias*. Lincoln and London: University of Nebraska Press, 1989.

Cannon, Walter. *The Wisdom of the Body*. New York: Norton, 1963.

Capra, Fritjof. *The Web of Life*. London: Flamingo, 1997.

Cilliers, Paul. *Complexity and Postmodernism*. New York: Routledge, 2000.

Davis, J. C. *Utopia and the Ideal Society: A Study of English Utopian Writing, 1516–1700*. Cambridge: Cambridge University Press, 1981.

Firestone, Shulamith. *The Dialectic of Sex: The Case for Feminist Revolution*. New York: Cape, 1972.

Gerber, Richard. *Utopian Fantasy*. London: Routledge & Kegan Paul, 1955.

Glorie, Josephine Carubia. "Feminist Utopian Fiction and the Possibility of Social Critique." *Political Science Fiction*. Ed. Clyde Wilcox and Donald M. Hassler. Columbia: University of South Carolina Press, 2011. 148–159.

Lefebvre, Henri. "Seen from the Window." *Writings on Cities: Henri Lefebvre*. Trans. and ed. Eleonore Kofman and Elizabeth Lebas. Oxford: Blackwell, 1996. 219–227.

Lewin, Roger. *Complexity: Life at the Edge of Chaos*. Chicago: University of Chicago Press, 2000.

Maturana, Humberto R., and Francisco J. Varela. *Autopoiesis and Cognition: The Realization of the Living*. Dordrecht: D. Reidel, 1980.

McLeod, Mary. "Henri Lefebvre's Critique of Everyday Life: An Introduction." *Architecture of the Everyday*. Ed. Steven Harris and Deborah Berke. New York: Princeton Architectural Press, 1997. 9–29.

Merrifield, Andy. *Henri Lefebvre: A Critical Introduction*. New York: Routledge, 2006.

Moylan, Tom. *Demand the Impossible: Science Fiction and the Utopian Imagination*. Ed. Raffaella Baccolini. Oxford: Peter Lang, 2014.

Piercy, Marge. *Woman on the Edge of Time*. London: Del Rey, 2016 [1976].

Russ, Joanna. "Recent Feminist Utopias." *To Write Like a Woman: Essays in Feminism and Science Fiction*. Bloomington: Indiana University Press, 1995. 133–148.

———. *The Female Man*. London: Women's Press, 1994 [1975].

Sargisson, Lucy. *Contemporary Feminist Utopianism*. London: Routledge, 1996.

Somay, Bülent. "Towards an Open-Ended Utopia." Ed. R[obert] M. P[hilmus]. *Science-Fiction Studies* 11.1 (March 1984): 25–38.

Suvin, Darko. *Metamorphoses of Science Fiction*. New Haven, CT: Yale University Press, 1979.

Toffler, Alvin. "Foreword: Science and Change." *Order Out of Chaos: Man's New Dialogue with Nature*. London: Heinemann, 1984. xi–xxvi.

Wiener, Norbert. *Cybernetics, or, Control and Communication in the Animal and the Machine*. Mansfield Centre, CT: Martino, 2013.

Yaszek, Lisa. "Science Fiction." *The Routledge Companion to Literature and Science*. Ed. Bruce Clarke and Manuela Rossi. New York: Routledge, 2012. 385–395.

MARIA VARSAM

# A Quantum of Hope?

## J.M. Coetzee's (Post)Colonial Dystopia *Life & Times of Michael K*

Having left his native South Africa to take up residence in Australia, J.M. Coetzee expresses through his fictional alter ego, Elizabeth Costello, part of the difficulty of imagining not only a better future for societies in the postcolonial era, but also of narrating one, indeed, creating one in a fictional form: "What is the future after all, but a structure of hopes and expectations? [...] We do not possess a shared story of the future [...] compared with our fiction of the past, our fiction of the future is a sketchy affair, as visions of heaven tend to be. Of heaven and even of hell" (*Elizabeth Costello* 38). Coetzee, however, has not shied away from imagining such fictional futures in several of his novels, and they are neither sketchy nor bloodless.

Indeed, the nightmarish setting of his 1983 Booker Prize winning novel, *Life & Times of Michael K* (hereafter *LTMK*), stands in the pantheon of twentieth-century postcolonial/dystopian fiction not only for its treatment of the genre's conventions expressed in unprecedented formal innovations but also for its engagement with the specific *topos* of South Africa. As a dystopia, *LTMK* forms a companion novel to its predecessor, *Waiting for the Barbarians* (1980), by referencing institutionalized modes of violence and oppression while simultaneously proposing its main protagonist as a model of resistance. Yet, this enigmatic character, Michael K, has baffled critics with his insistence on silence, fasting, idleness, and an unwillingness to conform to the rules of a postcolonial, dystopian society (Chesney 307; Adelman 609; Babcock 893). Others downplay the utopian/dystopian dimension for a more philosophical approach in an attempt to clarify the ethical ramifications of representing society's dispossessed (Monson 97, 102). In the often-quoted review by Nadine Gordimer, who finds the protagonist's ethic of "gardening" an inadequate model of resistance, the question which persists is whether his responses constitute a desirable ideal of ethico-political agency (143). My purpose is to show how reading this novel within the context of dystopian fiction and utopian theory illuminates aspects of the novel which do not suit the conventions of realist aesthetics. Furthermore, I argue that a realistic depiction of oppositional action is neither necessary nor desirable within the context of the given text since "realization or realizability" (Sargisson, *Fool's* 15) is not always among the conventions of fictional utopias/dystopias but rather, belongs to what Lucy Sargisson calls "the myth of utopia," which assumes a vision of utopia as blueprint (*Contemporary* 39). In order to disentangle and illuminate a hereto neglected perspective on Coetzee's poetics, ethics, and aesthetics, I apply Sargisson's theory of "utopian transgression" to a series of tropes, modes, and conventions. More specifically, Sargisson's theory, as developed in *Utopian Bodies and the Politics of Transgression* (2000), will direct attention to aspects of the narrative that otherwise frustrate straightforward interpretation, not least because of the seemingly "idiotic" behavior – from the Greek "idiotes" meaning private, common, or apolitical – of Michael K (Bolin 363), in particular his perceived "idleness" and persistent "reverie" (Adelman 609).

Although the origin of his textual existence was as a "suburban bandit" (Atwell 129), Michael K is not a conventional hero of classical dystopian plots, that is, the protagonist as a traditional hero of resistance, rebellion, and revolt (Barnett 296). But he does, as I will demonstrate, remain a utopian hero, not in the conventional sense as a man of action but as a nonwhite subject, the "obscurest of the obscure" as he is called (*LTMK* 195), who inhabits a postcolonial, post-apocalyptic space/time which necessarily determines his scope for meaningful action but suggests nonetheless, other modes of resistance. Specifically, both as allegory (Chesney 316) and as a model of goodness (Dragunoiu 85), Michael K's actions suggest modes of being that disrupt the hegemonic order and undermine its power over the human and non-human domains in order to experience, at the very least, the "thrill of being free" (Moses 133). The single mention of his identity as "CM" (*LTMK* 96) – colored male – and his lack of surname make him a member of the most dispossessed of society, the subject of Gayatri Chakravorty Spivak's "subaltern" (Boehmer 353–354). A reading, therefore, from the viewpoint of utopian thought and its relationship to postcolonial fiction brings to light aspects of the dystopia and the postcolonial which are mutually elucidating.

Within this broad outline, Coetzee's postcolonial dystopia presents a special case, in that it is written by a descendant of South Africa's Dutch settlers but with a protagonist who is one of the oppressed and marginalized. The shared motif of the landscape as promised land expresses itself generically in the literary genre of the pastoral that the text of *LTMK* also references, specifically the Dutch settlers' *plaasroman*, albeit with self-reflexive ambivalence, within the framework of the poetics of the post-pastoral. Coetzee has written that for the early South African writers, the "retrospective gaze of the pastoral is more reassuring than the prospective gaze of its twin genre the utopia," as their ownership of the land is at best, provisional (*White Writing* 4). From an ecocritical point of view, the conflicting desires of those who claim the land and those who dwell on it converge in so far as the land invokes the desires and hopes of the oppressors as well as the oppressed. Since colonial expansion justified itself through the hierarchical conceptualization of nature as *other* which extended to human *others*, postcolonial texts cannot easily represent nature's needs as above human needs or oppression (DeLoughrey and Handley 21).

Unfortunately, there has been little in the way of dialogue between postcolonial theory and ecocriticism (Lousley 319). What does exist points to a general discord between the two (Vital 91) because of the emphasis on the human in the former, and the non-human in the latter; though what links them is the common evil of the loss of harmonious co-habitation (Stableford 260). *LTMK* proposes another solution, one which attempts to consider the needs of the human and non-human equally. This is reflected in the centrality of the gardening motif which Michael K insists on and turns to repeatedly to justify his choices. Indeed, his attitude toward place is key to establishing a common ground between postcolonial and ecocritical perspectives.

Postcolonial fiction, however, shares many common elements at the level of content with dystopian fiction. In the postcolonial novel, as Elleke Boehmer explains, the cultural critique of empire leads to "experiences of exclusion, denigration, and resistance under systems of colonial control," and these texts are also preoccupied with injustice and inequality and thus seek out a "politics of transformational resistance" (340). As well, they express opposition to colonial oppression which includes responses which are "subtle, sly, oblique, and apparently underhand in their responses," and not only "contestatory" (Boehmer 340). Since the oppositional strategies postcolonial fiction suggests refer to real historical conditions whereas dystopias often offer future alternatives to an imaginary hypothesis as well as extrapolating from real events (e.g., apartheid), *LTMK* is situated at the crossroads of these two genres. Despite the vague coordinates of the novel's space/time parameters, its reference to a historical country with known injustices perpetrated against a minority, native population qualifies it as depicting a "concrete dystopia" (Varsam 209) where fictional storylines extrapolate from real historical events characterized by oppression, domination, and injustice. In his Jerusalem prize acceptance speech, Coetzee describes how distorted relations issue from the conditions of colonialism and apartheid: "The deformed and stunted relations between human beings [...] have their psychic representation in a deformed and stunted inner life. [...] All expressions of that inner life, suffer from the same stuntedness and deformity" (*Doubling* 98). As if to materialize this point, Michael K is born deformed, with a harelip which also constrains his speech and induces racist reactions. The protagonist's main desire, then, is to live outside oppressive structures, outside alienated relationships of inequality, in harmony with himself, others, and nature since, as Coetzee continues "fraternity [...] ineluctably comes in a package with liberty and equality" (*Doubling* 97) – in fact, the very conditions lacking in both the dystopian and the postcolonial narrative context.

This is nowhere more true than in this quasi/post-apocalyptic, postcolonial dystopia, the opposite of what Jacqueline Dutton calls an example of "intercultural imaginaries of the ideal" (224), set in an unknown future time within the special boundaries of the southern Cape of South Africa in the midst of a civil war. Michael K sets off with his mother from their basement flat in the city to travel to the latter's ancestral home, St. Albert, in the Karoo. Her death in the early section of part one provokes in her son a desire to bury her ashes where she once lived as a happy child. This initiates a series of ordeals for a young and innocent Michael K, ostensibly for the purpose of "education" but in fact, seeking to restrict and institutionalize his existence, something which he repeatedly resists at every encounter with his determination to reject the position of slave vis-à-vis any potential master (personal or political) at the level of both discourse and action. The lessons he learns through repeated trial and error conclude with his self-identification as a gardener (Coetzee, *LTMK* 248). Part quest, part coming-of-age, and part traveler to strange lands reminiscent of utopian fiction, the text of *LTMK* poses questions until the very last page, particularly, how to proceed through life (and wartime) with correct action. The hybridity of the thematic conventions parallels a series of transgressions at the stylistic level that jolt readers into a more careful reading experience and asks them to consider whether the text really is "about the failure to imagine a future" which includes liberty, equality, and fraternity (Atwell 106).

Both dystopian fiction and postcolonial writing share a relatively short literary history, having developed primarily in the twentieth century, but they also share overlapping interests in the motif of the "promised land/Arcadia" with its utopian overtones. But while there has been, and still is, an abundance of postcolonial theory and literature produced in the past six decades, there has been little comparatively work produced on what can be called postcolonial utopias or dystopias (Dutton 223). This is despite the fact that literary postcolonial utopias are on the rise in all former colonial nations, just as utopian works written by the original settlers of these lands abound. According to Lyman Tower Sargent, utopias had been initially written by the settlers of these lands but following their overthrow were supplanted with writing by the indigenous populations seeking to establish for themselves a new, self-defined identity. These postcolonial utopias, when written by the indigenous, are often dystopian representations of the past and the future, whereas the settlers and exploiters have presented the same space/time positively (Sargent 213–214). There is, nonetheless,

an overlap in the depiction of nature by settlers and indigenous populations: settlers "produced works that describe the future of the colony in
utopian terms" and the landscape in terms of "earthly paradise and arcadia,"
while indigenous peoples describe an idealized past, "which stresses closeness to nature" (Sargent 213). The relevance of an ecocritical approach is
equally important in *LTMK* since both the utopian notion of "arcadia" and
the colonial *plaasroman* (the farm novel typical of early colonial settlers)
continue to partake in the (imperialist) symbolism/mythology of colonial
and postcolonial fiction. Here, again, Sargisson's work will illuminate how
the post-pastoral conventions used in *LTMK* serve the purpose of blurring generic codes in the interest of invoking new ways of thinking on the
uses of the pastoral in Coetzee's postcolonial – yet heavily influenced by
modernist sensibility (Easton 598) – dystopia.


## Utopian Transgression: Theory, Practice, and Value


Sargisson's work has always insisted on the function of utopia as a process
with transformative potential (*Contemporary*, *Utopian Bodies*, "Strange,"
"Curious," "Green," "Reflections," *Fool's*, "A Democracy"). In particular,
in *Utopian Bodies*, her theory of the utopian transgression of boundaries
has consequences for a wide array of phenomena, including the reading
of utopian texts and the utopian impulse within the text. Her concept is
critical for its ability to delineate and demystify the binary oppositions
which take up residence in literary projections of an idealized land and
how they function to buttress the logic of domination, possession, and
exploitation. Thinking differently necessitates an approach which seeks
"tools that enable a paradigm shift in consciousness" (*Utopian Bodies* 3).
There are three essential components to utopian transgression. First, it
"steps over boundaries that order and separate," such as "boundaries that
establish the norms of social behavior." Second, and as a consequence, "it
renders them meaningless or emphasizes their porosity." And third, it subsequently "permits the creation of a space [...] in which new and different

ways of relating to the world can be practiced" (Sargisson, *Utopian Bodies* 10). One of the most important sites of contestation, then, is the relation between self and other, whether animate or inanimate, since it is here that relations of domination take place. Within the limits of dualistic thought which structures this hierarchy, the "other" than the self is always of less value and thus open to exclusion, oppression, or violence. Whether the other is a woman, the land or nature itself, such binaries facilitate "some fundamental inequalities and exclusions" (*Utopian Bodies* 125–126). In a utopian or dystopian narrative, the perspective is of the estranged "malcontent" who channels the viewpoint of the reader through his/her critical stance on the present "norms, values and structures" ("Curious" 36). This in turn will lead to what Sargisson identifies as the "twin activity of criticism and creativity, that is, the potentially destructive function of criticism leads to the creative function of imagining alternative futures" ("A Democracy" 125).

The literary devices employed in *LTMK* slowly unravel the series of dualisms which buttress this dystopian/postcolonial world but also lead to the gradual unveiling of glimpses of the future outside these harmful modes of thought and action. In *LTMK*, the mother's role seems initially confined to one that sets the plot into motion and renders her son, Michael K, both homeless and jobless. Once her ashes are buried in what Michael K believes to be her childhood homeland, the Karoo, he decides this also will be his new home, a place she was happiest and where he may live off the earth in peace, away from the civil war raging all around him. It is in this physical space that Michael K attempts to carve out a psychic space beyond the constraints of the institutionalized life he has led, first as an abandoned boy with a deformed face in a hospice and later as a gardener for the city council. According to Ralph Pordzik, the protagonist's quest appears to be "an odyssey [...] of hopeful beginnings, failures, and escapes that constantly refuel his quest for another world where he will be able to lie unimpaired by the misconceptions of the society he rejects and in turn rejects him" (70). Yet the narrative throws up a series of obstacles which force Michael K to leave the place where he has created a burrow to sleep in while at the same time shifting the point of view from an omniscient third person to the point of view of a medical officer who becomes interested in his plight and attempts, in vain, to help him and "interpret" his behavior. Michael K's persistent silence and short, enigmatic responses to his would-be benefactors and/or captors function as the main point of interrogation and serve to puncture the text with literal and metaphorical gaps that demand attention to the allusions and symbolisms of the text. For example, when asked about his mother's burial place, Michael K replies that she "makes the plants grow" (Coetzee, *LTMK* 178). He repeatedly refuses to engage even with the discursive terms imposed on him, that is, to acquiesce to the position of slave which would necessarily render him complicit with the system's institutions. When the doctor impatiently attempts to provoke a response by saying "we haven't got all day, there is a war on," Michael K answers "I am not in the war" (*LTMK* 189). To bring the point home, the second section of the novel, narrated by the benevolent medical officer, ends almost unambiguously with an either/or choice of interpretation: "Have I understood you? If I am right, hold up your right hand, if I am wrong, hold up your left!" (*LTMK* 229). Although his attempts to understand Michael K are well-meaning, he too fails to comprehend Michael K's desire to live outside the camp and go hungry rather than to enter into a logic of exchange where food is paid for by the harsh labor of camp life, concluding that perhaps "he only eats the bread of freedom" (*LTMK* 200). He does not know that Michael K's quest includes the desire for "forgotten corners and angles and corridors between the fences, land that belonged to no one yet" (*LTMK* 64). Finally, the doctor's verdict is that Michael K is an "escape artist" (*LTMK* 228), thus failing to comprehend the latter's ultimate desire to return to his vegetable garden: "So what is it, he thought, that binds me to this spot of earth as if to a home I cannot leave?" (*LTMK* 171).

Bill Ashcroft usefully enlists the term *Heimat*, Ernst Bloch's concept for home, because "*Heimat* becomes the utopian form in postcolonial writing that replaces the promise of nation. It may lie in the future but the promise of *Heimat* transforms the present" (5). In literary expressions of postcolonial hope, *Heimat* is conceived of as a disruption of conventional boundaries (6) and "in most postcolonial writing the idea of utopia can be an image of possibility in place [...] the metaphoric site of freedom itself. Postcolonial utopianism is, therefore, grounded in a continual process, a process of emancipation without teleology" (8). In the Karoo of his mother's past and his own personal utopia, or "intopia" as Leah Hadomi describes "the quest for an alternative inner reality" (110), Michael K is able to experience his contentment by "wanting nothing, looking forward to nothing" (Coetzee, *LTMK* 94) and subsisting on very little while subjecting the earth that nourishes him to scarce exploitation. Consequently, Michael K inhabits the burrow he built as the "creation of beauty [...] the beauty of dwelling in a home" (Meljac 73). Even though his choice of home is officially "owned" by a family of white settlers, it has long been abandoned in the aftermath of war, leaving it "available" for cultivation by Michael K, rather than exploitation by its "legal" owners, thus signaling the blurring of hereto rigid demarcations of land.

Furthermore, *LTMK* borrows from the conventions of the *Bildungsroman* where "actions, thoughts and reflections" are equally treated in order to expose a "total personality: physical, emotional, intellectual and moral" in order to "maintain a balance between the social and the personal" and explain their interaction (Gottfried and Miles 122). In keeping with his poetics of subversion, the protagonist does indeed acquire a kind of education, one which, however, leads to his progressive isolation from society (Bolin 357). The reader is periodically informed of the "lessons" he learns. More akin to a protagonist of dystopias, his main desire is to live freely, even at the cost of his well-being, deciding that it is enough to "be out of the camps, out of all the camps at the same time" (Coetzee, *LTMK* 248). Part *Bildungsroman*, part postcolonial dystopia, this hybrid novel represents the "mini" concrete dystopias of encampment which make slaves of unwanted populations and attempt to institutionalize hierarchy, violence, and racism by creating camps for all "categories" of people (*LTMK* 248). As a consequence of his resistance, that is, of his desire to inhabit a spatio/temporal plane outside physical and psychological restrictions, Michael K's near constant fasting constitutes a metonym for his refusal to subject himself to even physical needs, thus transforming the body into a metaphor for the pain endured by the dispossessed and consequently breaking the mind/body barrier where the mind contradicts the body's need for nourishment. When the doctor contemplates that "the body contains no ambivalence. The body [...] wants only to live" (*LTMK* 224) it is because he cannot understand the causes of self-imposed starvation. As Daniele Monticelli argues, Michael K's progressive renunciation of food is "the most radical way of making inoperative the biopolitical mechanisms for the appropriation of life" (630). At the same time, it hints at a pessimism toward the future which suggests a form of "inconsolable mourning" (Durrant 437) as a reaction to his exclusion from the symbolic order which prevents him from attaining true emancipation. Is there nothing, then, that offers a glimmer of hope in Michael K's silences, withdrawals, and obfuscations? Or is the doctor's formulation of Michael K's indeterminacy the final word on "how scandalously, how outrageously a meaning can take up residence in a system without becoming a term in it"? (Coetzee, *LTMK* 228)

## The Post-Pastoral, Arcadia, and Natality

Graham Huggan, unlike most postcolonial critics writing on the environment, asserts that "postcolonial criticism has effectively renewed, rather than belatedly discovered, its commitment to the environment" (702). He points out that "the utopian aspirations of postcolonial criticism might well conflict, rather than coincide, with those of ecocriticism, while the early history of the twenty-first century [...] might well suggest that there is little room left for utopian thoughts" (720). Coetzee has written, nonetheless, a type of postcolonial pastoral novel which defies traditional western notions of property and instead proposes an ideal of dwelling in harmony, without "patriarchal or colonial domination" (Barnard 204) which becomes, instead, a relationship of "filiality" (Monson 94). In fact, Timothy Wright sees two forms of utopia co-existing/clashing in the novel, one as a "political project of the South African state with its pastoral-utopian ideological underpinnings" and the other as "the perpetually shifting and elusive utopia sought by Michael K" (73). A discussion, therefore, of the conventions of the pastoral enlisted, only to be subverted in *LTMK*, helps decode central concerns of the narrative's development and further illuminates Michael K's evolution into maturity.

According to David Atwell, Coetzee "would not allow the novel to end up as a justification of pastoralism" and felt "that he ought to keep K as an indeterminate figure who had no natural or cultural home" (145). However, the pastoral as a genre is traditionally related to most utopian fiction in that the earliest visions of utopia in the West were that of an earthly paradise or Arcadia. Terry Gifford writes that this is important because included in the pastoral are "those utopian Arcadias that project into an idealized future, a restoration of rural values" (20). Furthermore, his argument has relevance for the depiction of the environment in postcolonial literature, including *LTMK*, as he develops a theory of the post-pastoral which includes six features beyond the fundamental trope of "retreat and return" (Gifford 1). These include: first, "the ecofeminist realization that the exploitation of the planet is of the same mindset as the exploitation of women and minorities" (165); second, respect for "the immanence of all things" (152); third, the acceptance of the cycle of creation/destruction in an equal balance of "birth and death [...] rebirth, growth and decay" (153); fourth, the acknowledgment that the inner life of a human being can be "understood in relation to external nature" (156); fifth, the "interdependence of nature and culture" (162); and finally, our responsibility toward nature in our conscious behavior, thus acknowledging that "with consciousness comes conscience" (163). This last criterion, in particular, links to Michael K's ethic of dwelling, one that presupposes that the land belongs to no one and whose significance does not lie in its use value to humans. Thus, he tells the doctor: "What grows is for all of us. We are all the children of the earth" (Coetzee, *LTMK* 190). In realizing his alienation from the land, Michael K chooses to develop a non-alienating relationship through his new-found respect for nature, which expresses itself in his identification with its creatures, animate and inanimate: "He thought of himself as a termite boring its way through a rock" (91); a "lizard under a stone" (159); and "Perhaps I am the stony ground" (65). Thus, the human/ non-human divide is transgressed so that a non-hierarchical relation to the environment may emerge.

Arguably, the most important lesson Michael K learns is to dwell ethically: "The figure of dwelling is crucial as it inflects nature as the troubled ground of work, knowledge, economy and responsibility" (Garrard 134).

This upsets the usual binary between city/dystopia and countryside/utopia and though it may begin as a preoccupation with human relations to nature, it extends to all habitats, thus reversing the hierarchy between city and country but also suggesting real practical consequences. Michael K cannot live in the camps, but the country is also a site of contention, first, because of its previous occupants (the colonizers), second, because of the warring factions (army and rebels), and third, because of the initial hardness of the land itself. Mother earth, in short, is no more hospitable than his neighbors in the city but harboring the potential for new life means it is also a space of rebirth, spiritually, if not physically. For Martin Heidegger, "the real plight of dwelling lies in [...] that mortals ever search anew for the nature of dwelling, that they must ever learn to dwell" (161). But whereas Heidegger links this capacity to build homes where we dwell to our consciousness of mortality, Coetzee's text replaces the teleology of death with the model of natality, which not only pertains to women but to all humanity, and to nature itself, in the shared experience of (re)birth, expressed in the novel in the perennial act of gardening (Coetzee, *LTMK* 249). According to Hannah Arendt, the particularity of humans, of natality, is our ability to reproduce, to begin, to start again, to take action (Hayden 18). As Patrick Hayden explains, "the relationship between natality and action, points, in turn, to the potential for human freedom" (16). As such, it constitutes a prerequisite for the experience of a shared political *praxis* (16).

Natality is also useful in undoing the gender binaries based on rigid dualisms by splitting them into three in the narrative: his mother, beyond childbearing, the young mothers at the camps, and the young women in the city, possibly prostitutes. What binds these three archetypes is natality, not maternity, but this principle includes the masculine, as it is not their prerogative to begin again, to produce life or initiate action, as shown in the many references to pumpkin seeds that Michael K has planted, seeds he plans to nourish and call "his children" (Coetzee, *LTMK* 87). And when he contemplates his maternal genealogy, he identifies with a series of children, not fathers "I come from a line of children without end" (160), thus asserting his commitment to new life and beginnings amid death and destruction.

Derek Wright links the figure of Michael K to the novel's preoccupation with an earth myth: "Michael K is [...] a spirit of ecological endurance,
a Gaian ideograph, it remains to ask wherein lies his relevance, whether to
the contemporary political situation of South Africa or to the ecological
one of the African continent at large" (439). His verdict is that the mytho-
logical use of the earth mother motif is "primarily ecological, not political" and worse, questionable in itself as it proceeds from a white writer
expressing his anxieties about the myths of western industrialized cultures
(440). More positive toward the gardening motif is Erin Mitchell, who
believes that "K becomes his own narrator and thus transforms a binary
opposition between the maternal or 'feminine' and paternal or 'masculine'
into a both/and logic" (87–88). She concludes that the ending of the novel
suggests "that post-apartheid society can be a 'garden' in which the ethic of
mutual care can coexist with subjects' agency over space, time and narrative" (100). More skeptical is Michael Moses who argues that the ultimate
aim of Michael K's solitary life serves "no communal end" (137). In fact, he
concludes that "gardening is neither so innocent nor so free of social and
political consequences as it first appears" (151). But to posit the maternal
earth symbol against the paternal sky is far from what Coetzee's poetics
suggests and far from being apolitical, the text puts forward a much more
radical symbolic. Michael K's status as undecipherable "other" appears irreducible but the "other" is always premised "on a relation" as Derek Attridge
writes, which means there is a shared minimal framework of understanding.
Thus applied to *LTMK*, the figure of Michael *K* is always an "other" that
threatens to turn something unknown into something known (29). When
Michael K decides not to join the rebels (Coetzee, *LTMK* 150), it is because
of his commitment to the seeds he has planted and that need his care, for
he contemplates that if he neglects the earth too long, the umbilical cord
which links human to non-human will be broken and "the earth would
grow hard and forget her children" (*LTMK* 150). His commitment, therefore, is primarily to the needs of the land and not of society but for the
ultimate good of society which by extension reveals his commitment to
the future of humanity as well as the essential interdependence between
humanity and the environment.

In part because Michael K is presented as subjectivity in process, and in part because he is unsophisticated, the dialogues he engages in, whether with representatives of the State (the army, the hospital, the camp doctors, and policemen) or their antipodes (the vagrants in the city, the rebels, and the deserters) resist the position of complicity with the oppressor or identification with the oppressed. The former often implore/demand that he speak, the latter are placated with less, but in both cases Michael K chooses to inhabit a third space and hesitates (the word "baulk" is often repeated) to internalize their interpretation of the world, thus inviting the reader to also question these versions. When he does ponder on their insistence that he tell his "story," he asserts that either he does not have one worth telling or that he cannot narrate one: "I am not clever with words" (*LTMK* 147, 190). This again points to the narrative's resistance of simple either/or solutions and instead raises the issue of storytelling itself and, more specifically, the story of oneself. Is Michael K's story too insignificant to tell – as he insists toward the end, he is merely a gardener – or is he incapable/reluctant to narrate it in discursive norms that have been determined by the dominant, white/western, colonialists who have inhabited his space/home? This transgression of codes, storytelling, and narration is yet another level at which the novel provokes readers into questioning accepted knowledge, even as it writes the story of an individual deemed insignificant within the grand narrative of History.

At its most conceptual, *LTMK* begins with a questioning of space and extends to the notion of time, placing both under scrutiny for their practical and philosophical demarcations in the construction of selfhood. Place becomes re-interpreted as a space of dwelling with respect, that is, as a dynamic relationship rather than a static setting, whereas time becomes re-interpreted as a mode of narration, that is, without causality. When Michael K is happiest, and freest, he loses track of time, he has no interest in segmenting time, even the difference between night and day is overcome. With no interest in "keeping track" of time, and/or no great events to punctuate the passing of time, Michael K, concludes that his story is of no interest to anyone. What overcomes and supplants the heuristic use of categories for each term is in re-instating their intrinsic value, as Michael K recognizes "there is time enough for everything" (Coetzee, *LTMK* 249) and this in one of his final realizations. Not surprisingly, the three most important lessons he learns are linked inextricably together: that he is a gardener, that there is no scarcity to the fruits of the land, and that time itself is in abundance. Once more, the boundaries that bind the physical and conceptual binaries together are transgressed by the inscription of a third term which subverts and overthrows the rigidity and oppressiveness of the original binary, thus producing a sense of self outside the normal conventions/constraints of narration. In other words, as Adriana Cavarero states, "the ontological status of the narratable self becomes distinguished [...] from the text" of the story, "even if it is irremediably mixed up with it" (35).

Furthermore, by blurring the conventional boundaries of other literary traditions – *Bildungsroman*, pastoral, dystopia – in order to foreground and question standard ethico-political norms, Coetzee also upsets readers' expectations of these genres and norms and it is this "genre blurring" which, according to Raffaella Baccolini, constitutes "an oppositional writing practice and an opening for utopian elements in [...] dystopian fiction" (13). In short, both at the level of content and form, *LTMK* opens up a space for questioning accepted beliefs and expectations while simultaneously commenting, self-reflexively and philosophically, on the narrative's "innovations and processes" (Leist and Singer 6–7). At the level of narrative point of view, the three sections suggest three perspectives: the master narrative, the counternarrative, and a third that immediately disturbs the potential binary by presenting yet another perspective. In short, this particular text is especially conducive to an analysis from within the prism of utopian transgression as it already promotes its hybridity at the level of content and form.

## Conclusion: The Re-education of Perception and the Importance of Endings

The application of a utopian transgressive model to this postcolonial dystopian novel has elucidated aspects of Coetzee's aesthetics which usually frustrate readers. In part, this is due to their neglect of the utopian aspect of the text, because of its pessimistic outlook toward successful resistance to oppression. In part, it is due to the many innovations Coetzee employs, often elusive and indirect, in order to draw readers' attention toward a careful reading and necessary re-readings of his text. His subversion of traditional literary boundaries is in itself a utopian transgressive practice, since it resists easy classification and accepted codes and genres and produces a sense of defamiliarization in the reader through Michael K's experience of their oppressive nature and untenable implications. The importance of estrangement has been emphasized as essential in utopian narratives and by extension in *LTMK*, because, as Sargisson writes, "it has potentially liberating, critical and political functions [...] and stems from an epistemological lineage of pain, loss, and exclusion" ("Strange" 416). In seeing things differently, the reader begins thinking differently, and I would add, these two stages are mediated by a middle stage, that of renewed perception (Varsam 206–207). The multiple narrative viewpoints in the novel as well as the perspective of an ignorant/ innocent protagonist assist in this sharpening of the readers' perception toward awareness of oppositional tactics. Without direct reference to utopian textual conventions, Jan Wilm has illustrated how an essential component of Coetzee's poetics nonetheless provokes a key effect of utopian narrative conventions, that is, to defamiliarize readers' expectations by utilizing the formal strategy of slow reading. Slow reading foregrounds the protagonist's sense of alienation and similarly, estrangement is highlighted by textual slowness. The process of the readers' renewed perception is aided by what Wilm points out as the "sense of defamiliarization [...] through [...] formal slowness," which "motivates the reader to assume a similarly estranged and estranging comportment towards the text" (13). Wilm illustrates how the subsequent effect on readers provokes a self-reflective way of reading; in my analysis, this facilitates the process of utopian transgression.

A few critics have remarked on the possible utopian aspect of the text, albeit with ambivalence. Michael Marais concludes that the novel "evokes the utopian in a negative way" because Coetzee "excludes the utopian from the social domain [...] the utopian's only possibility lies in the aesthetic domain" ("From the Standpoint" 239). Derek Wright believes that by the end of the novel, "the epistemologically bleak conclusion has become inescapable" (439). This appears to be the case, as Michael K's dream of returning once more to the countryside seems unlikely, if only due to his emaciated body. Yet a careful reading at the level of linguistics at the end of the novel reveals another dimension. As Wilm points out, Coetzee's novels end by "indicating a soft announcement of hope that mandates further reflection by the reader [...] by situating the possibility for a character's transformation at the latest moment in a narrative," which then invites "further reflection" (184–185).

On the very last page, readers notice a transgression, this time, at the level of grammar. When Michael K returns to his flat in the city, he immediately begins planning his return to the country, realizing his greatest problem will lie in how to acquire water for his vegetable garden. His surprising solution is to imagine lowering a spoon into a well with a string attached. But whereas most of Michael K's thoughts here are expressed using the conditional structure of "would," the very final line does not end in the conditional form but, incorrectly, in the present simple tense, indicating real possibility or perhaps even probability: "and in that way, he *would* say, one *can* live" (Coetzee, *LTMK* 250, my emphasis). This deliberate choice of tense presents another instance of the transgression of boundaries which has persisted at all levels throughout the narrative, and suggests hope in the future, if only at the quantum level, of the seeds he hopes to plant upon his return. Is this final sentence an indication of opened-ended hope in the future or escapist delusion, merely compensatory in its function? As far as the physical state Michael K has reached, readers understand he is near death, yet he has endured everything that has attempted to suppress his freedom, compromise his autonomy, and render him complicit in the war machine. Psychologically, he may be hallucinating the presence of the old man in his city flat – perhaps a metaphor for the past he cannot return to – and this too, may be a consequence of his emaciated body, yet he perseveres in his desire to look toward the future with hope. Rather than reading this passage as the final stage in the countdown to his death, the grammatical form suggests that it is yet another stage in a series of beginnings – the political act of natality – which illustrates the presence of the utopian impulse at work by foregrounding hope.

This final epiphany on his journey of education signals once more, at the textual level, what Coetzee has been suggesting from the start and what Sargisson's utopian transgression confirms throughout, that is, that all physical or conceptual boundaries are constraining and debilitating (*Utopian Bodies* 126). What begins with the dualism of nature/body/matter versus humanity/mind/spirit ends in legitimizing the demarcation and appropriation of the land and facilitating exclusion, in this case of the indigenous "other" by the colonial settler. The end result of the exploitation of property on human relations, as Sargisson concludes, is dehumanizing (*Utopian Bodies* 97). Thus, the first step toward thinking a different and better world/future is to first "stay outside" of these confinements, physically and psychologically. To the degree that this is possible, one may begin to first perceive differently, then to think differently, finally, to act differently. Like a modern-day Sisyphus (Camus 175), Michael K is content with the outcome of his struggle because he has achieved mental and emotional freedom. The cost he has had to bear may be physical depletion, but it is a small price to pay for such freedom and autonomy. Like all dystopian heroes, his desire for freedom is primary and primal and though he, a gardener, may not act as savior for the world he escapes, in the context of the postcolonial society that has oppressed him his pacifism reflects a model of a war-free world. Likewise, the utopian setting of the pastoral "suggests the possibility of a relational mode that is wholly different" from the colonial history that has shaped him (Marais, *Secretary* 37). He may not be a conventional hero, but he is, significantly, in Coetzee's definition of a hero, "a paragon, a model [...] of resistance against [...] accepted ideas of the heroic" (*Doubling* 206). His adherence, furthermore, to an ideal of gardening foregrounds an ideal of prefiguration, the process which brings together the means with the ends, and this may become a global vision, one with far-reaching effects if applied as a universal ideal for non-violent co-habitation with the natural world.

The transgression of traditional binaries takes place, I have argued, at every level in Coetzee's text. It begins with the inter-textual dialogue between the genres of *Bildungsroman*, pastoral, and dystopia; it proceeds to experiment with narrative style in terms of the change in perspective and point of view; it interrogates itself at the level of literary motifs with regards to self/other relations; and it ends in the transgression of grammatical forms, at the very level of the sentence. It suffuses the text at every level to the degree that it seems to be the main purpose of Michael K's – and Coetzee's – story, that is, the importance of subverting existing binary pairs in order to perceive, then think of the world differently. Michael K's education is the reader's re-education, in that it mirrors a journey from alienation to knowledge and wholeness; that is, the reader, too, perceives the world anew, as a child, or a traveler in a strange land. As the personification of the "simple"/innocent man, Michael K is able to perceive, simply because they make no sense to him, beyond the complex, manipulative discourses of the state ideological apparatuses which marginalize, exclude, and oppress him and gradually, while recovering from mourning the loss of his mother, discovers what constitutes a "good life." Whether it is a compensatory dream, wishful escapism or a realistic life plan is not of importance because the text itself has warned against either/or dualist thought throughout. What is of importance is leaving a space open for imagining differently and, consequently, (re)acting differently, thus combining the two functions of criticism and creativity by allowing a space for "imagining alternative futures" as Sargisson proposes ("A Democracy" 125).

As a classic dystopia, it issues warnings, as an atypical dystopia it warns against the dangers of binary thought, and as a postcolonial novel it seeks to give voice to society's most excluded. As a function of utopian desire, it suggests that one requires only a quantum of freedom – conceptual, physical, and ideological – to stand outside these binaries/boundaries in order to see, feel, and think for oneself. As Sargisson writes, transgressive utopianism breaks rules, challenges paradigms, and "creates new conceptual" spaces (*Utopian* 4). The conceptual space Coetzee's *LTMK* opens up addresses a warning to the reader to beware of both literal and conceptual fences. Consequently, like Italo Calvino's *Invisible Cities*, *LTMK* implores the reader to "seek and learn to recognize who and what, in the midst of the inferno, are not inferno, then make them endure, give them space" (Calvino 165). Coetzee's utopian vision is neither a blueprint nor a strategy for action but it is a small step in the direction of change, a step in the direction of a vision of a better way of living, by posing questions that readers must deliberate over in good faith individually. By partaking in Michael K's journey, readers may realize that an individual need not suffer alone, and it is the sharing of this suffering that forms the basis of the relationship between readers and writer. This may confer a metafictional dimension to Aristotle's famous dictum "man is a political animal" (1253a) but it remains true to the original which emphasizes language and emotion in the creation of sociality. This ideal may not be sustainable at the global level, since occupying the position of the subaltern is not in itself revolutionary; but the figure of the gardener sets up the application of prefiguration as a model of agency, and endurance as a practice of resistance is an ideal to aim for that offers a glimmer of hope that, for the future of humanity, all is not lost.

# Bibliography

Aristotle. *Aristotle in 23 Volumes*, vol. 21, Trans. H. Rackham. Cambridge, MA: Harvard University Press; London, William Heinemann. 1944. Online. <http://www.perseus.tufts.edu/hopper/text?doc=Perseus%3Atext%3A1999.0 1.0058%3Abook%3D1%3Asection%3D1253a>. Accessed May 2019.

Adelman, Richard. "Ventriloquism and Idleness in J.M. Coetzee's *Life & Times of Michael K.*" *Textual Practice* 30.4 (2016): 599–619.

Ashcroft, Bill. "Introduction." *Postcolonial Utopianism*. Special Issue of *Spaces of Utopia*. 2nd edn. Ed. Lyman Tower Sargent, Bill Ashcroft, and Corina Kesler. Series II, no. 1 (2012): 1–17. Online. <https://ler.letras.up.pt/uploads/ficheiros/10634.pdf>. Accessed May 2019.

Attridge, Derek. *The Singularity of Literature*. London: Routledge, 2004.

Atwell, David. *J.M. Coetzee and the Life of Writing: Face to Face with Time*. Oxford: Oxford University Press, 2015.

Babcock, David. "Professional Subjectivity and the Attenuation of Character in J. M. Coetzee's *Life & Times of Michael K.*" *PMLA* 127.4 (2012): 890–904.

Baccolini, Raffaella. "Gender and Genre in the Feminist Critical Dystopias of Katherine Burdekin, Margaret Atwood and Octavia Butler." *Future Females, The Next Generation: New Voices and Velocities in Feminist Science Fiction Criticism*. Ed. Marleen S. Barr. Lanham: Rowman and Littlefield, 2000. 13–34.

Barnard, Rita. "J.M. Coetzee's *Disgrace* and the South African Pastoral." *Contemporary Literature* 44.2 (2003): 199–224.

Barnett, Chris. "Constructions of Apartheid in the International Reception of the Novels of J.M. Coetzee." *Journal of Southern African Studies* 25.2 (June 1999): 287–301.

Boehmer, Elleke. "Postcolonialism." *Literary Theory and Criticism: An Oxford Guide.* Ed. Patricia Waugh. Oxford: Oxford University Press, 2006. 340–361.

Bolin, John. "Modernism, Idiocy, and the Work of Culture: J.M. Coetzee's Afterlife of Michael K." *Modernism* 22.2 (2015): 343–364.

Calvino, Italo. *Invisible Cities.* Trans. William Weaver. London: Vintage, 1997 [1974].

Camus, Albert. *The Myth of Sisyphus.* Trans. Justin O'Brian. London: Penguin, 1975 [1942].

Cavarero, Adriana. *Relating Narratives, Storytelling and Selfhood.* Trans. Paul A. Kottman. London: Routledge, 2000.

Chesney, Duncan McColl. "Towards an Ethics of Silence." *Criticism* 49.3 (2007): 307–325.

Coetzee, J.M. *Doubling the Point, Essays and Interviews.* Ed. David Atwell. Cambridge: Harvard University Press, 1992.

——. *Elizabeth Costello.* London: Vintage, 2003.

——. *Life & Times of Michael K.* London: Penguin, 1983.

——. *Waiting for the Barbarians.* London: Vintage, 1980.

——. *White Writing, On the Culture of Letters in South Africa.* New Haven, CT: Yale University Press, 1988.

DeLoughrey, Elizabeth and George B. Handley. "Introduction: Towards an Aesthetics of the Earth." *Postcolonial Ecologies: Literatures of the Environment.* Ed. Elizabeth DeLoughrey and George B. Handley. Oxford: Oxford University Press, 2001. 3–39.

Dragunoiu, Dana. "J.M. Coetzee's *Life & Times of Michael K* and the Thin Theory of Good." *Journal of Commonwealth Literature* 41.1 (2006): 69–92.

Durrant, Samuel. "Bearing Witness to Apartheid: J.M. Coetzee's Inconsolable Works of Mourning." *Contemporary Literature* 40.3 (1999): 430–463.

Dutton, Jacqueline. "'Non-Western' Utopian Traditions." *The Cambridge Companion to Utopian Literature.* Ed. Gregory Claeys. Cambridge: Cambridge University Press, 2010. 238–258.

Easton, T. Kai Norris. "Text and Hinterland: J.M. Coetzee and the South African Novel." *Journal of Southern African Studies* 21.4 (1995): 585–599.

Garrard, Greg. *Ecocriticism: The New Critical Idiom.* London: Routledge, 1991.

Gifford, Terry. *Pastoral.* London: Routledge, 1999.

Gordimer, Nadine. "The Idea of Gardening." *Critical Essays on J.M. Coetzee.* Ed. Sue
    Kossew. New York: G.K. Hall, 1998. 139–144.
Gottfried, Marianne Hirsch and David H. Miles. "Defining Bildungsroman as a
    Genre." *PMLA* 91.1 (1976): 122–123.
Hadomi, Leah. "From Technological Dystopia to Intopia, Brave New World and
    Homo Faber." *Utopian Studies* III. Ed. Michael S. Cummings and Nicholas
    D. Smith. Lanham, MD: University Press of America, 1991. 110–117.
Hayden, Patrick. "Introduction." *Hanna Arendt: Key Concepts.* Ed. Patrick Hayden.
    Durham, NC: Acumen, 2014. 1–19.
Heidegger, Martin. *Poetry, Language, Thought.* Trans. Albert Hofstadter. New York:
    Harper and Row, 1971.
Huggan, Graham. "'Greening' Postcolonialism: Ecocritical Perspectives." *Modern
    Fiction Studies* 50.3 (2004): 702–733.
Leist, Anton and Peter Singer. "Introduction." *J.M. Coetzee and Ethics: Philosophical
    Perspectives on Literature.* Ed. Anton Leist and Peter Singer. New York: Columbia
    University Press, 2010. 1–15.
Lousley, Cheryl. "Home on the Prairie? A Feminist and Postcolonial Reading of
    Sharon Butala, Di Brandt, and Joy Kogowa." *The Isle Reader: Ecocriticism,
    1993–2003.* Ed. Michael P. Branch and Scott Slovic. Athens: Georgia University
    Press, 2003. 318–343.
Marais, Michael. "From the Standpoint of Redemption: Aesthetic Autonomy and
    Social Engagement in J.M. Coetzee's Fiction of the Late Apartheid Period."
    *Journal of Narrative Theory* 38.2 (2008): 229–248.
———. *Secretary of the Invisible: The Idea of Hospitality in the Fiction of J.M. Coetzee.*
    Amsterdam: Brill/Rodopi, 2009.
Meljac, Eric Paul. "The Politics of Dwelling: A Consideration of Heidegger, Kafka,
    and Michael K." *Journal of Modern Literature* 32.1 (2008): 69–76.
Mitchell, Erin. "Towards the Garden of the Mothers: Relocating the Capacity to
    Narrate in J.M. Coetzee's *Life & Times of Michael K.*" *THEORIA* 91 (June
    1998): 87–101.
Monson, Tamlyn. "An Infinite Question: The Paradox of Representation in *Life &
    Times of Michael K.*" *Journal of Commonwealth Literature* 38.3 (2003): 87–106.
Monticelli, Daniele. "From Dissensus to Inoperativity: The Strange Case of J.M.
    Coetzee's Michael K." *English Studies* 97.6 (2016): 618–637.
Moses, Michael Valdez. "Solitary Walkers: Rousseau and Coetzee's *Life & Times of
    Michal K*" *The South Atlantic Quarterly* 93.1 (1994): 131–156.
Pordzik, Ralph. *The Quest for the Postcolonial Utopia, A Comparative Introduction to
    the Utopian Novel in New English Literatures.* London: Peter Lang, 2001.

Sargent, Tower Lyman. "Colonial and Postcolonial Utopias." *The Cambridge Companion to Utopian Literature*. Ed. Gregory Claeys. Cambridge: Cambridge University Press, 2010. 200–222.

Sargisson, Lucy. *Contemporary Feminist Utopianism*. London: Routledge, 1996.

——. "The Curious Relationship between Politics and Utopia." *Utopia Method Vision. The Use Value of Social Dreaming*. Ed. Tom Moylan and Raffaella Baccolini. Oxford: Peter Lang, 2007. 25–46.

——. "A Democracy of All Nature: Taking a Utopian Approach." *POLITICS* 33.2 (2013): 124–134.

——. *Fool's Gold? Utopianism in the Twenty-First Century*. Basingstoke: Palgrave Macmillan, 2012.

——. "Green Utopias of the Self and Other." *The Philosophy of Utopia*. Ed. Barbara Goodwin. London: Routledge, 2007. 140–156.

——. "Reflections: Can Utopianism Exist Without Intent?" *Journal for Cultural Research* 13.1 (2009): 89–94.

——. "Strange Places: Estrangement, Utopianism, and Intentional Communities." *Utopian Studies* 18.3 (2007): 393–424.

——. *Utopian Bodies and the Politics of Transgression*. London: Routledge, 2000.

Stableford, Brian. "Ecology and Dystopia." *The Cambridge Companion to Utopian Literature*. Ed. Gregory Claeys. Cambridge: Cambridge University Press, 2010. 259–281.

Varsam, Maria. "Concrete Dystopia: Slavery and its Others." *Dark Horizons: Science Fiction and the Dystopian Imagination*. Ed. Raffaella Baccolini and Tom Moylan. London: Routledge, 2003. 203–224.

Vital, Anthony. "Toward an African Ecocriticism: Postcolonialism, Ecology and *Life & Times of Michael K*." *Research on African Literatures* 39.1 (2008): 87–104.

Wilm, Jan. *The Slow Philosophy of J.M. Coetzee*. London: Bloomsbury, 2016.

Wright, Derek. "Black Earth, White Myth: Coetzee's *Michael K*." *Modern Fiction Studies* 38.2 (1992): 435–444.

Wright, Timothy. "The Art of Evasion: Writing and the State in J.M. Coetzee's *Life & Times of Michael K*." *Journal of Literary Studies* 28.3 (2012): 55–76.

ALMUDENA MACHADO-JIMÉNEZ

# Bleak Bodies: Genetically Engineered Women in Louise O'Neill's (Anti-)Utopian Patriarchal Satire *Only Ever Yours*

Utopian desire, inherent in human behavior, brings forth many kinds of utopias that can collide or ally to forge alternatives to a grim present. In her latest book *Fool's Gold? Utopianism in the Twenty-First Century* (2012), Lucy Sargisson offers the following examples of utopianism: apocalyptic, escapist, hierarchical, practical, speculative, and prefigurative utopias. Apart from these cases of utopia, I focus on another utopian model which has been persistent throughout history: the patriarchal utopia. Sargisson states at the beginning of her book that "utopianism is everywhere but not everything is utopian," and patriarchal utopias are highly representative examples of such a contradiction (6).

This utopian mode has been present from the beginning of the genre in Thomas More's *Utopia*. It can fit in many of Sargisson's categories: it can be escapist, in its attempt to find a lost paradise where women are never corrupted (in all senses); it can be practical, implementing an ideal conception of woman as reflected in religious or pseudoscientific gender essentialism. Patriarchal utopias can be speculative, inasmuch as they can actually provoke thought by posing alternatives to contemporary society. However, as Chris Ferns points out, "although utopias may sweep away such fundamental existing institutions as private property, money, or the Christian religion, they rely as heavily on the maintenance of patriarchy for their distinctive character as on the abolition or transformation of other aspects of society" (64). In this sense, I will refer to patriarchal utopias as any manifestation of utopian thought, fictional or real, that presents dominance over women, regardless of other possible sets of relations among their inhabitants.[1] Patriarchal utopias are highly hierarchical, at least on one axis, male/female gender, similar to the utopianism that feeds the organization of religious fundamentalism (see Sargisson, *Fool's* 43). Such an unequal arrangement of reality based on dualistic opposition is what makes this utopianism anti-utopian.

Although this social phenomenon does not need to be dystopian per se, it eventually "resists the utopian impulse" – particularly, the impulses which dissent from the masculine heteronormative standards (Sargisson, *Fool's* 22). Moreover, patriarchal utopias coincide with Sargisson's notion of anti-utopianism insofar as they deride female desires as naïve and ideal (and, needless to say, dangerous). This underestimation comes not only from the compliant members of the regime, but can come also from other male dissidents. Examples of such female degradation are the twentieth-century dystopias *Brave New World* by Aldous Huxley, with Lenina's ambivalent feelings being disregarded, and *Nineteen Eighty-Four* by George Orwell, with Julia's revolution being doubted and ridiculed by her comrade Winston Smith – "You're only a rebel from the waist downwards" (Orwell 179). Even though these novels have traditionally been catalogued as dystopias for their depiction of a worse society, they are also patriarchal utopias, given the manifest interdependence and conformity between the system and the male dissenter to control the female body. As long as male privileges are not questioned and patriarchy is left uncontested, the anti-utopian triumph of this social mode of organization is what, paradoxically, lets patriarchy reach a utopian state from a male point of view.

It is at this point that patriarchal utopias differ from Sargisson's interpretation of utopianism in *Utopian Bodies and the Politics of Transgression*, for these utopian conceptualizations are perfection-seeking indeed. However, such a claim does not fall under a simplistic understanding of perfectionism. Quite to the contrary, perfection-seeking in patriarchal utopia becomes a lifelong process imposed upon women to achieve an

---

1    Hartmann identifies patriarchy as a system based on male interdependence and solidarity against women: "Though patriarchy is hierarchical and men of different classes, races, or ethnic groups have different places in patriarchy, they are also united in their shared relationship of dominance over their women; they are dependent on each other to maintain that domination" (219).

unrealistic ideal state of being. Of course, these utopias are full of (un)intended imperfections, but the idea of female perfection-seeking remains constant despite variations. From the figure of the virgin-mother to more contemporary photoshopped models that defy aging and gravity, women have been represented as unrealistic patriarchal conceptions of the ideal woman in order to be socially acceptable. This failed attempt to reach female perfection is what makes women enter in a static cycle of despair that supports male dominance.

The determining factor in the perpetuation of a fool's paradise comes with what Sargisson, in *Fool's Gold*, calls sham utopianism. Particularly, this phenomenon of an enslavement that conspires with the patriarchal regime has a dramatic impact on the female body. Women then feel pressure to become themselves utopian products. In our global competitive market, each woman becomes a passive producer and consumer, as it is patriarchal capitalism that establishes the market conditions, and, in so doing, the female body and desire are commodified. Sarah Sceats broadens the paradox of perfection-seeking in patriarchal utopias in her analysis of female images in the media:

> The implication of such advertising (for its purpose is to foster discontent and a sense of lack) is that our bodies are deficient, requiring the intervention of whatever is being offered [...] We are constantly bombarded with images urging consumption and promising instant gratification [...] We are simultaneously exhorted to be thin and to consume, to be hedonistic and virtuous, to worship the body and punish the body. (6)

When approached from the point of view of patriarchal essentialism, the natural female body presents limitations on its configuration and is exploited as a utopian space without barely any possibility of agency.

But, what happens with female bodies and patriarchal utopias in the twenty-first century? With the coming of the posthuman as a real possibility, there have been many authors who have escaped from the patriarchal mold as the only possible social configuration, and in doing so, they have also explored other bodily configurations as a source of transgressive utopianism. Paramount examples are Joanna Russ's Whileaway, Marge Piercy's Mattapoisett, and Octavia E. Butler's Earthseed. Other authors have opted to fight patriarchal utopia from within: by de(con)structing its foundations with a female rebel who exposes it as a feminist dystopia, as it is the case of Offred in Margaret Atwood's novel *The Handmaid's Tale*; or by appropriating previously oppressive features as empowering tools, such as technoscience (see, e.g., Ellen Ripley in Jean-Pierre Jeunet's film *Alien Resurrection* and, more recently, Imperator Furiosa in George Miller's film *Mad Max: Fury Road*). All these works are clear representations of a militant feminist utopianism that sternly criticizes the monolithic tradition of the anti-utopian patriarchal utopia. Nonconformity emanates from the internal dissident of the story as well as the external dissident – the reader/spectator – who together reveal the system as a feminist dystopia. However, such mutual correspondence is not always evident, which makes the novel's position toward patriarchal utopia more complicated.

This is the case in *Only Ever Yours* (2014), the first novel written by the Irish author Louise O'Neill. This feminist contemporary dystopia obscures the boundaries between what is utopian and what is anti-utopian. The blurring of conceptual opposites does not entail a transgressive action nor enacts a utopian drive, but rather leaves the audience moved and deflated, with an emptiness that invites confessional criticism.

*Only Ever Yours* presents a theocratic patriarchal society in which natural women have ceased to exist, as daughters are unwanted beings because "a female baby was an invader, come to steal her mother's beauty. A female baby was dangerous" (O'Neill, *Only* 49). Hence, society creates gynoids, that is, female androids, for the species' survival – "eves." Traditional sexual intercourse applies only to the conception of sons, as eves are designed and assembled by Genetic Engineers in their laboratories. After this artificial genesis, eves are confined within the School until they reach seventeen when at this stage their future lives will be arranged in a Ceremony. After this event, eves will be assigned a function in society when joining one of the thirds within which they have been trained: they can become companions, who have to "obey their husbands and to bear as many sons as their wombs will hold" (364); concubines, devoted to "the physical gratification of the good men" (365); or chastities, who are actually the leftover eves: "In the uncommon event of an eve failing to prove attractive to the Inheritants, said eve will be inducted into the third of the chastities"

(150). The triquetra symbolizes the three thirds, as "separate entities, but inextricably linked": the ivory triangle represents the companions, the scarlet is for the concubines, and the ebony stands for the chastities (36). The story is narrated through the life of eve #630, freida, in her last year of school. Through her experience, the reader has an overall view of the eves' indoctrination and (re)formation in a posthuman patriarchal utopia that satirizes the Generation Z.

Throughout her narrative, O'Neill exposes the toxicity of romantic love and the trivialization of rape culture in the patriarchal system. Accordingly, she reveals the fatalist perfectionism distinctive of patriarchal utopias: "It has created a situation where we are held up to such a more rigorous standard of moral behaviour than men are, that it is we that are somehow to blame when our bodies have been violated without our consent" (O'Neill, "Why" online). She also exposes the illusion of contemporary sham utopianism compliant with patriarchy, and how viral and devastating the pathological results of nurturing it are, even for feminist thinking. As many feminists, O'Neill has experienced the revelatory need to deconstruct the most ordinary, realizing how rooted this patriarchal perfection-seeking feeling is in every member of the patriarchal utopia: "I called myself a feminist, but in truth, I was buying into the patriarchy. I was internalising all of that misogyny, making it my own, making it my truth, and I didn't even realise it" (O'Neill, "My Journey" online).

The present study ponders O'Neill's destabilizing vision on utopianism in an anti-utopian setting. The appalling demystification of patriarchal utopia as a feminist dystopia is two-fold. On the one hand, freida is a compliant member of the Inheritants' regime – a very obliging one indeed, but she ends up devastated when her uncontrollable love collides with the system's brutality. On the other hand, the mockery of the Generation Z under new estranged parameters and the subjugation of freida and her friend isabel to the patriarchal system shockingly displays a bleak future brought about by the global latent passivity of the new millennium. Particularly, the notion of the posthuman and the cyborg are brought into the discussion as ambivalent ingredients in utopianism – in transgressive feminist utopianism or in the hierarchical patriarchal utopia. As Patricia Melzer argues, "the cyborg [...] can be both a patriarchal fantasy of dominating technologies and a feminist tool of resistance" (25). O'Neill's patriarchal utopia ensures the eradication of the eves' utopian desire from the moment they are designed and assembled. And yet, their posthuman condition is not the conditioning factor that guarantees their subjugation; rather, it is a dormant transgressive quality that never comes to eruption. This way, the (re)formation process of the eves undergoes two phases: a *pre-natal* stage, concerning the criteria of the Genetic Engineers in the conception of gynoids, and a *post-natal* stage, which involves their subsequent indoctrination at the School Centre.

The *pre-natal* stage opens the debate on the figure of gynoids as a positive/negative portrait of women. Donna Haraway states that "a cyborg is a cybernetic organism, a hybrid of machine and organism, a creature of social reality as well as a creature of fiction" (5). If we consider that, paraphrasing Haraway's own words, a social reality is a political construction based on specific lived social relations, then the eves of *Only Ever Yours* are the creatures resulting from a globalized millennial patriarchal utopia. This statement can be validated considering that, according to Melzer, "globalization is driven by technology, and late capitalism is defined by the commodification of biotechnologies such as genetic engineering" (19). The use of genetic engineering in the process of creating eves supposes a tragic, albeit deliberate, flaw, seeing that they are conceived and trained as consumer goods. In spite of this, the damnation of eves in O'Neill's patriarchal (anti)-utopia is not a result of the intervention of biotechnologies on the female body, but rather of the continuance of certain natural female qualities.

As if working for a dolls' catalogue, the Genetic Engineers beget eves following specific beauty samples which will constantly surround the girls during their upbringing as a crucial part of the construction of their identities: "S41 Delicate Iced Chocco Hair. #66 Chindia Yellow eyes. *That's me. That's what people see when they look at me*" (O'Neill, *Only* 13). The novel presents an obvious resemblance between eves and Barbie dolls. The similitude is accentuated when the laboratories in the Underground, where the Genetic Engineers carry out their research, are described: "Lining the other wall is a row of clear boxes, each containing a naked sleeping woman. They are bald too, held in a standing position by white belts secured around their feet, waist and head" (389). Posing obediently in plastic boxes and grasped by plastic wires, these half-formed eves await their moment to become of some use for society, that is, to become sham consumers and sexual objects.

In this creative process, Genetic Engineers play with the posthuman and have at their disposal the chance of materializing the patriarchal utopia's ideal woman because, "since they had the opportunity, it would have been foolish not to make necessary improvements in the new women, the eves" (O'Neill 49). Technological advances in the posthuman make possible what Thomas More once said – "that nature's defect may be redressed by industry" (199), in the form of alternative embodiments. The gynoid has the potential of reconciling women and technology as a form of resistance within and against patriarchy. Haraway suggests how the transition of power in the posthuman era can leave behind the comfort ensured by the old white capitalist patriarchy and with it a sexual hierarchy based on natural determinism. Instead, postmodern society is ruled by the informatics of domination, characterized by the infinite and polymorphous potentialities of genetic engineering. This transformation in the posthuman era also entails a shift from reproduction to replication. Thus, the application of genetic engineering in the creation of eves could result in the end of gender essentialism. Particularly, it could lead to the end of the reproduction of the species and motherhood as a state duty, because such labor is unnecessary thanks to replication. Genetic engineering could actually bring equality between the eves and the men of the regime – the Inheritants – but in fact it only augmented the gender gap in the system.

Posthuman women in this society are trapped in a submissive position regarding the male, despite all improvements: she is more beautiful, but also weaker, duller, and more self-conscious. Like Barbies, these "mechanical dolls" are created to be pleasing to the eye and with limited ability to communicate (O'Neill 46). Moreover, both female simulations are characterized by a dependence on consumerism. Despite this correspondence, one cannot blame the new plastic posthuman eve. Focusing on images from popular culture and, in particular, on the figure of the Barbie doll, Kim Toffoletti claims the transformative and transgressive potential of the dolls' plasticity, because this material is highly malleable and resilient. Rather than being merely a product of patriarchy, the plastic body "serve[s] as a strategy to hack into the phallogocentric codes that structure ideals of femininity, and scramble interpretations of embodiment that reinscribe an unchanging and essentialised myth of woman as tied to nature" (Toffoletti 79).

The replacement of the natural woman by the eves exposes their parallelism with Fenichell's characteristics of plastic: "artificiality, disposability, and synthesis" (qtd. in Toffoletti 69). Curiously, this is a persistent pattern in patriarchal utopias, where female plasticity combines women's capacity for resilience with their disposability by the system and their lack of transcendence of the body. Particularly, the complex identities found in female bodies are reshaped in a single yet contradictory ideal of woman. The posthuman plastic self of *Only Ever Yours* enables the embodiment of such incongruity thanks to the material. Nevertheless, it is the dolls' creative process that leaves them rigid and without any possibility of articulation. Sherryl Vint observes that "what needs to be transcended in a move from humanism to posthumanism is not the human body but instead the narrow vision of humanity that has been characteristic of humanism as a discourse" (137). Hence, the conception of eves as posthuman beings exposes the work of the Genetic Engineers as biased toward a normative version of patriarchal femininity.

A process of intended uglification is carried out in the laboratories: despite eves' original attractive condition, the deliberate remnants of a primitive and dynamic female nature ensure the eternal quest for perfection and eves' constant unhappiness. Such bodily features aim to be selective as it depends on the fashion or necessities of the different Zones of the world (the Euro-Zone, the Chindia-Zone, and the Americas-Zone). Apart from the factors of aging and weight, two salient female features of a pre-existent natural condition and which persist in the creation of eves are "body hair" and "womenstruation." The former differs across the Zones' fashions and is exposed as an inconsistency in the Engineers' initial design: " 'I don't understand why we can't have laser treatment like the eves in the Americas do' 'Or better yet, be designed without body hair at all, like in the Chindia Zone' " (O'Neill, *Only* 20). However, the latter condition is left as an aberrant, albeit necessary, element for the perpetuity of patriarchal utopia, as only by having womenstruation can eves engender sons naturally: "We knew this [womenstruation] was our curse. We knew it had to be hidden"

(196). Paradoxically, Haraway's transition of reproduction into replication is only applied to eves, while reproduction is maintained as a symbol of biological fundamentalism that establishes hierarchical relations of power between men and women, but also between the human and the posthuman. O'Neill's novel evidences Sargisson's idea of patriarchal difference as a deviance from the norm, which "legitimises treatment aimed at inequality" and has a universalizing function. Concurrently, this patriarchal utopia marks another binary opposition between human/posthuman (*Contemporary* 74). So, the condition of eves as posthuman women supposes a double threat which has to be restrained. In the end, it is not nature's or technology's fault that causes gender stratification, but rather a mischievous misuse of power based on the essentialism of the former and the gendering of the latter in order to maintain the privileges of the male. Patriarchal utopia is unveiled as a dystopia, for it is exposed as "a utopia that functions only for a particular segment of society" (Gordin, Tilley, and Prakash 1).

Body imperfections are perceived negatively after a severe conditioning process of shame and disgust. By perceiving womenstruation as impure – "chastity-ruth hung the tainted sheets outside my cubicle for the five days that I bled as a sign that I was unclean" – eves end up abhorring every trace of naturality (O'Neill, *Only* 196). The reason for such contempt relies not in the source *per se*, but in the subsequent sacrifices made in order to overcome them. This supposes an exhausting feeling of self-consciousness due to social pressure, as can be appreciated in the motto "you may be perfectly designed, but there is *always* room for improvement" (38). This eternal quest for female perfection is what characterizes patriarchal utopias, and yet, the reader witnesses how tiring it becomes for eves to become perfect:

> They have told us that in order to succeed we need to be good girls, we need to follow the rules, we need to look pretty and speak nicely and be pleasant. I've tried. I've waxed every last hair on my body. I have taken my pills. I have gone to bed hungry every night since I was four years old. I've done everything they have told me to do and here I am, ten days left, and I don't know if it's enough. (283)

The novel offers a more complex identification of the utopian flaw: eves' utopian desires are not eradicated at their birth. The process is far slower and persistent, as if it were a dripping water torture. During the *post-natal* stage, there exists at the School a wide range of techniques of indoctrination which have as an ultimate goal the submission of eves through paradoxical (de)sexualization, emotional censorship, and sororities without solidarity. Since eves are in a boarding-school, indoctrination can be utilized inside and out of the academic life. Within the school there are a number of subjects that bolster patriarchal domination: PE, unacceptable emotions, organized recreation, calorie calculation, comparison studies, little mama, social graces, and sex-ed (O'Neill, *Only*).[2] These subjects are compulsory to all the eves, regardless the third they will later join. Ironically, eves do not receive any instruction about chastity-life when it is precisely chastities who are in charge of the School's education. But, as has been aforementioned, they "are not wanted like the concubines are. They are not necessary like the companions" (39). O'Neill uses the farcical to display the grim reality in an imperceptible manner. She portrays the fearful consequences of making fun of the trivialities that hide the darkest and most difficult weeds that need to be eradicated from patriarchy.

To understand the paradoxical (de)sexualization I examine Organized Recreation and Sex-Ed.[3] Organized Recreation is aimed at combating "female hysteria syndrome [...] until the urges dissipate" by introducing eves in glass coffins (O'Neill, *Only* 43). Paradoxically, freida affirms that it is in the coffin with the mist choking her that she feels free. Whereas the idea of death as a possible utopian transgression will be readdressed, it is striking how the repression of their sexual arousal – considered to be an infection between eves – is combined with an education based on

2    The hilarious word game reminds us of another peculiar school, that of the Mock Turtle from *Alice's Adventures in Wonderland*: "Reeling and Writhing, of course, to begin with [...] and then the different branches of Arithmetic — Ambition, Distraction, Uglification, and Derision [...] there was Mystery [...] ancient and modern, with Seaography: then Drawling — the Drawling-master was an old conger-eel, that used to come once a week: he taught us Drawling, Stretching, and Fainting in Coils" (76–77).

3    I prefer the term "desexualization" to terms like "asexuality" or "asexualization" as many patriarchal utopias restrain female sexuality while they still consider female sex essential for the continuation of their utopias. Indeed, many patriarchal utopias have a religious influence, and consequently, their female ideal is a virgin-mother – contradictory in her asexuality and unfeasible for female humans.

mainstream pornography. In order to be perfect concubines, eves must be assimilated by an oversexualized culture where their bodies are commodified. For this, they ironically must act sexual, even though they do not know how to: "Make noise. Make sure that you *look like* you're really enjoying it" (216, emphasis added). Another manifest contradiction in eves' sexuality is associated with their education being based on rape culture. eves are taught to always be willing, but at the same time they must maintain their purity until the Ceremony in order to reach the most elevated third, that of the companions. However, freida is bewildered by such ambiguity: "We have never had a class on how to say no to men while simultaneously never saying no to them" (186). In their last year, eves are trained in the final Inheritant Module where the Inheritants begin the courting, that is, hunting. The coercion of eves by men to have sex is so burdensome that eves realize they do not have any other choice in this society: "What difference does it make anyway, freida? It's not like we can say no" (220).

Oversexualization influences not only their physical reality but affects the configuration of their virtual selves on social networks. At the same time, the exposure of their bodies and their overdependence on online opinions affects the eves' perception and configuration of their physical selves. As Haraway says, the posthuman shows a fluctuation being between reality and virtuality that can expand the corporeal limits. With it, communications technologies, together with biotechnologies, are "crucial tools recrafting our bodies," insomuch that they embody new alternative social relations for women (33). In this way, the posthuman fluctuates between reality and virtuality. Nevertheless, even though it could be another transgressive form to overcome the imprisonment of eves, social networks are also dystopified, as the eves' judgments are devoid of self-love and female solidarity. In addition, instead of being used as an extension of the body, the virtual realm functions as a distorted mirror where the real eve is confronted with the virtual eve. Such confrontation results in a feeling of distress due to the impossibility of achieving that perfection of their own virtual selves.

Social networks such as MyFace become a space for eves to exercise their rivalry and contempt for their sisters. Contests like *Your Face or Mine* or *Who Wore It Better* are a continuation of the female failure of solidarity that can be found in the subject of Comparison Studies or the weekly ranking of the School. Eves with a higher position can achieve popularity and have higher chances to be the companion of the most important Inheritant. As if competing for the title of prom queen, eves acquire an egotistic drive that can only be satisfied by the humiliation of their sisters:

> These tasks *are* preparing us for our lives after School, a life in which concubines and companions might share their men but are otherwise eradicated from one another's existence. We may be sisters, but in the future we will not associate with each other. We will not speak to one another. We will be invisible to each other. That is the way it has always been. (O'Neill, *Only* 186–187)

The expected result is what I call sororities without solidarity, or hereafter, patriarchal sororities. The lack of empathy and understanding between eves and their superficial conversations evince the bleakness of this sorority – in the sense of social organization of women – and leave this collective body at the mercy of patriarchy. But still, the sacrifice of the sororal community does not assume individual mindfulness, as eves' narcissistic desires originate from the commodified happiness of sham utopianism.

Under the name of Disneyfication, Darko Suvin explains how the commodification of desire serves as a strategy for capitalist patriarchy's sham utopianism to ensure infantilization, "an infantile 'security blanket'" that impedes any kind of transgressive construction of the self and the community ("Theses" 194). Like Barbies, eves' understanding of the pursuit/purchase of happiness, that is, the accomplishment of their utopian desire, is reduced to the selection of clothes, drugs, and beauty products. eves are besieged with advertisements which stress the need for these goods as if they were miraculous. The ultimate improvement of eves comes with re-design (i.e., plastic surgery), as it not only camouflages eves' changing age and weight but brings about the belief in the genuine possibility of retrieving their unaltered default image. This is the most longed-for commodity, as it grants women the distinctive perfectionism of patriarchal utopias. Infantilization of consumers in this sham utopianism turns literal with anti-age re-designs or, more concretely, with companion vaginal re-design, as any physical trace of maternal experience is regarded as disgraceful.

Plastic surgery holds a transgressive potential because of its possibility of creating multifaceted alterations. Nonetheless, this potential utterly fails, because, by defying aging and weight changes, women embody perfectionism and fixity and conform to the normative standards of patriarchal utopia. eves can undergo anti-age re-designs and evade the passing of time. This action has a utopian drive that can actually be achieved with the posthuman. The anti-utopian patriarchal utopia of the Inheritants sees the danger of the ever-lasting women, as it breaks the rule of plastic disposability. Hence, eves are programmed with a termination date when they become forty, since they are no longer functional for the patriarchal utopia. This form of life expiration is only applied to companions and concubines, as these two thirds are in contact with the Inheritants. The termination date is also commodified, and the impossibility of chastities to reach this good causes them anxiety: "As if anyone would want to become a chastity, faced with a lifetime of caring for newer, more nubile students as you grow old and decrepit, without the *luxury* of a Termination Date appointed to preserve your beauty" (O'Neill, *Only* 51, emphasis added).

Re-designs also stabilize possible weight changes. However, eves are constantly pressured beforehand to abstain from eating the temptations found at the section of the FatGirl Buffet at the Nutrition Centre. Anorexia is praised as a symbol of strength, but it serves as a means of achieving submission. Actually, Sceats argues that anorexia's refusal of food implies a refusal of social connection due to the fact that "food is a weapon and a means of communication in this world. But more than this, forbidden foods themselves become a measure of delight, of transgression" (112). freida's best friend isabel is a habitual consumer of the FatGirl Buffet. She is marginalized and criticized as a weak girl, though this weakness is actually a site of resistance against patriarchal beauty standards. Her fatness becomes an act of rebellion. However, isabel unavoidably yields to authority when she is obliged to undergo a re-design. As one of the eves asserts, "they did it to *control* her. It's so weak" (O'Neill, *Only* 181).

In a posthuman world entirely dominated by patriarchal utopia, suicide proves the only effective act of utopianism, but it never becomes a turning point in the system's stability. isabel's behavior about her external image is a transgressive attempt to defy the system. And yet, her transgression is futile in that isabel is amended to a default form by the Genetic Engineers. Such physical improvement is a gesture of forgiveness from the leaders, but not because of compassion (such flaunting of the laws would not be permitted in any case), but rather, it is the infatuation of the Original Father with isabel that keeps her alive, for she will become the Father's companion. Shortly after she starts her new life, she kills herself. Since they were friends, isabel's suicide means the end of immunity enjoyed by freida, who is accused of being defective and sent to the Underground to go through genetic testing. Together with other lifeless naked bodies, she will be reprogrammed to finally "be of some use" for further research by the Genetic Engineers (389). Together with isabel's suicide, freida's passive, albeit willing, acceptance of her death is the most transgressive act in the novel, accomplishing what Sargisson labels as "ironic utopia" through death. Such contradiction is even more accentuated when analyzing suicide: "the ultimate self-destruction is the subject permitted agency. Only in this act of transgression can one assert one's will" (*Utopian* 141). eves' regained agency through death leaves readers in a quandary: either to live selflessly and devoid of utopian desires or to die trying to reach one's utopian aspirations. These are the only possible alternatives found in *Only Ever Yours*, and both of them promote somehow the anti-utopianism of patriarchal utopia.

Patriarchal utopias offer bleak futures to bleak bodies. Such bleakness can be understood in its most literal sense, as can be inferred from eves' pallid faces and bony structures. Their corporeal inhibition is the result of other simultaneous manifestations of bleakness: their dullness and desolation are the side effects of a body without culture, confidence, self-awareness, and sisterhood. Likewise, the notion of the body presents multiple interpretations: bleakness affects the individual body, the collective body, and the narrative body (see Sargisson, *Contemporary* and *Utopian*). The conditioning of eves' bodies as living corpses enables the creation of patriarchal sororities, where the feeling of female solidarity cannot grow as a result of a noxious competitiveness. O'Neill plays the macabre satirist by burlesquing the Inheritants' phallocentric regime. Tragic death functions as the turning point of the story, where patriarchal utopia turns into feminist dystopia, inasmuch as the textual body of this form of utopianism offers death as the only utopian alternative. Despite all this, the reading and deconstruction of patriarchal utopias and dystopias is very important, because, as Sargisson affirms, "notwithstanding the overwhelming bleakness that pervaded these texts, they almost all contained some glimmer of hope, and *more importantly*, I suggest, they stimulate thought" ("Dystopias" 41). After reading *Only Ever Yours*, the easy-going attitude of the Generation Z crashes into a wall of reality. The impact is so tremendous that it leaves us too damaged to keep on moving. And yet, there is an uneasiness that urges the reader to overcome such paralysis. Women in O'Neill's patriarchal utopia are condemned to a bleak life of commodified happiness, but she invites the reader to defy such conformism. If only we cooperated actively in (de)constructing our contemporary reality differently, this invitation could become a utopian transgression on behalf of those who never learnt to dream.

# Bibliography

Atwood, Margaret. *The Handmaid's Tale*. London: Vintage, 2010 [1985].

Butler, Octavia. *Parable of the Sower*. New York: Seven Stories Press, 2016 [1993].

———. *Parable of the Talents*. New York: Seven Stories Press, 2016 [1998].

Carroll, Lewis. "Alice's Adventures in Wonderland." *Alice in Wonderland. A Norton Critical Edition*. Ed. Donald J. Gray. New York and London: Norton, 1992 [1865]. 1–100.

Ferns, Chris. *Narrating Utopia. Ideology, Gender, Form in Utopian Literature*. Liverpool: Liverpool University Press, 1999.

Gordin, Michael D., Helen Tilley, and Gyan Prakash. "Introduction: Utopia and Dystopia beyond Space and Time." *Utopia/Dystopia: Conditions of Historical Possibility*. Ed. Michael D. Gordin, Helen Tilley, and Gyan Prakash. Princeton: Princeton University Press, 2010. 1–14.

Haraway, Donna J. "The Cyborg Manifesto: Science, Technology, and Socialist-Feminism in the Late Twentieth Century" [1985]. *Manifestly Haraway*. Minneapolis: University of Minnesota Press, 2016. 5–90.

Hartmann, Heidi. "The Unhappy Marriage of Marxism and Feminism: Towards a More Progressive Union." *Feminist Theory Reader: Local and Global Perspectives*. Ed. Carole R. McCann and Seung-Kyung Kim. New York: Routledge, 2017. 214–228.

Huxley, Aldous. *Brave New World*. London: Vintage, 1994 [1931].

Jeunet, Jean-Pierre (Dir.). *Alien Resurrection*. United States: 20th Century Fox, 1997.

Melzer, Patricia. *Alien Constructions. Science Fiction and Feminist Thought*. Austin: University of Texas Press, 2006.

Miller, George (Dir.). *Mad Max: Fury Road*. Australia: Warner Bros, 2015.

More, Thomas. "Letter to William Gonell, the Teacher of More's Children" [1518]. *Thomas More Source Book*. Ed. Gerard B. Wegemer and Stephen W. Smith. Washington, DC: Catholic University of America Press, 2004.

O'Neill, Louise. *Only Ever Yours*. London: Quercus, 2014.

——. "Louise O'Neill: My Journey to Feminism." *The Guardian*, 21 January 2015. <https://www.theguardian.com/childrens-books-site/2015/jan/21/teenager-feminism-louise-o-neill-only-ever-yours>. Accessed 3 April 2020.

——. "Why I Explore Rape Culture in my New Book for Teens." *The Guardian*, 02 September 2015. <https://www.theguardian.com/childrens-books-site/2015/sep/02/rape-culture-teen-book-louise-oneill>. Accessed 3 April 2020.

Orwell, George. *Nineteen Eighty-Four*. London: Penguin Classics, 2000 [1949].

Piercy, Marge. *Woman on the Edge of Time*. New York: Random House, 2016 [1976].

Russ, Joanna. *The Female Man*. London: Orion Publishing Group, 2010 [1975].

Sargisson, Lucy. *Contemporary Feminist Utopianism*. London: Routledge, 1996.

——. "Dystopias Do Matter." *Dystopia(n) Matters. On the Page, on Screen, on Stage*. Ed. Fátima Vieira. Newcastle on Tyne: Cambridge Scholars, 2013. 40–41.

——. *Fool's Gold? Utopianism in the Twenty-First Century*. Basingstoke and New York: Palgrave Macmillan, 2012.

——. *Utopian Bodies and the Politics of Transgression*. London: Routledge, 2002.

Sceats, Sarah. *Food, Consumption and the Body in Contemporary Women's Fiction*. Cambridge: Cambridge University Press, 2000.

Suvin, Darko. "Theses on Dystopia 2001." *Dark Horizons: Science Fiction and the Dystopian Imagination*. Ed. Raffaella Baccolini and Tom Moylan. New York and London: Routledge, 2003. 187–202.

Toffoletti, Kim. *Cyborgs and Barbie Dolls. Feminism, Popular Culture and the Posthuman Body*. London and New York: I. B. Tauris, 2007.

Vint, Sherryl. *Bodies of Tomorrow: Technology, Subjectivity, Science Fiction*. Toronto: University of Toronto Press, 2007.

DUNJA M. MOHR

# Entangled Utopianism in the Anthropocene

## The Dystopian Spirit of the Twenty-First Century

Twenty-first century speculative fiction has taken a prominent and widely visible dystopian turn – dystopia "defines the spirit of our times" (Claeys 498). As Jill Lepore writes in a piece titled "A Golden Age for Dystopian Fiction" in *The New Yorker* in 2017, "[d]ystopias follow utopias the way thunder follows lightning" and relates this upsurge of dystopian fiction to a distinct disappointment with the political promises of the twenty-first century, for example, an open society, individual economical gains, and beneficial technological progress. Reading Barack Obama's 2008 speech in New Hampshire about the utopian impetus of the American creed, "Yes, we can heal this nation. Yes, we can repair this world. Yes, we can," as the "lightning, the flash of hope, the promise of perfectibility" then halted by the new presidency, Lepore relates politics to the reading of dystopian literature, where "polarized politics" are expressed in a "duel of dystopias," "a proxy war of imaginary worlds." When Obama publicly criticized a politics of objectivism, an individualism severed from relationality, his referencing of Ayn Rand's *Atlas Shrugged* (1957) resulted in an upsurge of interest in Rand's book, while Donald Trump's election triggered a renewed interest in George Orwell's *Nineteen Eighty-Four* (1949) and in Margaret Atwood's famous *The Handmaid's Tale* (1985). The latter gained momentum as a prophetical political allegory of twenty-first century American politics with a surprising fan following, including admonitory dress-ups in Handmaiden gowns, popularized by the multi-Emmy and Golden Globe award-winning Hulu TV series adaptation (2017–) of the novel.[1] In fact, inspired in part by "the world we've been living in," as she writes in a Penguin press release, Atwood has announced a sequel called *The Testaments* (2019).

More surprisingly perhaps, young adult (YA) fiction prominently features dystopian series (often turned into successful films), such as Suzanne Collins's *The Hunger Games* trilogy (2008–2010); James Dashner's *Maze Runner* series (2009–2011) and its prequels *The Kill Order* (2012) and *The Fever Code* (2016); Scott Westerfeld's *The Uglies* tetralogy (2005–2007) and its sequel tetralogy just started with *Impostors* (2018); or Lois Lowry's *The Giver Quartet* (1993–2012). In an essay with the rather sermonizing title "Our Young-Adult Dystopia" in the January 2014 edition of *The New York Times Magazine*, Michelle Dean critically comments on the rise of "hastily assembled" YA fiction series – often written by very young authors, cashing in on the success of J.K. Rowling's *Harry Potter* series and Collins's books – referencing Veronica Roth's *Divergent* series (2011–2013) in particular for its flat reworking of *The Hunger Games*, lacking Collins's round, ambivalent characters. While the literary quality might be a matter for critical debate, the topics and the critical impetus many of those YA dystopian novels take find their equivalent in the themes established, award-winning authors employ, for example, in Larissa Lai's *Salt Fish Girl* (2002) or Atwood's *The MaddAddam* trilogy (2003–2013), Kazuo Ishiguro's *Never Let Me Go* (2005), Cormac McCarthy's *The Road* (2006), Dave Egger's *The Circle* (2013), or, most recently, John Lanchester's post-Brexit eco-dystopia *The Wall* (2019). Similarly, in *The Guardian*, Damien Walter argues that "young adult fiction is the most serious literature in contemporary culture" – possibly providing the best guidance for "the dysfunctional reality of adult life" – pushed by "the rise of sci-fi and fantasy in popular culture" as "both employ the same tools of allegory and metaphor."

---

1    In 2017, *The Handmaid's Tale* was on the *Sunday Times* bestseller list for sixteen weeks and, according to the publisher Vintage, saw a 670 percent year-on-year increase in sales.

## Transgressive Utopianism

But is this true? Is the twenty-first century the age of exclusively *dystopian* speculation? Has utopia evaporated, has the "utopian spirit [...] vanished" (xi) as Russel Jacoby gloomily had suggested in his study *The End of Utopia* (1999) at the end of the last millennium? Or has utopia, as Anahid Nersessian recently claimed, not only "always been a dirty word" but has "effectively [become] anathema" (91)? From a classical point of view, generic dystopia, as Gregory Claeys maintains, merely "describes negative pasts and places we reject as deeply inhuman and oppressive, and projects a negative future we do not want but may get anyway" (498). Tracing the genre's historical trajectory, Claeys emphasizes its "paradox of impotence of an apparently omnipotent humanity" that oscillates between "renegerat[ing] humanity" and "revert[ing] to monstrosity" (498) and sketches the genre's prospective twenty-first century move toward narratives of chaos, global climate crisis, species extinction, and the erasure of humankind with the decadent affluent few furiously partying in the face of the approaching apocalypse (cf. 499–501). A bleak outlook indeed. Yet the generic clear-cut taxonomies that Claeys, Lepore, or Dean use have been contested in the past. With the late twentieth century's turn to postmodernism and its rupturing of binaries and boundaries, the speculative genre underwent a process of dissolution and cross-fertilization, culminating in generically fluid speculative fiction – hard to classify as either distinct utopia or distinct dystopia – or science fiction for that matter. Sarah Lefanu was among the first to recognize a "hidden utopian streak" in feminist dystopian novels of the late 1970s, what Lyman Tower Sargent then termed "critical dystopias," following Tom Moylan's terminology of "critical utopias" for those feminist utopian texts that "reject [classical] utopia as a blueprint" of perfection and stasis and instead improvise imperfect dynamic utopias (Lefanu 75; Sargent 7; Moylan, *Demand* 10). Liberated from classical notions of utopia as the unattainable place and societal form safely located in political, philosophical, and literary imagination, critical utopia evidently leans more to the *possible* than the impossible. Contemporary taxonomies then stress the fuzziness and hybridity of the

genres, emphasize interrelations rather than distinct separateness, and essentially underline the ongoing exchange and openness between the utopian and the dystopian genres that Raffaella Baccolini has identified as a
generic "opening for utopian elements," a "utopian horizon," or Moylan
calls "an open form" (Baccolini, "Gender" 13; "Persistence" 518; Moylan,
*Scraps* xiii; see also Baccolini and Moylan 2003).

In addition to the generic crossovers and "the ambiguous, open endings
[that] maintain the impulse *within* the work" as utopian impulses within
contemporary critical dystopia, I have argued that particularly feminist
dystopian texts of the late twentieth century (and cross-gender texts of the
twenty-first century) contain a "utopian subtext [...] interwoven as a *continuous* narrative strand within the dystopian text" (Baccolini, "Persistence"
520; Mohr, *Worlds* 53). Similarly, Atwood, with her term "ustopia," suggests
such an integration of utopian elements into dystopian narratives, "each
contains a latent version of the other" (Atwood, *In Other* 66). Drawing on
Lucy Sargisson's well-known *Contemporary Feminist Utopianism* (1996)[2]
where she explores the radical shift from conventional utopia as the per-
fected ideal to the imperfect, processual utopian spaces open for renegoti-
ation and continuous change in postmodern, feminist, and poststructuralist
theories as well as in (feminist) literary texts, I have termed these dystopian
texts that displace binary thought "transgressive utopian dystopias" (see
Mohr, *Worlds*; "Transgressive").[3] Rejecting a language and thought practice

---

2    Addressing "the question of agency" in *Utopian Bodies and the Politics of
     Transgression* (1999), Sargisson further explores "transgressive utopianism" as a
     political project and an enabling creative practice in a multiplicity of "bodies of
     thought and bodies of people," environmentalism in particular (4, 1). While trans-
     gression must remain an elusive concept to a certain extent, given its rejection of
     the fixed and the static, Sargisson defines transgressive utopianism as "the product
     of an approach to utopian thinking that does not insist upon utopia as blueprint
     [...] of perfection" and the necessity "to break free of mental constraints and think
     differently" (2, 3).
3    The concept of transdifference contains a similar critique of binarisms and also
     practices transgression (cf. Mohr, "Elements"). In contrast to other concepts
     stemming from cultural, political, and postcolonial discourses that describe fluidity
     and dynamic interaction between groups – implying either a permanent cultural
     synthesis (syncretism, transculturalism, creolization, mélange), or a permanent

along the "complex and hierarchical system of binary opposition" failing to value the relationality and multiplicity contained in difference, Sargisson's pioneering work shifts the focus instead on fluidity and relationality and how such a perspective expands the binary of either/or to a plurality of choices (*Contemporary* 4). If we temporarily "transgress the binary position of either/or and say both, neither and more[, ...] thus creating a new space [...] in which something else (the unforeseeable) can be foreseen. Thus we neither (fully) accept nor (fully) reject, and either/or is no longer a meaningful position" (Sargisson, *Contemporary* 95). Transgressive utopianism describes then a constant and imperfect transformative process toward an *evolving* alternative social vision that seeks to move beyond the exclusory choices of binary logic. Twenty-first century critical utopian visions located within dystopian narratives describe then a fragmented fragile processual *becoming* navigating a shifting dystopian-utopian continuum. As much as this creative utopian view has shifted utopian thinking toward ambiguity, openness, and process, it has, however, largely retained an anthropocentric focus.

Evidently, critics have rightly noted a distinct dystopian turn over the past two decades, and it is probably not surprising that we have turned to dystopia, or more generally speaking, to speculative fiction as a means of aesthetically topicalizing our radically changing world. With the twenty-first century's increasing awareness of the fast progressing ecological crisis, the promises of and anxieties about (bio)technological advances, and the growing unease about present and future AI potentialities, not only temporalities but also literature and science increasingly coalesce, as both address similar themes and share concerns.[4] Interestingly, this shift also

---

deconstruction of dualism (hybridity) – transdifference covers a wide range of *temporary* loopholes, where boundaries zigzag and spill in any context or discourse, that *momentarily* dissolve binaries, addressing "a simultaneity of – often conflicting – positions, loyalties, affiliations and participations" (Breinig and Lösch 21). While transgression addresses more the *act* of moving across binaries, transdifference describes the ongoing elusive *process* of temporarily suspended binarisms, of ambivalent or paradoxical phenomena that dislodge but do not permanently deconstruct or harmonize binaries.

4  Noting that "environmental nonfiction draw[s] increasingly on themes and narrative strategies of speculative fiction" while "the Anthropocene itself can usefully

includes a turning away from science fiction and its often technophilic and anthropocentric (if not androcentric) narrations as a generic denominator toward speculative fiction, an "inherently plural category" (Oziewicz),[5] as an umbrella term to comprise utopia, dystopia, sf, cli fi, and the new genre of Anthropocene fiction,[6] possibly indicating a turning away from sf's technological solutions while sharing an interest in science. As "a mode of thought-experimenting" speculative fiction's narrations about the future, whether it be a utopian or dystopian one, involves the narrative strategy of estrangement, the rhetoric of "making strange," to defamiliarize and reimmerse readers in new worlds, mindsets, and relationalities to critically reflect back on their own world (Oziewicz). It is this critical distancing from one's own world and mindset that provides the fissure where change may occur. Speculative fiction's impetus is then perhaps much less a drive to defamiliarize us, but *familiarize* us with new perspectives, similar to Simon Spiegel's claim that "naturalization" is sf's real objective, "sf does not estrange the familiar, but rather makes the strange familiar" (372).[7] Roughly a hundred years ago the Russian formalist Viktor Shklovsky explained in "Art as Technique" (1917) how *ostranenie* (estrangement) disrupts everyday perception, dislocates our pre-existing perception of objects and relations,

be understood as a science fiction trope," Heise, for instance, calls for a more productive dialogue between the entangled stories of species, ecology, and human stories in *Imagining Extinction* (18).

5     Marek Oziewicz's definition of speculative fiction as a Bourdieusian "cultural field" and "a fuzzy set super category that houses all non-mimetic genres" includes such a broad range of genres (slipstream, fantasy, ghost stories, fairy tales, etc.) that indeed it *only* serves as a non-mimetic denominator.

6     In *Anthropocene Fictions*, Adam Trexler argues that cli fi invests in a hypothetical future, while Anthropocene fiction is grounded in factuality, that is, in the "scientific theory" of the "geological process" of the Anthropocene (5). SF's planetary geoengineering tends to perpetuate anthropocentrism, enforcing "planetary adaptation [...] of alien planets for habitation by earthbound life," "modifying a planet's climate, atmosphere, topology, and Ecology" (Pak 1). On the subgenre of environmental sf, see Otto.

7     See Spiegel (cf. 369–374) for a cogent analysis of Shklovsky's *ostranenie* in the light of Bertolt Brecht's V-Effekt and Suvin's inconsistent generic use.

and breathes new life into automatized views and experience of objects and relationalities. Applying Shklovsky's *ostranenie* to genre, Darko Suvin was the first to define sf as the "literature of cognitive estrangement," exploring "a realistic irreality, with humanized nonhumans, this-wordly Other Worlds[, ...] the space of a potent estrangement" (viii) with an "interest in a strange newness, a [scientific] novum" (4). A hundred years onward from Shklovsky, I would argue, the interest in a novum has decidedly shifted from science – although narratives are grounded in scientific facts, for example, the Anthropocene[8] – to relationalities, to a distinctly utopian interest: how could we relate to the world around us that is also part of us and how does it relate to us? Turning the essentially anthropocentric to a postanthropocentric perspective, this involves the uncomfortable, but, from a planetary point of view, essentially utopian question: how will the world look like without us?[9] Writing about a postanthropocentric world thus necessitates a *speculative* dimension, "as it [the world] will be when it has become the past[, ...] imagining this world after humans" (Colebrook 24).

Some dystopian novels and films employ these post-apocalyptic settings, yet not only include a perhaps sometimes overlooked discrete turn toward a critical utopianism that seeks to destabilize a persistent binary thinking continually creating the dystopian present (cum near future) we live in, but a *postanthropocentric critical utopianism* that expands beyond the binary human/animal, culture/nature divide, reflecting the twenty-first century postanthropocentric theoretical shift toward Anthropocene studies, critical animal studies, critical posthumanisms, and new materialisms. The inclusion of such postanthropocentric perspectives opens up new creative spaces for a transgressive critical utopianism rethinking our world in terms of relationalities.

---

8    In 2016 the International Commission on Stratigraphy confirmed the Anthropocene as the new geological time.

9    Weisman's non-fictional *The World Without Us* extrapolates how the planet might survive, where after human extinction "life still goes on" and nature returns to wilderness. albeit loitered with human-made non-biodegradable rubble (214).

## Entangled Utopianism in the Anthropocene

Geology (Anthropocene), biology (microbiome), and physics (diffraction) empirically point toward shared materialities and dynamic
relationalities, and critical theory – for example, Anthropocene studies,
critical posthumanisms, and new materialisms – interrogate humanism's
dominance, puncturing the traditional humanist human vs. nature/
animal/machine/object oppositions. Boundaries, it seems, are far more
permeable and binary thinking becomes obsolete. Clearly, we need
to renegotiate our relationalities to the world in new ways, in a transgressive move that reaches beyond either/or dichotomies, as hard scientific facts and theoretical thinking urge us to do: the recognition of
the Anthropocene as our new geological age accepts that humans have
both changed nature and *become* a geological force; metaorganism and
microbiome research evidences the symbiotic cooperative interaction of
(multi-)organisms as part of the human self, composed of human self and
nonself (cf. Rees, Bosch, and Douglas); matter must be recognized as a
participant "in its intra-active becoming, not a thing but *a doing, a con-
gealing of agency*" (Barad, "Posthumanist" 828; my emphasis). With the
Anthropocene, diffraction, and the metaorganism suggesting dynamic
interactive relationalities between humans and non-humans, inhuman,
and animal others, between humans and machines and other life-forms,
Anthropos no longer maintains a meaningful central organizing position. This is essentially a form of postanthropocentric transgressive utopian thinking that merges futurity with reality which we find reflected in
recent twenty-first century critical theory that dislodges binary thinking,
namely, in Donna Haraway's Chthulucene as a messier term moving away
from the Anthropocene's Anthropos and in Karen Barad's agential new
materialism broadened by N. Katherine Hayles's "planetary cognitive
ecology" and "cognitive nonconscious." Similarly, ustopian texts imagine
multispecies societies, negotiations of more just environmental relations
and forms of existence of non-human, inhuman, and human, or a beneficial future planetary existence sometimes entirely without humans or
populated by posthumans or posthuman-human hybrids.

Known for her advocacy of interconnections, coevolution, and cohabitation, Haraway's recent turn to the Chthulucene, "sympoetic systems," and symbiotic "living across species," addresses the messy entanglement of humans and the "wild category" of "oddkin," requiring "tentacular thinking" (3). Essentially, Haraway locates the human as part of heterogeneous multispecies socialities similar to Ursula Heise's multispecies "environmental world citizenship" (*Sense* 10). As "[o]ntologically heterogeneous partners [...] in relational material-semiotic worlding," she ascertains, we must act out our "response-ability" (Haraway 12–13, 12). In contrast to the Anthropocene's nihilistic future, Haraway maintains, the Chthulucene grinds us in "the thick present," shifting the anthropocentric story to postanthropocentric "multispecies stories and practices of becoming-with," where the "order is reknitted: human beings are with and of the earth, and the biotic and abiotic powers of the earth are the main story" (Haraway 55), what Bruno Latour calls the "Earthbound" network of entangled non-humans and humans in *Facing Gaia*. The Chthulucene thus contains a deeply utopian impulse of transgression, "We are humus, not Homo, not anthropos; we are compost, not posthuman," gesturing toward a different imagining of our future (and present) that begins to tell enabling stories about shared materialities, transgressions of making kin and oddkin, and entanglement of species (Haraway 55).

This acknowledgment of material interdependence reverberates with new materialisms' exploration of fuzzy boundaries, what Barad terms the "connections and responsibilities to one another – that is, entanglements" (*Meeting* xi). Delineated from quantum physics and the dynamic ontological indeterminacy of matter, Barad's "entanglement" of all matter is grounded in a relational ontology of emerging being with indeterminate boundaries that (re)mixes and interacts with other intra-active entities in the process of becoming, formed during momentary ontological "cuts," the acts of observation and measurement. Observed object and observing subject intra-act where matter participates in "the world's becoming," refracting (species) determinant boundaries (Barad, "Posthumanist" 803). In such a logic of porosity, we cannot exist outside of or separate from matter, "we are part of that nature we seek to understand," and enmeshed in a material-discursive entanglement in an intra-active relational quantum reality we cannot step outside of matter (Barad, "Posthumanist" 828).

In *Unthought*, Hayles argues along deeply postanthropocentric and transgressive lines, vigorously emphasizing the shared nonconscious cognitive capacities of humans, animals, plants, and machines, forming a "planetary cognitive ecology" (8). Seeking "to locate the human on a continuum with nonhuman life and material processes," she argues for a "reevaluation of cognition as distinct from consciousness" (65, 19).[10] Her key concept "nonconscious cognition," the titular "unthought," describes "a kind of thinking without thinking [...] a mode of interacting with the world enmeshed in the 'eternal present' that forever eludes the belated grasp of consciousness" but is a pre-requirement for its function (Hayles 1). Ascribing cognition to all life-forms, as artificial intelligence, cognitive biology, and the human microbiome evidence "provides a bridge between human, animal, and technical cognitions [...] locating them on a continuum" (Hayles 67).

What all three approaches offer is a different kind of perceiving reality and a thinking that refuses humanisms bizarre paradigm of either/or and instead invite us to recognize the connectedness of humans with nature, animals, plants, the environment, and technology – our interdependence. All three approaches share a potential to shift the perception of experienced materiality and of lived temporality, what Anticipation Studies call a "thick present" (see Poli, ch. 8), the overlapping of the present with an imagined (ustopian) future shaping the present time and the present and constructing the understanding of the past, while knowledge of the past informs ideas of future possibility. In short, the human experience of temporality virtually conflates past, present, and future. Firmly grounded in the experience of the present time, these theories supplement Sargisson's transgressive utopianism with an impetus of temporality that locates the anticipated changed relationality of the imagined future in the present, the past, and the future. Speculation about the future, dystopian, utopian, or ustopian, is thus grounded in a recognition of the plurality of simultaneous overlapping stories of oddkin, planetary cognitive ecology, and the

10    According to Hayles, the cognitive nonconscious framework could break new ground for new materialisms and rescue their (Deleuzian) concepts from self-enclosure, allowing for a more constructive conversation with other knowledge practices (see ch. 3).

pervasive material-discursive entanglement of materialities in the present. Thus, we can perceive narratives of future ustopian change as located in our contemporaneous experienced (dystopian) realities. Indeed, "[t]he task of the literary dystopia [...] is to warn us against and educate us about real-life dystopias. [...] Here, then, is a genre, and a concept, whose hour has come" (Claeys 501). A meaningful notion of future needs to contain hope, but it is perhaps less helpful to just "pass through the critical dystopias of today to move toward a horizon of hope" (Baccolini, "Persistence" 521), but to turn to explorations of alternative trajectories in the present, emerging new realities, extrapolate from there, narrate different stories that ambivalently are neither about the future nor about the present, neither fully dystopian nor fully utopian, but emergent narratives of entangled transformation and creative adjustments.

## Imaginative Explorations

How do texts narrate such "entangled utopianism," the agency of matter, sympoetic systems, cognitive assemblage, and oddkin? From dystopian settings of multiple crises, of domination, colonization, capitalist exploitation, pollution, species and habitat extinction, social, gender, ethnic, as well as species segregation – extrapolated from our lived already dystopian present – utopian transgressions and connectedness emerge. Margaret Atwood's *MaddAddam* trilogy (2003–2013), for instance, addresses the legacies of the Anthropocene and human (self-)annihilation via a designed biogenetic pandemic to save the depleted and overpopulated earth. Oblivious to Anthropos dwindling into irrelevance, "[n]othing in the material world died when the [human] people did" (*MaddAddam* 33), nature adapts and replenishes, overgrowing the remnants of the human wasteland and its plastic pollution. The utopian element is contained in the re-membering of material and species connectivity. Gradually, a postanthropocentric communal network of species co-evolves, characterized by transgressive multiple origins refuting either/or categorizations.

The bioengineered posthumans are of multiple origins, sharing animal, human, and other spliced transgenes. As an eco-friendly species devoid of grand master narratives, these posthumans practice caring and response-ability toward all other species.[11]

Larissa Lai's *Salt Fish Girl* (2002) similarly foregrounds material and species relationalities. The female characters transgress the human/non-human binaries and leak over material and species boundaries as their wild "messmating" of oddkin, species, and matter, recombine human genes with animals, water, and plants. Messy "putrid origins" and mixed temporalities result in reincarnated selves and multiple lives (253). These posthumans "are the new children" of the earth, "Once we stepped out of mud, now we step out of moist earth, out of DNA both new and old. [...] By our difference we mark how ancient the alphabet of our bodies. By our strangeness we write our bodies into the future" (259). Lai's novel explores relationality through "shared [sensory] experiences" and materialities (4). Olfaction fuses human, animal, plant, and posthuman. "On the day of my conception, there was a [strange] scent in the air," both "familiar" and "illicit," stemming from "wild things," the protagonist Miranda narrates (13, 14). In a sensuous entanglement of wild durian fruit and parents, the postmenopausal mother is impregnated by human and fruit, giving birth to a "reeking bundle" nine months later (15). The novel connects human, plant, and animal materialities, poetically highlighting how the leaves of the durian tree resemble human body parts with the "faint red of their veins as though blood flowed from the trunk"; the durian fruit "nestled in the dark foliage [...] distinctly lizard-like" "as though blood flowed from the inside to the pointed tips" (221). Feeling "the tree pulling" at her, Miranda picks a fruit resembling "a small corpse" with freshly cut "yellow pieces" that resemble "fresh organ

11    While the last book foregrounds these ustopian aspects, *Oryx and Crake* and *The Year of the Flood* are firmly set in a dystopian frame of species divide, class segregation, and an all-encompassing binarism that rips up the environment and social as well as gender relations. I have investigated various aspects of the trilogy elsewhere, see Mohr, "Anthropocene," for a reading of the Anthropocene, things, and what I termed "heterophoric posthumanism"; see Mohr, "When Species," for multispecies justice and entanglement; and Mohr, "Missing Link," for interspeciesism in correlation with multiculturalism and interculturalism in Canadian literature.

meat" (221, 223). Eating becomes a form of self-harm, it seems "cannibal-istic" to devour the fruit, "as though I'd bitten my own tongue" (224).

In Jeff VanderMeer's *Southern Reach* (2014) trilogy, the Chthulucene's infusion of materialities describes a "thick present" of multiple tempor-alities. Although narrated by alternating human focalizers, Area X is the trilogy's real protagonist, a self-sealed off wild territory exceptionally pris-tine and fertile, an area strangely inhabited by an unknown environmental system that disintegrates and transforms any matter coming into contact with its border into a new transgressive form. Here, nature vibrates in a constant state of becoming. It is strangely alive (intra-active), radically inex-plicable, incomprehensible, *intelligent*, and profoundly affecting. It clones, but also mysteriously merges with, those scientists on research expeditions who venture into the system, seeking to understand the iridescent sphere that dissolves the human/non-human gap, "Membranes and dimensions. Limitless amounts of space. Limitless amounts of energy. Effortless manipu-lation of molecules. Continual attempts to transform the human into the non-human" (*Acceptance* 491), infiltrating plants and animals with human cells, retaining human memory in living plants arranged in hallucinatory literal writing on the wall. As an ecological allegory of anthropocentric interference and (self-)annihilation, Area X effectively suffuses a potentially paradisiacal landscape with (body) horror as it remixes all life-forms' DNAs, molecules, and materialities. It is both a simulation of a pastoral idyll and a horrific site of extinction with only architectural monuments commem-orating former human existence. Poetically conveying the eerie fascination with both the beauty and the horror of a morphing metaorganism's own reality, indifferent to humans, and beyond our comprehension, Area X is a posthuman landscape beyond postanthropocentrism and a poetic image for nature's fight for survival, herbaforming *us*. Area X is a transgressive utopian world without us, where planetary cognitive ecology intra-acts as an un/natural transformative metaorganism and can only be understood in a mode of "nonconscious cognition" or "unthinking." The trilogy often verges on the experimental, with poetic passages of a dreamlike uncertainty suggesting messy material entanglements beyond established conceptual categories and diluting the boundaries between human and non-human/inhuman, the inside and the outside, and self and other. It intertwines border breaching, interpenetration, infection, webbed hybridizations, oddkin remix, and entanglements.

Infected by Area X, the ecosystems biologist describes how her senses and reflexes adapt and intensify, her skin becomes phosphorescent, leaving her with an awareness of Area X's "brightness," a feeling of kinship (*Annihilation* 55). Transformed into a post-inhuman entanglement, a "vast bulk" of "emerald luminescence" expanding "[i]n all her glory and monstrosity" (*Acceptance* 492, 493, 492), she retains a nonconscious cognition, sensing her environment that is herself, "the brightness washed over me in unending waves, and connected me to the earth, the water, the trees, and the air, as I opened up and kept on opening" (*Annihilation* 106), which is, of course, a conscious description of a sensed nonconscious cognition. Transmorphed into a "mountain that *was* the biologist" (*Acceptance* 493; my emphasis) with "many, many glowing eyes that were also like flowers or sea anemones spread open [...] all across its body. [...] Her eyes. [...] As it smashed into the lower floor, seeking something. As it sang and moaned and hollered" (*Acceptance* 494), the biologist comes with a "seeking" and "questing," a "communication or communion" (*Acceptance* 493), metaphorically signifying nature's desperate attempts to communicate with humanity through its sheer force (avalanches, climate change, rising sea levels, etc.). Mutated into a "multiplicity," the mountain fuses with others in moments of "unthought," "there was connection, there was *recognition*," and shares her mountainous perspective of "now exist[ing] across locations and landscapes" (*Acceptance* 494). As the boundaries dissolve, the human contacted feels "[s]omething like an eclipse in his head, a thick, tactile eclipse, pushing out his own intent. Questing through his mind" (*Acceptance* 502). Ultimately, Area X remains radically impenetrable from an anthropocentric perspective. Impaired by "a lack of imagination, because human beings couldn't even put themselves in the mind of a cormorant or an owl or a whale or a bumblebee" (*Acceptance* 490), those protagonists who do not willingly enter the cycle of annihilation, sensing Area X's authority, and then accepting it, are incapable of deciphering a world independent of humans for a lack of reference points, ignoring the vibrant communication all around them, "What if an infection was a message, a brightness a kind of symphony? As a defense? An odd form of communication" (*Acceptance* 490).

All three novels end ambiguously, leaving tentacular ends, a multiplicity of versions, or thick presents that stress the transgressive utopian impetus. In the final part of Atwood's *MaddAddam* trilogy humans have receded and with the advent of a new generation of interspecies post/humans transgression is literally embodied, "we [...] are all people [...] though we have different gifts" (*MaddAddam* 386). Lai's *Salt Fish Girl* also ends with fusion, where humans temporarily become fish and, as the lovers "coils interlocked and slid through one another," one of them gives birth "from an opening in my scaly new flesh" to a human baby girl (269). The *Southern Reach* trilogy opaquely references our dystopian Anthropocene present, or the novel's present world, or Area X's Chthulucene webbing, "[t]he world we are part of now is difficult to accept. [...] But acceptance moves past denial, and maybe there is defiance in that too" (*Acceptance* 593). Moving past denial means investing in "critical hope" (Ojala 78), a hope that is enabling through the acceptance of crisis and coping through cognitive restructuring. These utopian stories invite us to question separateness, rigid categorizations, and fixed solutions, instead reading about enmeshed inter-acting, fused existences, and widened kinship increases our awareness about the rich abundances of entanglements and collisions of the present temporality. Such stories dissolve antagonisms and indeed familiarize us with the strange. Our minds can hold both, "the beautiful awful brightness of the world. Before you are nowhere. Before you are everywhere" (*Acceptance* 592). Transgressive entangled utopianism in the Anthropocene gives us critical hope to cope with the complexities of our dystopian realities and world them into livable future utopian ones.

# Bibliography

Atwood, Margaret. *In Other Worlds: SF and the Human Imagination*. Toronto, ON: McClelland & Stewart, 2011.

———. *MaddAddam*. London: Bloomsbury, 2013.

Baccolini, Raffaella. "Gender and Genre in the Feminist Critical Dystopias of Katherine Burdekin, Margaret Atwood, and Octavia Butler." *Future Females, the Next Generation: New Voices and Velocities in Feminist Science Fiction*. Ed. Marleen S. Barr. Boston, MA: Rowman and Littlefield, 2000. 13–34.

———. "The Persistence of Hope in Dystopian Science Fiction." *PMLA* 119.3 (2004): 518–521.

Baccolini, Raffaella, and Tom Moylan, eds. *Dark Horizons: Science Fiction and the Dystopian Imagination*. New York: Routledge, 2003.

Barad, Karen. *Meeting the Universe Halfway: Quantum Physics and the Entanglement of Matter and Meaning*. Durham, NC: Duke University Press, 2007.

———. "Posthumanist Performativity: Towards an Understanding of How Matter Comes to Matter." *Signs: Journal of Women in Culture and Society* 28.3 (2003): 801–831.

Breinig, Helmbrecht and Klaus Lösch. "Introduction: Difference and Transdifference." *Multiculturalism in Contemporary Societies: Perspectives on Difference and Transdifference*. Ed. Helmbrecht Breinig, Jürgen Gebhardt, and Klaus Lösch. Erlangen: Universitätsbund Erlangen-Nürnberg, 2002. 11–36.

Claeys, Gregory. *Dystopia: A Natural History*. Oxford: Oxford University Press, 2016.

Colebrook, Claire. *Death of the PostHuman: Essays on Extinction*. Vol. 1. Michigan: Open Humanities Press, 2014. Online. <http://dx.doi.org/10.3998/ohp.12329362.0001.001>. Accessed 10 January 2019.

Dean, Michelle. "Our Young-Adult Dystopia." *The New York Times Magazine*, 31 January 2014. Online. <https://www.nytimes.com/2014/02/02/magazine/our-young-adult-dystopia.html>. Accessed 15 December 2018.

Haraway, Donna. *Staying with the Trouble: Making Kin in the Chthulucene*. Durham, NC: Duke University Press, 2016.

Hayles, N. Katherine. *Unthought: The Power of the Cognitive Nonconscious*. Chicago: University of Chicago Press, 2017.

Heise, Ursula K. *Imagining Extinction: The Cultural Meanings of Endangered Species*. Chicago: University of Chicago Press, 2016.

———. *Sense of Place and Sense of Planet: The Environmental Imagination of the Global*. New York: Oxford University Press, 2008.

Jacoby, Russell. *The End of Utopia: Politics and Culture in an Age of Apathy*. New York: Basic, 1999.

Latour, Bruno. *Facing Gaia: Eight Lectures on the New Climatic Regime*. Cambridge: Polity, 2017.

Lefanu, Sarah. *Feminism and Science Fiction*. Bloomington: Indiana University Press, 1989.

Lepore, Jill. "A Golden Age for Dystopian Fiction." *The New Yorker*, 29 May 2017. Online. <https://www.newyorker.com/magazine/2017/06/05/a-golden-age-for-dystopian-fiction>. Accessed 15 December 2018.

Mohr, Dunja M. "Anthropocene Fiction: Narrating the 'Zero Hour' in Margaret Atwood's *MaddAddam* Trilogy." *Écrire au-delà de la fin des temps? Les littératures au Canada et au Québec. Writing Beyond the End Times? The Literatures of Canada and Quebec.* Ed. Ursula Mathis-Moser and Marie Carrière. Innsbruck: University of Innsbruck Press, 2017. 23–43.

——. "Elements of Transdifference in Canadian Women Writers' Fiction." *Zeitschrift für Kanada-Studien* 24.2 (2004): 49–61.

——. "The Missing Link: Bridging the Species Divide in Margaret Atwood's *MaddAddam* Trilogy." *Canadian Science Fiction, Fantasy, and Horror: Bridging the Solitudes.* Ed. Amy J. Ransom and Dominick Grace. Basingstoke: Palgrave Macmillan, 2019. 239–256.

——. "Transgressive Utopian Dystopias: The Postmodern Reappearance of Utopia in the Disguise of Dystopia." *Zeitschrift für Anglistik und Amerikanistik* 55.1 (2007): 5–24.

——. "'When Species Meet': Beyond Posthuman Boundaries and Interspeciesism – Social Justice and Canadian Speculative Fiction." *Zeitschrift für Kanada-Studien* 37 (2017): 40–64.

——. *Worlds Apart? Dualism and Transgression in Contemporary Female Dystopias.* Jefferson, NC: McFarland, 2005.

Moylan, Tom. *Demand the Impossible: Science Fiction and the Utopian Imagination.* New York: Methuen, 1986.

——. *Scraps of the Untainted Sky: Science Fiction, Utopia, Dystopia.* Boulder, CO: Westview, 2000.

Nersessian, Anahid. "Utopia's Afterlife in the Anthropocene." *The Routledge Companion to the Environmental Humanities.* Ed. Ursula K. Heise, Jon Christensen, and Michelle Niemann. New York: Routledge, 2017. 91–100.

Ojala, Maria. "Hope and Anticipation in Education for a Sustainable Future." *Futures* 94 (2016): 76–84.

Otto, Eric C. *Green Speculations: Science Fiction and Transformative Environmentalism.* Columbus: Ohio State University Press, 2012.

Oziewicz, Marek. "Speculative Fiction." *Oxford Research Encyclopedia of Literature*, 2016. DOI: 10.1093/acrefore/9780190201098.013.78. Accessed 10 January 2019.

Pak, Chris. *Terraforming: Ecopolitical Transformations and Environmentalism in Science fiction.* Liverpool: Liverpool University Press, 2016.

Poli, Roberto. *Introduction to Anticipation Studies.* New York: Springer, 2017.

Rees, Tobias; Bosch, Thomas, and Angela E. Douglas. "How the microbiome challenges our concept of self." *PLOS Biology* 2018. Online. <https://journals.

plos.org/plosbiology/article?id=10.1371/journal.pbio.2005358>. Accessed 10 January 2019.

Sargent, Lyman Tower. "The Three Faces of Utopianism Revisited." *Utopian Studies* 5.1 (1994): 1–38.

Sargisson, Lucy. *Contemporary Feminist Utopianism*. London: Routledge, 1996.

——. *Utopian Bodies and the Politics of Transgression*. London: Routledge, 1999.

Shklovsky, Viktor. "Art as Technique" (1917). *Russian Formalist Criticism: Four Essays*. Ed. Lee T. Lemon and Marion J. Reis. Lincoln: University of Nebraska Press, 1965. 3–24.

Spiegel, Simon. "Things Made Strange: On the Concept of 'Estrangement' in Science Fiction Theory." *Science Fiction Studies* 35.3 (2008): 369–385.

Suvin, Darko. *Metamorphoses of Science Fiction: On the Poetics and History of a Literary Genre*. New Haven, CT: Yale University Press, 1979.

Trexler, Adam. *Anthropocene Fictions: The Novel in a Time of Climate Change*. Charlottesville: University of Virginia Press, 2015.

VanderMeer, Jeff. *Acceptance*. New York: Farrar, Straus and Giroux, 2014.

——. *Annihilation*. New York: Farrar, Straus and Giroux, 2014.

——. *Authority*. New York: Farrar, Straus and Giroux, 2014.

Walter, Damien. "Young adult fiction is loved because it speaks to us all – unlike adult stories." *The Guardian*, 19 September 2014. Online. <https://www.theguardian.com/books/booksblog/2014/sep/19/young-adult-fiction-speaks-to-all>. Accessed 15 December 2018.

Weisman, Alan. *The World Without Us*. New York: Thomas Dunne, 2007.

JOSÉ EDUARDO REIS

# Literary Utopianism and Ecological Literacy

In *Ecological Literacy*, David W. Orr, following a critical essay on the model of liberal education proposed by Allan Bloom, presents a list of books and articles he considers essential for establishing an interdisciplinary model for ecological education. Without denying the contribution of the western literary tradition for a plan of higher education suitable to build a project for a globally sustainable society, Orr highlights the bibliographical contribution made by what he calls the "utopian tradition" (124). This tradition is related to the ideal of living within a harmonious, integrated society, the world of nature, or, in less ambiguous terms, the principles of ecosystem organization. What could be called "ecological utopianism" is embedded within the complex, tense, continuous, and discrete tradition of western ideal thinking, which is, in turn, inseparable from the intellectual and ideological history of its civilizing process.

Its literary sources are to be found in such fundamental texts as the biblical *Genesis*, the *Epic of Gilgamesh*, and Homer's *Odyssey*. Rather than present here a genealogy of the ecological strand within literary or philosophical utopianism, whose imaginary or conceptual representations can sometimes be seen extending into the social sphere or in the form of community experiment, it is important to begin by highlighting both the contributions and, indeed, some of the tensions in the thematic content of these two texts, so as to throw some light on this ecological-utopian tradition.[1] In

1   Community examples are, among others: Francis Bacon's 1627 scientific utopia, *New Atlantis*, which inspired the foundation of scientific academies in Western Europe, beginning with the British Royal Society in London; James Harrington's 1656 political treatise, written in the form of a utopian novel, *The Commonwealth of Oceana*, which contains a political draft constitution subsequently adopted as a model by the constitutions of the independent states of Massachusetts, New Jersey, North Carolina, and Pennsylvania; the psychologist B.F. Skinner's 1948 utopian

the course of this chapter, and in support of its argument, relevant passages of other canonical texts – More's *Utopia*, Bacon's *New Atlantis*, Morris's *News from Nowhere*, and Huxley's *Island* – will be critically analyzed as well.

Thus, if we consider the cosmogonic narrative found in the Bible, we see that the two versions narrating the process of God's creation of "heaven" and "earth," corresponding to the first two chapters of the book of *Genesis*, which seek to reflect the perfection and harmony of the created world, describe events differently. The first chapter outlining the sequence of creation follows somewhat of an evolutionary logic, that is, plants, animals, and human beings (male and female). The second chapter reiterates the account of the act of *Genesis* but follows a heteroclite irregular order of events governed by the hierarchical importance given to the male anthropocentrism, that is, man, plants, animals, and woman. This iterative and disparate narrative recounting of the alpha moment of the universe is due to editorial criteria and results from the likely juxtaposition of different documentary sources, written at different times, together constituting the first five books of the Bible. According to the aptly named Documentary or Graf-Wellhausen hypothesis, formulated in the nineteenth century by the German Orientalists Heinrich Graf and Julius Wellhausen, who sought to elucidate criteria based on a theory of textual ordering, what these two versions of the creation story share is that they reveal a harmonious original state of life wherein the human creature is represented both as bringing an end to the phased process of creation and as the primal being from whose centrality God conceives the design of the entire natural world.[2] It is in this chapter that the description of the earthly paradise appears, the place conceived to welcome and secure Adam, the man formed "out of the dust

---

novel *Walden Two*, which inspired American intentional communities such as *Twin Oaks* in Virginia.

2    In accordance with this hypothesis, chapter 1 of *Genesis* contains the P version (abbreviation for its authors, priests, and clerics) from the Torah/Pentateuch, roughly dating from the fifth century BC, and written subsequently to chapter 2, which is the J version (J being the abbreviation of the German pronunciation of the first letter of YHVH, translated in English as Lord), the original text from the tenth century BC.

from the ground," and to provide a nurturing environment to assist the primordial being in all his needs and functions (Gen. 2.7).

In both of the discrete versions of this myth, the prevailing representation is one of complete benignity regarding the original conditions of human life, but comparison of the two reveals a productive tension concerning humanity's ontological status. While the first narrative points to man's position of supremacy in the whole of nature's creative symphony of invention, the second narrative makes him an absolute protagonist/soloist, separate from the orchestration of other forms of nature. The P version of *Genesis* is not only more intuitively logical than the J version in the evolutionary description of the process leading to the emergence of intelligent life, but also, when it comes to describing the creation of human beings, conveys a lesson in the ontological balance and complementarity between their male and female qualities. Created in the image and likeness of God, this androgynous human appointed to have dominion over nature, and, in a way, this is because s/he is the co-participant in and co-beneficiary of the integration and sublimation of other living beings – among all the elements that support his/her life – into a single homeostatic ontological constitution. "So God created [...] male and female. God blessed them, and God said to them, [...] 'Rule the fish of the sea, the birds of the sky and every creature that crawls on the earth'" (Gen. 1. 27–28). Yet the paradise described in the J version reflects a notion of general integration of nature subordinated to the vital hegemony of the human male: "The Lord God formed out of the ground every wild animal and every bird of the sky, and brought each to the man to see what he would call it. And whatever the man called a living creature, that was its name" (Gen. 2–19). Although predominantly anthropocentric in conception and counter to holistic views of nature, both versions of biblical cosmogony present the idea of a naturally perfect condition. In particular, the version describing the earthly paradise is established, within the context of western culture, as one of the most ancient literary testimonies of an idealizing representation of the general conditions of life. Therefore, notwithstanding the ontological hierarchy attending its design, it nonetheless conveys the image of a harmonious and balanced ecological whole.

There is an even more ancient text than the Hebrew *Genesis*, the Sumerian *Epic of Gilgamesh* (third millennium B C). What is of interest here is to examine it as an ancient witness to the human aspiration to preserve its unalienated position within the general structure of nature. Though it does not display an explicit affinity with utopianism, this epic does, none-theless, outline some of its recurrent or subsidiary motifs, such as the de-sirable good government of the city of Uruk, presided over by Gilgamesh, "the shepherd of the city, wise, comely, and resolute" (4), albeit in such a way as to require restraint; the fraternity of human relationships (rep-resented by the friendship between Gilgamesh and Enkidu); the journey in search of the island where a wise policy is preserved, or an inaccess-ible commodity, the land of Dilmun, the dwelling place of "Utnapishtim whom they call the Faraway, for he has entered the assembly of the gods" (16). Although a superficial reading of this narrative symbolically assigns the antithesis culture/nature to the characters of Gilgamesh and Enkidu, a closer analysis reveals that this duality is not narratively represented in a sealed and irreducible way. The course of Enkidu's acculturation begins with the overcoming of the solipsistic nature of his savage state by means of sexual union with a prostitute-instigator and concludes with defeat in the fight he engages in with Gilgamesh. The complementary reverse side of this process is the moderation of the autocratic excesses of Gilgamesh by integrating the benign qualities of nature given through the friendship that he shares with Enkidu: "So Enkidu and Gilgamesh embraced and their friendship was sealed" (6). We can discern in this bond a principle of mutual cooperation between irreducible phenomena; a kind of ideal harmonization or utopian synthesis between the civilizing process and the organizing principles of natural ecosystems; and an overcoming of the an-tagonism between civilized and pre-civilized man, between the ideal city and the Edenic primitive space.

In this most ancient work in the western literary canon, the human non-human tension has plainly been blurred. It prefigures the (re)valu-ation of the instructive qualities of nature, the mastery of its language, achieved in another literary classic, the *Odyssey*, where the clash between the human and the non-human is no longer a wild spontaneous manifest-ation, but is embodied in its cultivated, humanized mode. In the *Odyssey*, there also appear descriptions of utopian places (the island of Ogygia, the land of the Phaeacians) and narratives recounting situations of consummate human happiness (Odysseus's return to Ithaca and the passionate reunion with Penelope), but almost at its climax, in the final canto (XXIV), something happens that helps us, readers living in the twenty-first century, to relearn from Homer the instructive value of cultivated nature as a plainly idealized space of civic education, and to prepare ourselves for initiation into ecological literacy. Odysseus finds his father Laertes "alone on the vineyard terrace hoeing round a tree" (Homer 225) and does not disclose himself at once. After witnessing his father's distress at not knowing of his whereabouts, Odysseus reveals his identity to Laertes through signs that show that he is his son. The most decisive of these signs is when he recalls a moment they once experienced together. Odysseus says to Laertes: "I can tell you all the trees you gave me one day on this terraced garden. I was only a little boy at the time, trotting after you through the orchard, asking about this and that, and as we wound our way through these very trees you told me all their names. You gave me thirteen pear-trees, ten apple-trees, and forty fig-trees" (227).

Rather than a fleeting instant of complicity between father and son, Odysseus's evocation of that past moment marks his recognition that the essential lesson of life that he gleaned from the fruits of the earth and his father's knowledge of farming – knowledge that had guided him in the command of his companions at sea and had helped him return to Ithaca – was that introduction to arboreal nomenclature, to the characteristics of the biodiversity of cultivated nature. Pietro Citati writes:

> Father educates the child, not by moral codes, social customs, philosophical sentences or poetic stanzas, but through nature, teaching him the names of the plants and how to treat them and make them grow. The king-gardener taught his son the art of nature and of power because the art of ruling is justly, as Odysseus said, the art of making the land produce wheat and barley, and making the vines, fig trees and apple trees bear fruit. (265, my translation)

Nature forms the basic support necessary to life in general and to communities, and its organizing patterns appear to be of immense organic complexity. As such, nature, whether in its pure state or subject to cultivation, symbolizes, as shown above, attributes that represent it as a model example of education, an inexhaustible source of lessons in cooperation.

So it is that at the advent of modernity, Thomas More in his *Utopia* takes nature not only as an integral part of the design of the ideal city of Amaurot, model for all the cities of the "Best State of a Commonwealth," but also as a practical guide to cultivate a socially committed and ethically conscious way of living. In fact, in the ordered and walled city of Amaurot, there are discontinuous portions of land for agriculture and gardens that complement and mitigate the geometrics of the urban space:

> The streets are conveniently laid out for use by vehicles and for protection from the wind. Their buildings are by no means paltry; the unbroken rows of houses facing one another across the streets through each ward make a fine sight. [...] Large gardens, which extend the full length of the street behind each row of houses, form the centre of the blocks. (More 46–47)

In his detailed description of the political order of the utopian city, More introduces a sort of parallelism between the rhythms of work in the fields, defined by the renewal of crops and improvements in farming techniques, and the mandatory refinement of social housing regulations. In doing so, he seems to express, through the voice of the narrator Raphael Hythloday, the same idea of harmonization or complementarity between the essential teachings of nature and its adaptation to civilized life that were seen in the *Epic of Gilgamesh* and in Homer's *Odyssey*. Thus, like the rotation of crops in order to guarantee the fertility of soils, on the island of Utopia likewise "the houses themselves change hands every ten years" (298) as an effect of a social regulation intended to dissipate attachment to private ownership of property among the Utopians, banned for reasons of economic and social justice. And because the indicator of highest quality in the Utopian society was measured by the devotion shown by its citizens in the attention given to cultivating nature – "The Utopians are very fond of these gardens of theirs. They raise vines, fruits, herbs and plants, so thrifty and flourishing such care and handling [so that] you will find nothing else in the whole city that is so useful or more pleasure" (47) – also the quality of their homes, which at first "were low, like cabins or peasant huts, built slapdash out of any sort of lumber with mud-plastered walls and steep roofs, ridged and thatched with straw" (48), improved dramatically with the contribution of architecture and the improvement of construction techniques: "Today their houses are all three storeys high and handsomely constructed" (48).

As for the ethical doctrine, the stoic model that was to guide the conduct of Utopians was also inspired by verifying the principle of the interdependence of the organic activity of nature, measured by the agency of reason, taken as a pure human faculty, divinely enlightened and ideally inclined to seek the general good:

> [The Utopians] define virtue as living according to nature. [...] And as nature bids men to make one another's lives cheerful, as far as they can, so she repeatedly warns you not to seek your own advantage in ways that cause misfortune to others, And this is right; for no man is placed so far above the rest that he is nature's sole concern; she cherishes alike all those living beings to whom she has granted the same form. (More 69–70)

Another classic utopia is *New Atlantis* by Francis Bacon. It is a kind of allegorical fiction about the different stages in the inductive and experimental method of scientific research, which Bacon conceptually developed in his treatises *The New Organon or Aphorisms Concerning the Interpretation of Nature, The Great Instauration*, and *Advancement of Learning*. Although *New Atlantis* presents an anthropocentric vision that legitimizes the absolute dominion of man over nature, this has not prevented it from being seen by scholars, such as Frank E. and Fritzie P. Manuel, as a consecrated object, revealing the omniscient divine intelligence (257). In fact, *Salomon's House*, built on the island of Bensalem, which could be likened to a college campus or contemporary technology park, is described as a place ruled by an elite of thirty-six male elders, responsible for a society geared to the continuous pursuit of scientific experiments, undertaken not so much in order to dominate, but to reveal the secrets of nature itself. The environment of religious veneration toward forms of matter as a physical manifestation of transcendent creativity, cultivated by a society of observers, experimenters, and theorists disciplined by strict rules of functional ordinance, indicates the theoretical position that Bacon's philosophy of nature attaches to the meaning, purpose, and limits of objective investigation. Allegorizing civilized questioning in *New Atlantis* is unclouded by prejudices – "idols," in his terminology – and guided by reverent awareness of the limits to understanding the mechanisms and processes of the language of the natural world. The description of the solemn manner in which members of *Salomon's House* move across the island of Bensalem to give their public audiences is identical to the ritualized way that ecclesiastical dignitaries hold religious services. As well as indicating the equivalence between the heuristic function pursued by the scientist of nature and the revelatory function mediated by the priest of transcendence, this description also seems to illustrate the assumption of an ethical awareness of restraint and modesty, regulating and even limiting scientists braving the unknown in their incursions into the world of nature, as Bacon recommends in the preface to his *Great Instauration*: "that they [philosophers of nature] consider what are the true ends of knowledge, and that they seek it not either for pleasure of the mind, or for contention, or for superiority to others, or for profit, or fame, or power, or any of these inferior things; but for the benefit and use of life; and that they perfect and govern it in charity" (16). Bacon embraces a religious attitude, or militant conscience, enlightened by the discovery and disinterested promotion of the objective knowledge of nature's laws in view of the general good. Over the centuries to come, this Baconian religious conception of nature has evolved into a materialistic view of the physical laws of nature and of the fabric of society.

Vigorously expressed, this philosophy permeates the thought of the utopian Marxist of the second half of the nineteenth century, William Morris. In the context of one of his numerous newspaper articles, he exhorts "fellow-workers [to] devote yourselves to the spread of the religion of Socialism" (Morris, *A Factory* 13). Morris, true to his aesthetic and libertarian conception of socialism, proved in his fiction, essays, and pamphleteering to be a tireless thinker on the possibilities of a better world without human exploitation and injustice. He continued his prospective work under the aegis of an unwavering romantic spirit and a paradoxical medievalist nostalgia, tinged with idealism for a human order more in harmony with the language of nature. Thus, in the short essay *A Factory as It Might Be*, Morris foretells a future society configured by the dominating presence of industrial structures and reverberating with the dramatic technological changes witnessed in his own time. He proposes a socialist factory model backing ingenuity, education, and supporting human solidarity, all in contrast with the brutalizing reality of the inhospitable and inhumane places representative of the nineteenth century with their mechanized and exploitative working conditions. Setting forth his vision in three articles published between May and July 1884, in *Justice, Organ of the Social Democratic Federation*, Morris envisions a factory model fully integrated within the landscape, built according to the same criteria of beauty and under the same sophisticated and delicate handcrafted building techniques used by medieval monks and craftsmen – "nor do I see why [...] we should not emulate the monks and craftsmen of the Middle Ages" (Morris, *A Factory* 17). A factory whose spatial integration would benefit the surrounding landscaped nature and with an almost identical atmosphere (almost, on account of the unpredictable and slightly disturbing effect of the weather in the British Isles) to the mythical image of an idyllic place: "our factory stands amidst gardens as beautiful (climate apart) as those of Alcinous" (Morris, *A Factory* 15). For this utopian, who had witnessed the dramatic ecological impact of the industrial revolution on nature in parts of nineteenth-century Britain, the future regeneration of the environment would have to involve a return to the slow rhythms of a pre-industrialized order, which were ecologically more sustainable. Such a return, regarded paradoxically as a condition of human progress, would welcome technological advances in industry but duly cleansed of their harmful effects on the environment and the welfare of the community.

The beginning of William Morris's famous utopia, *News from Nowhere* (1890) illustrates this question when the protagonist, William Guest, after returning home at night through the suburbs of "shabby London" is projected via a dream into the twenty-second century and is surprised at the crystalline state of the waters of the river Thames and the absence of polluting factories along its banks (Morris 7–8). This is the first sign of the harmonious social and environmental order of the socialist and libertarian England that, as champion of this ideal, he longed to see in real life: "How clear the water is this morning! [... H]ow all was changed from last night! The soap-works with their smoke-vomiting chimneys were gone; the engineer's works gone; the lead-works gone;

and no sound of riveting and hammering came down the west wind from Thorneycroft's" (9–10).

Finally, changing literary landscape once more, another revealing example from the utopian genre that helps in constructing a program of ecological literacy, is Aldous Huxley's final work, *Island* (1962). The island Pala, located somewhere in the Indonesian Sea, serves as the setting for the representation of an ideal society. It was conceived by Huxley as a fictional projection of his psychedelic experiences and idiosyncratic assimilation of thought from Eastern philosophies. Protected from the outside world by its geological configuration and separated from it by the secessionist free choice of its citizens, Pala can be interpreted as a place of synthesis between the pragmatic sense of objective thought and Western science and the subjective spirituality of Eastern philosophical inspiration. The first is exemplified by the self-sustaining food project carried out by the Agricultural Experimental Station, while the second is expressed in the cultivated pedagogy of conscious individual attention given to the circumstances of the present life. With its model of detached and frugal living as practiced by its citizens, Pala also emerges as being a place of ideal synthesis between a refined culture of spiritual brotherhood and a luxuriant and pristine natural landscape. It is in this sense that the dominant directive of the community of self-sufficient and self-governing citizens of Pala have opted not to proceed with the exploitation of the oil wealth in the surrounding seabed. Thus the preservation of the ecological balance is guaranteed together with the relative harmony of the individual and collective psyche of the citizens, who are trained in transpersonal awareness, aided by *moksha* medicine. This is a kind of hallucinogenic to be administered under special conditions of initiation, and which can open the "doors of perception" and provide access to the infinite reality of the world beyond our senses. And herein lies one of the traits of originality in this utopian narrative: what Huxley most wishes to communicate is not so much the message that it is desirable to maintain the natural conditions of an island territory spared from the ferocity of human exploitation and greed. Rather it is an appeal to reflect on the possible conditions necessary to form an eco-conscious society, that is, a society made up of individuals who mentally practice the same principles of harmony and ecological balance that they advocate and exercise in environmental conservation. While Huxley does not exclude reality as it is, paradoxically perceived as a flickering sequence of undetermined events – "Mysteries of Darkness" and "Apocalypses of Light" (Huxley 213) – in Pala the emphasis on the quality of social life is understood to derive from the quality of the mental life of its citizens. Hence, the importance is given to practices of unlimited training of consciousness, with yoga occupying a central role in this process of inclusive and integrative education in experiencing the real world in its totality. As a result, great attention was paid to the practice not only of "yoga of love" or "yoga of the summit" or of "yoga of rest and letting go" or "yoga of complete and total receptiveness," as psychomotor luminous relaxation techniques, but also to "yoga of danger" and "yoga of the jungle," as exercises in consciously integrating feelings of fear and perceptions of horror (208, 194). There is a passage early in the narrative that illustrates the educational scope of this inclusive practice of yoga, involving the protagonist, the cynical journalist Will Farnaby, and a psychologically mature child of Pala, Mary Sarojini, who is instructed in the principles of this spiritual discipline. After being shipwrecked off the island of Pala and hurting himself as a result of a fall caused by the horror of being confronted with a snake when he was attempting to climb the island's steep cliffs, Will, in a state of anxiety and suffering, engages in a conversation with Mary. So as to ease him from the obsessive and nauseating image of his encounter with the reptile, she encourages him to confront this memory, in a practical application of the knowledge she possesses of the yoga of horror:

> "Listen Will: there was a snake, a big green snake, and you almost stepped on him. [...] Now say it yourself – say it!" [...] All the horror of it came back to him [...] "Say it again – "I almost stepped on him. [...]" He heard himself whimpering. – "That's right, Will. Cry – cry!" The whimpering became a moaning. Ashamed he clenched his teeth. "No, don't do that," she cried. "Let it come out if it wants to. Remember that snake, Will. Remember how you fell." [...] Gradually the sobbing died down. The words came more easily and the memories they aroused were less painful. (18–19)

In that mentally confused state of a wounded castaway in an unknown and apparently hostile land, Will is further tormented by remorseful hallucinations of the image of his abandoned partner dying beside him in a car accident for which he was responsible. But what proves to be most effective for his complete physical and mental recovery is the practice of "yoga of love" under the guidance of Mary's mother, Susila Macphail. This passage is highlighted because in it we find once more the ideal integration of the classical antinomy, already observed in Gilgamesh, between culture and nature, town and country. Still in a state of physical and psychological suffering, Will enters a trance state in the presence of Susila, who, being aware of his nationality, tells him that in her youth she had studied in Wells, a small English town known for the magnificence of its cathedral. By recalling this place and the serene memories he has of it, Will is gradually drawn into a progressive state of relaxation. The evocative ability to form visual and sonic representations, as an integrative technique pursued by yoga so as to reach a sublime state of consciousness, initially causes Susila to recall the image of the cathedral of Wells, that magnificent feature of the city and architectural symbol of Christian civilization. She then immediately juxtaposes this image with the fluid description of elements of nature that, spontaneously manifested, become harmonized with the solid and intransitive expression of medieval artistic genius:

> "Do you know Wells? [...] I used to love walking by the water," Susila went on, "looking across the moat at the cathedral," [...] The voice, it seemed to Will Farnaby, had become more musical and in some strange way more remote. The voice was almost chanting now, [...] "I can shut my eyes," it chanted on, "and see it all clearly. Can see the church – and it's enormous [...]. Can see the green grass and the water and the golden sunlight on the stones and the slanting shadows between the buttresses. And listen! I can hear the bells. The bells and the jackdaws. The jackdaws in the tower – can you hear the jackdaws?" (35)

This composite image is motivated by unselfish love for a stranger – a love which is all the more generous seeing as Susila, in the course of applying her yoga therapy, does not allow herself to be disturbed by her own suffering, caused by the recent death of her companion Dugald. It steadily gives way to a representation predominated by water, the natural fluid element, to induce a hypnotic state of floating in Will Farnaby:

"Floating," the voice softly insisted, "Floating like a white bird on the water. Floating on a greater river of life." [...] "Life flowing silently and irresistibly into ever fuller life, into a living peace all the more profound, all the richer and stronger and more complete because it knows all your pain and unhappiness, knows them and takes them into itself and makes them one with its own substance." (36–37)

In the novel's general structure, the mirroring actions performed by Mary and Susila function narratively as a core episodic device that reflects its utopian message about the value of mental harmonization as a condition of eco-social well-being. In other words, it is important to incorporate within the notion of ecology not only the balance between the dynamics and elements of nature, but also self-awareness of the balance between the impulses of consciousness.

By tracing a course through the long history of literary utopianism, we have seen the various ways in which nature has been represented idealistically. Beginning with the ancient literary allegories of Western civilization, we saw nature first represented as both an elemental foundation and a continuous system in the modelling of phenomena, as both a perfect whole and a harmonious partaker of human life (*Genesis*). We then saw nature as an ally or mentor of the civilizing process (*Epic of Gilgamesh*, Homer's *Odyssey*). We witnessed its apologetic appointment as a model of virtue (More's *Utopia*). We saw it identified as a manifestation of divine intelligence or creativity (Bacon's *New Atlantis*) and rehabilitated as the element compensating the imbalances caused by the dominating impact of human technology (Morris's *News from Nowhere*). Finally, we witnessed that nature can play a therapeutic and redemptive role in the delusions created by human consciousness (Huxley's *Island*).

The appreciation of utopian literature and idealistic thought demonstrates, through the classic examples analyzed here, a thematic tradition congenial with the essential lesson of ecological thinking, a lesson declaring and proving that a good and sustainable human community is based and conditioned upon an understanding of the language of nature.

# Bibliography

Alter, Robert. *The Art of Biblical Narrative*. New York: Basic Books, 2011, [1981].

*Christian Standard Bible*. Online. <https://biblehub.com/csb/genesis/>. Accessed January 2019.

Bacon, Francis. *The New Atlantis and the Great Instauration*. Ed. Jerry Weinberger. Arlington Heights, IL: Crofts Classics, 1989, [1627].

Citati, Pietro. *Ulisses e a Odisseia. A Mente Colorida*. Trans. Maria Jorge Vilar de Figueiredo. Lisboa: Livros Cotovia, 2005.

*Epic of Gilgamesh, The*. Trans. N. K. Sanders. Assyrian International News Agency Books Online. aina.org/books.html. Online. <https://archive.org/stream/TheEpicofGilgamesh_201606/eog_djvu.txt>. Accessed January 2019.

Homer. *Odyssey*. Trans. E. V. Rieu. Rev. Trans. D. C. H. Rieu. Intr. Peter Jones. London: Penguin, 2003.

Huxley, Aldous. *Island*. London: Grafton Books, 1976, [1962].

Manuel, Frank E. and Fritzie P. Manuel. *Utopian Thought in the Western World*. Cambridge, MA: Belknap Press of Harvard University Press, 1979.

More, Thomas. *Utopia*. Ed. George Logan and Robert M. Adams. Cambridge: Cambridge University Press, 1989, [1516].

Morris, William. *A Factory as It Might Be*. New York: New York Labor News Co., 1922, [1884].

——. *News from Nowhere*. Ed. Krishan Kumar. Cambridge: Cambridge University Press, 1995, [1890].

——. "Why Not." *Justice* 1.13 (April 12, 1884): 2. Online. <http://www.marxists.org/archive/morris/works/1884/justice/08why.htm>. Accessed January 2019.

Orr, David W. *Ecological Literacy: Education and the Transition to a Postmodern World*. Albany: SUNY Press, 1992.

Wellhausen, Julius. *Prolegomena to the History of Israel*. Trans. J. Sutherland Black and Allan Menzies. Pref. W. Robertson Smith. Online. <http://www.gutenberg.org/cache/epub/4732/pg4732-images.html>. Accessed January 2019.

Intentional Communities

CHRIS COATES

# On Being Studied: A Utopian Remembers

Hidden away in the news snippets page of a 1978 copy of *New Society* magazine was a warning to social scientists attempting to carry out research into intentional communities to "Beware the community that Bites Back!" The short piece warned that if you sent an enquiry to a small "Alternative-living-Working-Co-operative" in East Lancashire, instead of receiving a polite reply and invitation to visit, you were likely to get a reply printed on purple recycled paper requesting that you fill in a "Questionnaire for people who send out questionnaires." The paper sent out under the auspices of the QRU (Questionnaire Research Unit) started by asking: "How many questionnaires have you written? and How many questionnaires have you filled in? (approx.)," before going on to more searching topics with multi-choice answers such as:

Do you think researchers write questionnaires mainly for:

(a) Their own interest?
(b) To provide useful info for the people questioned?
(c) Amusement?

Why is it that we fill in so many questionnaires yet only get to see very few finished reports: Is it because

(a) People are only doing it as part of an examination course & the work fades into obscurity afterward?
(b) The work is presented in such a way that it is only of interest to academics?
(c) It gets lost in the filing system?

And perhaps most impertinently – "Why is seemingly so much money spent on researching things rather than doing them?"

Clearly something, or someone, had seriously annoyed me and my fellow communard in arms, Rod, to inspire us to compose such a response in the first place, let alone go to the trouble of printing off copies on our Gestetner duplicating machine and sending them out to anyone enquiring about studying People in Common (PIC), the commune we lived in in Burnley, Lancashire. Quite why we were so annoyed or inspired is lost to me in the mists of communal memory. All I have in my personal archive is a copy of the said questionnaire (see Appendix 1) and a cutting from *New Society*. I do remember that we did receive numerous letters from students requesting interviews and visits. What sort of response they got very much depended on how relaxed or overworked we were feeling at the time.

Like many members of intentional communities then (and now?), we were not very aware of any academic research or publications about communal living and if we had been, we might well have been skeptical as to their relevance to what we were trying to do. I do remember being intrigued by a copy of Dennis Hardy's *Alternative Communities in Nineteenth Century England* that I got out of the local library that started my fascination with historical intentional communities. I also avidly read a copy of Andrew Rigby's *Communes in Britain* that I came across on the communal bookshelves at Laurieston Hall. Here seemed to be a writer with a foot in both academia and the alternative society, which may have led to an occasional lapse of objectivity, even if that lapse could be inspirational to those of us "putting our bodies on the line":

> above all else, commune members are people who have begun to see through the fictions upon which our social order rests and who have sought to create their own modes of existence. The potential of this movement lies in the fact that through putting their bodies on the line, so to speak, through putting their ideals and beliefs into living practice, they can provide the spark to light the dreams of others and through their example can provide others with the courage to demand the right to decide for themselves the way they should lead their lives. It is this type of demand, crystallised in the stance of many communards, which lies at the heart of any true revolutionary process. (Rigby, *Communes* 148)

Looking back now, *Communes in Britain* seems to belong to an earlier period, the so-called heady days of the long sixties 1957–1973 (see Marwick) rather than the late 1970s onward of Thatcherism, urban decay, the miners' strike, and the poll tax riots. Rigby himself later remembered the time with a touch of nostalgia: "It was a wonderful time when, in a way it is hard to imagine now, considerable numbers of people enjoyed the space and the opportunity to experiment with their lives. It was a time of enormous creativity which stemmed from the utopian confidence that anything was possible" (Rigby, "Dig" 32).

Living communally back in the late 1970s, the nearest I got to any sort of theoretical thinking about the way we were trying to live was reading a copy of Murray Bookchin's *Post-Scarcity Anarchism*, which Derek, one of the members of PIC, had. And that was about it for my engagement with academic thought and its relevance to intentional communities during my first decade of communal living. We were much more interested in practical how-to-do-it books or networking through our own DIY newsletters, such as *Communes Network*, than we were in searching out the ideas and views of academia. I guess our comic questionnaire was in part a response to a frustration that we never seemed to see any results from the various en-gagements we had with anyone who claimed to be seriously studying us. In those early years (1978/1988), I can't recall the results of any research being shared with us after the event or any of it finding its way into publication, either in stand-alone book form or in any alternative magazines. Maybe it came out in academic journals, but on the ground, we didn't see anything.

The first "serious" academics that came to study us at PIC were David Pepper, principal lecturer in geography at Oxford Polytechnic and part-time geography lecturer, Nickie Hallam. They stayed with us for a few days at PIC and carried out a series of in-depth interviews with some members as part of a research project covering a dozen or so communes around the country with the aim of trying to answer the question: How important are communes in leading the way to a socially more just and ecologically more harmonious society? The results were published in 1991 as *Communes and the Green Vision: Counterculture, Lifestyle and the New Age*. When the book came out, I remember that members of other communities who had been interviewed were critical of it. They claimed that Pepper and Hallam had come with their own "Marxist agenda" and were just looking for evidence to prove a pre-formed view of communes and in some way had misrepresented groups. I don't recall that we felt PIC had been misrepresented. At the end of the book they said: "We have found that the communes we visited do have overwhelmingly green values and attitudes which they do try to put into practice. Therefore communes could be a significant, even major part of a green society – of Ecotopia. But they probably will not be so, nor are they likely to constitute a leading edge in any move towards radical social change" (Pepper 199), which seemed like a fair conclusion, both at the time and on rereading it now. If I have any criticism in hindsight, it is that the original research question seems flawed: I am not sure that at the time any of us thought we were trying to "lead" anybody anywhere in the classical political sense of leading a movement. I certainly thought we were just getting on with it, and if anyone wanted to follow our lead, that was entirely up to them.

In 1990 I was part of a small group of members of the UK *Communes Network* who decided to produce a publication to "dispel the myth that communes came and went with the 1960s" and at the same time to "bring the idea of communal living to more people" (5). And so, *Diggers & Dreamers: The Guide to Communal Living (D&D)* was conceived, as a journal and directory that would be the "public face" of communal living in the UK. Being part of the editorial and production team of what has become a highly successful series of publications cataloguing the up and downs of communal life in the UK, I slowly started to become aware of a whole range of different approaches to and aspects of communal living. Not just from the wide variety of communal groups that *D&D* was in touch with, but also from journalists, writers and, yes, academics who were covering communes. All with differing approaches depending on their particular interests, political persuasions or research backgrounds. This contact broadened my communal horizons somewhat and was to lead me down unsuspecting paths in the future.

In the mid-1990s, Bill Metcalf, from Griffith University in Australia, called in on us a couple of times in Burnley on his international research tours of intentional communities. I don't know if we were ever on the long list to appear in his book, *Shared Visions Shared Lives: Communal Living around the Globe*; if we were we never made the final cut – perhaps PIC wasn't "inspirational" or "new-age sexy" enough when compared to the likes of Findhorn. After having visited some 120 communities around the globe, Bill Metcalf seemed to have reached a similar point in his thinking as David Pepper before – that communes might change the world if only …

> Communal living has much to offer in terms of promoting sustainability, by resolving contemporary social and environmental problems. Communalism is increasing, but mainly in its least radical forms, and the more radical forms are being moderated. Have the millennia-old ideals of utopian communalism been subsumed by the dominant, capitalist paradigm, or is the survival of any communal activity a sign of hope for our sustainable future? (Metcalf, "Sustainable" 19)

Bill Metcalf was another academic with one foot firmly in the communal camp, having lived in communal groups in Australia. He was also a board member of the International Communal Studies Association (ICSA), which viewed from the outside looked like a rather smoke and mirrors academic body. The ICSA was started by the Kibbutz movement in 1981, following a conference held in Israel claiming to be the First International Conference on Communal Living, a claim hotly disputed by the International Communes Network (ICN), made up of a grouping of, mainly European, communities who were at the time busy organizing their second festival-cum-conference in Denmark. This clash of conferences led to something of a stand-off during the 1980s between the more academically minded ICSA and the more grassroots ICN. The ICN saw itself as being made up of and representing communes, at least in Europe, whereas it saw the ICSA, albeit through somewhat cliché-tinted spectacles, as a rarefied, stuffy, distant, and probably irrelevant ivory-towered academic association more interested in furthering their own rather obscure academic careers than being any actual help to communes on the ground. The ICN went on to organize eight festivals across Europe, the last in 1987, before it ran out of steam and money. The ICSA, with financial support from Kibbutz, fared better and continued to organize conferences hosted by various universities through the 1980s and 1990s. But the mistrust between communards and the world of academia continued to bubble away.

Bill Metcalf entered the fray of this divide when in 1998 he became president of the ICSA with responsibility for organizing the subsequent conference. Perhaps because of his background living communally, or maybe because he had visited so may communities around the world, he made the inspired decision to not hold the next ICSA conference at a university, but instead to persuade an intentional community to host it. Under the title "Communal Living on the Threshold of a New Millennium," the 2001 ICSA conference took place at the ZEGG Center for Experimental Cultural and Social Design in Germany.[1] While it was an inspired choice of venue from the perspective of building bridges to members of communes, it wasn't without its difficulties. Persuading some kibbutz members to visit Germany might have been a challenge in itself; inviting them to a site that had historical links to both German dictatorships proved nigh on impossible. Previous uses of the ZEGG property included: a Nazi SS base; an equestrian training center for the German military cavalry prior to the 1936 Munich Olympics; a Hitler Youth and League of German Maidens camp; and later both a training school for the East German trade union federation and an espionage school for the Stasi secret police. Add to this the ZEGG community's open approach to love and sexuality, and not only did it turn out to be an uphill struggle to get Jewish members of Kibbutz to attend, but also many of the more conservative Mennonite and Hutterite members in the USA that the ICSA had managed to make links with at previous conferences refused to come. Despite these problems the gathering of academics with many members of intentional communities was a resounding success. So much so that all future ICSA conferences have been hosted by communities.

Bill Metcalf invited me to the ZEGG conference, the first "academic" event I had ever attended. Diggers & Dreamers had just published my first book, *Utopia Britannica*, and I suddenly found myself rubbing shoulders with other members of – what shall we call us? – the communal jet set – maybe not. But I do recall realizing that I was part of something bigger, global, with a history, with a future? At the final conference plenary, in a roll call of communal experience, I found myself somewhat to my surprise

---

1    See the Zegg website: <https://www.zegg.de/en/>.

standing in the communal veterans' section of those with twenty or more years' experience of communal living along with born and bred Kibbutzniks and a few other of us 1970s survivors. Almost from then on, again much to my surprise, I have slowly morphed into being the unofficial historian of and occasional, and rather reluctant, spokesperson for UK intentional communities. Following publication of *Communes Britannica* and my involvement in the setting up of Forgebank Cohousing,[2] I have found myself attending ICSA and Utopian Studies conferences and various symposia on intentional communities to give papers and keynote speeches. I became along the way a self-taught, maybe somewhat fraudulent, but certainly a rather different sort of alternative member of academia.

From the very start Lucy Sargisson did seem to be a different sort of academic – I am not sure if this is actually true, or whether it is a fantasy I have made up since getting to know her, but I would swear that on her first visit to us at People in Common, Dr. Sargisson, Lecturer in Politics, and future Professor of Utopian Studies, arrived in deepest, darkest Lancashire on a large motorbike. If it is not true is could easily have been. Lucy visited us at People in Common a few times in 1997 during her yearlong sojourn around intentional communities in the UK. Individually we took part in in-depth open-ended interviews, being asked questions such as: what made you decide to live in this community? what, if anything, do you think is wrong with modern society and politics? and do you think intentional communities play any role in bringing about social and political change? At the time I don't think I could really make out what a Politics lecturer was doing coming and interviewing us in our little social experiment. What relevance did we have to political theories and ideas? Years later she explained her motivations:

> The idea was (basically) that utopias weren't just wishful thinking – fanciful escapist daydreams – but that they had an important political function: they broke the rules and created new spaces in which it was possible to think about the world differently. They were always created by people who were discontented with their present, who imagined a better tomorrow: a good life. So although I came at this from a highly theoretical standpoint, I wanted to see whether these ideas had any meaning in real

2    See <https://www.lancastercohousing.org.uk>.

life. I wanted to see whether intentional communities were utopian, in this sense, and whether these ideas about utopia made any sense in the real world. (Sargisson, "Do Intentional" 103)

We received a complimentary copy of the resulting publication from the year's research (one of the few times anyone sent us any results of their research). I don't know how many members of PIC actually managed to read *Utopian Bodies and the Politics of Transgression* from cover to cover. I guess we all flicked through to the bits about us and any of the other communities that we knew about and skimmed over a lot of the theorizing. Having said that, I have returned to the book over the years and found it remarkably thought-provoking, both in its attempt to frame intentional communities within a theoretical political context and in its recognition of their personal and political significance to those of us who live in them: "If composting domestic sewage, deciding where to live, using your home as a space of political opposition and creativity, using your home to host political gatherings and events, using your home as a showcase for inspiration ... if these activities are considered to be political, then these political agents might be reconceived as active citizens, rather than slothful dropouts" (Sargisson, *Utopian Bodies* 74).

I don't know whether it was Lucy's definite feminist perspective or her anarchist political leanings that warmed us to her more than other researchers. Or maybe it had something to do with her canny understanding of the potential antipathy and potential lack of understanding, even misunderstanding, between intentional community members and academics. I have come to view her work as containing some of the clearest bits of thinking about the role and function of intentional communities that I have come across. Both at a political level:

> ecologically informed intentional communities in the UK engage also in politics in the more conventional sense of the term. They are politicised spaces. They are mostly busy in terms that would be normally named political activity. Briefly – they offer to some a temporary resting place between engagement in direct action and eco-politics and often members have a (continuing) history of political activism. (Sargisson, *Utopian Bodies* 53)

And at a more personal level relevant to members living communally:

> Intentional communities are strange places, full of dreams, hopes and disappoint-
> ments as groups of individuals work collectively to realise a better life. In order to
> pursue their vision of the good life, these groups require space (in which to experi-
> ment), individual security, and group coherence [...] Intentional communities need
> to provide space inside which members can explore the good life. This exploration
> often involves deep experimentation with the self as members seek self-improvement,
> self-development and/or self-transformation in a search for a different ontological
> relationship with the world. (Sargisson, "Strange" 396)

It is a shame that, despite the efforts of the likes of the ICSA, the Utopian
Studies Society,[3] and others, many members of intentional communities are unaware of or uninterested in the not inconsiderable body of
academic work about them. Having said that, not many members show
much interest in any communities other than the one they live in either.
A bit of attention to what others have said and done might help us to
avoid repeating past communal mistakes either as tragedy or as farce.

So what have I learnt from my various encounters with academics and
academia? I've learnt to take myself more seriously. It was something of a
surprise to be taken seriously by the likes of professors and writers and to
be considered at least on some level as an equal and peer when it comes
to discussing communal living and utopian ideas. I've also learned not to
take some of the academic papers I have read too seriously! I learned as a
communard that our ideas sometimes (often?) were way ahead of our resources. Viewed from outside of our communal bubbles, we were so way
out of kilter, in fact, that it seems hard now to imagine how we thought
we were ever going to achieve them. And that it was often hard to see how
our idealistic "utopian" rhetoric was born out in practice.

I've learned to delve into and question seemingly impenetrable academic treatises on the basis that somewhere hidden away among all the
self-referential jargon might be some ideas worth thinking about. I have
gained the confidence to search out other thinkers and writers that I probably wouldn't have come across otherwise and considered how their ideas
relate to my experience and that of people living in intentional communities. Dinah Zohar's ideas about how quantum physics might relate to our
individual experience and how society works in her books, *The Quantum*

3    See <http://utopian-studies-europe.org/>.

*Self* and *The Quantum Society*, blew my mind. I have grappled with and been inspired by the works of David Graeber. I have revisited the works of Peter Kropotkin and Murray Bookchin. And through a throwaway line in a pamphlet I read, that said that he had been in part inspired by the example of European intentional communities, I was led to the ideas of Abdullah Öcalan about Democratic Confederalism and the Kurdish anarcho-feminist revolution taking place in Northern Iraq, Syria, and Turkey. All of which have chimed with the thoughts put forward by Lucy Sargisson and her colleague Lyman Tower Sargent about the relationship between intentional communities and utopian ideas.

None of these ideas have amounted to any sort of coherent set of conceptual/theoretical ideas within which I have been able to understand the role of intentional communities either in the past, present or future. The nearest I have come to a framework that seems to encapsulate my own thoughts is in the work of American blogger and writer John Michael Greer,[4] perhaps best laid out in his book, *The Ecotechnic Future: Envisioning a Post-Peak World*. In his book, he puts forward the idea that if human society is part of the natural world, then the "rules" of the natural world must in some way apply to human society. That you could conceive of the carbon-fueled capitalist civilization of the last couple of centuries as equivalent to an invasive species: fast growing, resource hungry, dominating all before it, until ecological limits are reached, and the system starts to collapse. He critiques various other ideas about the future of society, including what he refers to as "lifeboat ecovillages":

> It's all very reminiscent of the aftermath of the Sixties, when a great many young people headed back to the land with equally high hopes. Most of them straggled back to the cities a few months or years later with their hopes in shred, having discovered that fantasies of the good life in natures lap made poor preparation for the hard work, discipline and relative poverty of life as a subsistence farmer [...] it's one thing to leave the city behind for a rural commune when you're nineteen years old and can put all your worldly goods in a knapsack, with room left over for dreams. It's quite another to do so when you're 40 and comfortable, with a family, a career [...] There simply aren't that many people who can abandon their modern lifestyles, help

---

4   See <https://www.ecosophia.net/>.

pay for a rural community and support themselves for decades while the machinery of industrial society shudders to a halt around them. (Greer 181)

He then suggests a possible future path that would lead to an Ecotechnic future via an age of industrial scarcity and a salvage society. And that rather than be looking for a solution or set of solutions that will "save us" – we could view the myriad of small community-based experiments in sustainability: community-supported agriculture, transition towns, housing co-ops, worker co-ops, credit unions, alternative currencies, ecovillages, farmers markets, makerspaces, cohousing, community-owned renewables, food co-ops, intentional communities, and utopia experiments ... as the seeds of the new ecological society attempting to grow in the shade of the invasive civilization. Some will fail/die, others will go on to develop/ grow and form the basis of a new more ecological "climax" civilization – invasive species are never the long-term climax ecology in nature.

"The future is already here – it's just not very evenly distributed." William Gibson.

Ps. I did wonder about writing a paragraph or two about what I thought academics could learn from my experience. But then I thought that ought to be obvious from what I have written. If not – please fill in the questionnaire in Appendix 1.

## Appendix 1

Questionnaire for People who send out questionnaires.

1. How many questionnaires have you written?
2. How many questionnaires have you filled in (approx.)?
3. Do you think researchers write questionnaires mainly for
    (a) Their own interest?
    (b) Providing useful info for the people questioned?
    (c) Amusement?

4. Why are researchers not aware of other people doing almost identical research in the same field?

5. Why is it that we fill in so many questionnaires yet only get to see very few finished reports: Is it because
   (a) People are only doing it as part of an examination course & the work fades into obscurity afterward?
   (b) The work is presented in such a way that it is only of interest to academics?
   (c) It gets lost in the filing system?

6. Why is seemingly so much money spent on researching things rather than doing them?

7. Have you read the book *How to Lie with Statistics*?

8. Did you fill in this questionnaire while:
   (a) Sitting down?
   (b) Standing up?
   (c) Drinking coffee?
   (d) Taking a bath?
   (e) Other (Please state)?

9. Are you a:
   (a) Sociologist?
   (b) Psychologist?
   (c) Cooperative research worker?
   (d) Police officer?
   (e) Other (Don't bother)?

Thank you very much for your cooperation in filling in this questionnaire, the details you provide will be treated with the utmost confidentiality. When they have been handed to our secretary, handed back again, queried, lost, found, brought to a weekly meeting, lost again, found again and filed for three years we will send you a copy of the final report.

Yours sincerely Cathie Cross

Questionnaire Research Unit (QRU) c/o 2 Sussex st, Burnley, Lancs

# Bibliography

Bookchin, Murray. *Post-Scarcity Anarchism*. Berkeley: Rampart Press, 1971.

Coates, Chris. 2001. *Communes Britannica*. London: Diggers and Dreamers Pub., 2001.

Greer, John Michael. *The Ecotechnic Future: Envisioning a Post-Peak World*. Gabriola Island, BC: New Society Pub., 2009.

Hardy, Dennis. *Alternative Communities in Nineteenth Century England*. London: Longman, 1979.

Marwick, Arthur. "The Cultural Revolution of the Long Sixties: Voices of Reaction, Protest, and Permeation." *The International History Review* 27.4 (December 2005): 780–806.

Metcalf, Bill. *Shared Visions Shared Lives: Communal Living Around the Globe*. Findhorn, Forres: Findhorn Press, 1996.

——. "Sustainable Communal living around the Globe." *Diggers & Dreamers, 2000/2001*. Ed. Sarah Bunker, Chris Coates, David Hodgson, and Jonathan How. London: Diggers & Dreamers Publications, 1999. 5–19.

Pepper, David. *Communes and the Green Vision: Counterculture, Lifestyles and the New Age*. London: Green Print, 1991.

Rigby, Andrew. *Communes in Britain*. London: Routledge & Kegan Paul, 1974.

——. "Dig the Old Dreams, Man!" *Diggers & Dreamers 1998–99. The Guide to Communal Living*. Ed. Sarah Bunker, Chris Coates, Jonathan How, Lee Jones, and William Morris. London: Diggers & Dreamers Publications, 1997. 26–33.

Sargisson, Lucy. "Do Intentional Communities Matter?" *Diggers & Dreamers 2008/09*. Ed. Sarah Bunker, Chris Coates, and Jonathan How. London: Diggers & Dreamers Publications, 2007. 102–112

——. "Strange Places: Estrangement, Utopianism and Intentional Communities." *Utopian Studies* 18.3 (2007): 393–424.

——. *Utopian Bodies and the Politics of Transgression*. London: Routledge, 2000.

Zohar, Danah. *The Quantum Self: Human Nature in Consciousness Defined by the New Physics*. London: Flamingo, 1991.

Zohar, Danah and Ian Marshall. *The Quantum Society: Mind, Physics, and a New Social Vision*. New York: William Morrow, 1995.

SURYAMAYI CLARENCE-SMITH

# Auroville: An Experiment in Spiritually Prefigurative Utopian Practice

## Introduction: From Politically Transgressive to Spiritually Prefigurative Utopianism

In 1968 young people throughout Europe and North America insisted that "Another world is possible," and sought to claim and enact it. The spirit and culture of this revolution were in part informed by the concurrent popularization of Indian spirituality, which offered tools for individual emancipation that were seen as necessary to accompany and realize the transformation sought for society at large. In the years leading up to 1968, in India, two spiritual activists – Sri Aurobindo, a revolutionary in India's independence movement who had turned to spirituality to further the work of realizing an emancipated society, and The Mother (born Mirra Alfassa), his partner in this socio-spiritual undertaking – had begun (r)evolutionizing the yoga tradition. Rather than individual enlightenment achieved through ascetic withdrawal, the premise of Integral Yoga was the spiritualization of all aspects not only of self, but of society – and Auroville was founded in 1968 by The Mother as an experimental township dedicated to this endeavor.

This chapter seeks to further Lucy Sargisson's work on utopian practice in intentional community, as represented in *Utopian Bodies and the Politics of Transgression*, based on the case study of Auroville. Sargisson is one of the scholars to have undertaken field research on utopianism in contemporary intentional communities, and in so doing, has been key to furthering our present-day understanding of utopian practice (see Sargisson, *Utopian Bodies*; Sargisson and Sargent). She highlights how everyday life in intentional communities, in which personal and collective practices are loci of experimentation for alternatives to dominant societal paradigms, and boundaries between the public and the private spheres are challenged, constitutes a politically transgressive utopianism. Alternatives are not only imagined and explored, but are themselves open and subject to reformulation, giving permission for and contributing to "paradigm shifts in consciousness" (Sargisson 15).

Of scholarship on intentional communities in general, while the alternative practices they engage in are often well documented, why and how these are enacted, embodied, and sustained, and the meanings their members ascribe to this process, remain largely under-explored (see Brown; Pitzer; Sargisson and Sargent). I seek to offer an insight into the role of spirituality in informing such articulations in the Auroville context; Sargisson uses "consciousness" in the secular sense of the term, yet it is the promise and experience of a *spiritual* dimension of a paradigm shift of consciousness, and its allied social change, that inspires Aurovilians to invest their lives in this communal experiment, and which is key to sustaining its utopian practice.

The foundational worldview of the Auroville community – the philosophy and practice of Integral Yoga – is that the world is in a progressive trajectory of spiritualization, in which people can choose to actively participate, and thereby hasten, through the exercise of an applied spirituality in shaping and transforming both the individual and collective spheres of life. Auroville's experimental political philosophy and practice is congruent with Sargisson's framework of "transgressive utopianism," yet its embodied anticipation and intentional elaboration of a spiritualized society makes it future-facing and prefigurative. Research on Auroville thus offers a unique opportunity to further her work.

Furthermore, it is a comparable site to that at which Sargisson conducted a significant part of her ethnographic study for *Utopian Bodies and the Politics of Transgression*, the Findhorn Foundation. Both Auroville and Findhorn are among the most widely recognized intentional communities in existence today; they emerged within a year of each other, Findhorn in 1967, Auroville in 1968. Each is long-lasting, having in the last two years celebrated their golden jubilees, while 80 percent of intentional communities do not survive beyond two years (Reinhalter 11). They benefit from significant international recognition; Auroville is endorsed and funded by the Government of India and recognized by UNESCO, which has issued five resolutions on the community; Findhorn has been awarded the UN Habitat Best Practice designation, and regularly hosts sustainability seminars in affiliation with the United Nations Institute for Training and Research. Each is among the largest and most diverse of intentional communities, Findhorn with a membership of approximately 400 people of 40 nationalities, Auroville with a considerably larger population of 3,000, made up of over 50 nationalities. Significantly, both are spiritual communities founded by charismatic female mystics.

While Sargisson has also conducted research in other intentional communities, primarily in New Zealand (see Sargisson and Sargent), Auroville is not evoked in any of her work. A second-generation Aurovilian, who has formally studied the community as a social scientist since 2015, I find myself uniquely positioned to supplement Sargisson's rich legacy on utopian practice and intentional community. Crucial to yielding the insights I seek to contribute to this field are insider and subjective understandings of community members, which to date have remained largely absent from or under-analyzed in intentional community scholarship,[1] and to which I have rich access as an autoethnographer and highlight in my work.

1    Even the work of Barry Shenker, a former kibbutz member who felt that existing literature did not adequately capture his or his peers' experiences and thus sought to offer an "insider" view of communitarianism, is not significantly different from other work in that it remains a largely descriptive and theoretical account that lacks subjective experience and voices – including his own. Work – including by academics – in which the voices of community members are represented is often not academic, and does not include sustained analysis (e.g., work by Metcalf), or lacks grounding in thorough ethnographic fieldwork (Sargisson carried out only short-term ethnographic fieldwork, of several days to two weeks, in intentional communities). Significant exceptions are recent research on Auroville by Pommerening, Vidal, and Meier.

## On the Evolution of Utopian Practice and Its Theorization

While in recent years, a variety of social phenomena – social movements, protests, practices, performances – have increasingly been framed through the praxis lens of utopian scholarship, intentional communities, which had long been one of its primary loci, remain central to it by virtue of their potential to experiment with the transformation of societies as whole entities (Sargent 48; see Cooper; Dinerstein; Dinerstein and Deneulin). Many intentional community members, however, object to having their communities branded as utopian, Aurovilians among them. The reasons for this are the dominant identification of the concept of utopia with a fixed ideal of perfection, which many intentional community members feel they are far from, and its association with a detailed, pre-determined blueprint, toward which much sound criticism has been levelled (Sargent 34; see Kateb). Lucy Sargisson, however, states that inadequacy lies not with the state of realization of these communal experiments, but rather in the "mistaken reading of utopias as perfection-seeking, blueprinting and desirous of perfection and finality" (11). Based on her field research in utopian communities, she theorizes a "transgressive" utopianism that is "internally subversive" as well as "flexible and resistant to permanence and order" (2). She emphasizes that it does not "construct a blueprint for the ideal polity" (3); on the contrary, there is "no full-stop to the process of politics in this utopianism [...] It is, above all, resistant to closure and it celebrates process over product" (3).

In so doing, Sargisson squarely places her utopian scholarship within, and significantly contributes to shaping, a body of work spanning the last several decades in which utopianism has been re-evaluated and redefined in a radical move away from the idea of utopia as synonymous with perfection, fixity, and the intangible, toward the dynamic articulation of a utopian aspiration within and seeking alternatives to present mainstream conditions – or perfectibility rather than perfection. In the last thirty years, literary utopias emerged as "critical utopias," (Moylan 10) utopian practice as "concrete" (Dinerstein, "Concrete") and "transgressive" (Sargisson 1), and utopian social theory began to focus on the role of utopianism in "the education of desire" for a better way of life (Levitas, *Concept* 4). The concept of what could constitute a utopia became internally diverse and changeable, imperfect, and self-critical in terms of form and content. Thus reformulated, utopian better reflects the practice and experience of intentional communities – certainly the "second-wave" intentional communities founded in the 1960s and 1970s, Auroville among them (Schehr 44).

Key to this evolution of the conceptualization of utopianism was – and still remains influential – the groundbreaking work of Marxist utopian philosopher Ernst Bloch, *The Principle of Hope*, in which he elucidates the concepts of "utopian function" and "concrete utopia" (146). Unlike theoretically perfect, imagined utopian societies, a concrete utopia is rooted in present conditions, however limited these may be, seeking to perfect itself in an evolutionary process through the work of the utopian function, whose role it is to continually reach into future potential, the "Not-Yet-Become" (146). A concrete utopia is thus prescient but not pre-determined, centered on a process of dynamic perfectibility rather than seeking to fulfil a statically perfect outcome.

It is this body of work that I build on in examining Auroville as a utopian experiment, one I find to be congruent with the community's autochthonous ontological framework of Integral Yoga, which sought to hasten an evolution of spiritual consciousness through an applied, anticipatory embodiment in the present. Over the last fifty years, Auroville has developed collectively and experimentally as a participatory body politic dedicated to conscious evolution, in a perpetual learning process heightened by the integral nature of the evolution it aspires toward, in which every endeavor and interaction acts as a potential and applied site of transformation and reformulation.

## A Note on "Hope," Disappointment, and Criticism

> It is a question of learning hope. Its work does not renounce [... It] requires people who throw themselves actively into what is becoming, to which they themselves belong. (Bloch 3)

Following Bloch's *The Principle of Hope*, hope features strongly in the new body of theoretical and ethnographic work on utopian practice and prefiguration (see Dinerstein, *The Politics*; Dinerstein and Deneulin). While hope is certainly a primary driving and sustaining force for a utopian endeavor, from autoethnographic observation and experience, I insist on adding the dimension of disappointment, which I have found to be key to fostering ongoing mobilization for social change within Auroville. I would go so far as to extrapolate from it the theory that it is the tension between these two forces – hope and disappointment – that engenders the dynamism at the core of grassroots, concrete utopian practice.

Criticism is a natural ally to disappointment in this dynamic. Tom Moylan, among the contemporary scholars of utopianism, has defined some utopias as "critical," in both the "Enlightenment sense of *critique* – that is the expressions of oppositional thought, unveiling, debunking, of both the genre itself and the historical situation," and "in the nuclear sense of the *critical mass*" (10). To this double meaning of critical, I suggest we add the dimension of *self*-critique in order to better understand the subjective experiences of utopian practice in intentional communities, and thus complement our already existing understanding of what they represent: place-based, enacted critiques of the mainstream societies in which they are embedded.

The dynamic of self-critique within intentional communities has already been highlighted – in her work, Sargisson observes that intentional communities do not claim to be perfect, and that their members are "often excessively critical of their community" (29). This is certainly true of Auroville, and I would argue is key to fueling a continued process of perfectibility, while the fundamental, underlying, animating, and inspiring hope principle crucially serves to frame and activate disappointment to serve this process. In the Auroville context, the ideals of the community, as outlined in its founding texts (*The Auroville Charter, To Be a True Aurovilian,* and *A Dream*), articulate and inspire the collective hope of the community, yet, at the same time, they are a constant gage against which Aurovilians critique themselves, and each other. Of hope, Bloch says "it is in love with success rather than failure" (3), yet Fredric Jameson points out that utopias "have something to do with failure, and tell us more about our own limits and weaknesses than they do about perfect societies" (qtd. in Sargisson

122). Sargisson herself has remarked that they are "a mirror to the present designed to bring out flaws" (112).

Excessive criticism is a phenomenon that many within the Auroville community consider damaging to the fabric of our society – and in my own opinion and experience, rightly so – however, it is important to note that an elected lack or active repression of questioning and critique in utopian community projects served to deny any human failings and was responsible for the perpetuation of unjust and unethical behavior within them.[2] It is also worth highlighting that Auroville has a culture of satire that offers many a welcome respite from the high expectations we place upon ourselves: plays, skits, cartoons, videos, and articles produced by Aurovilians as a commentary on various aspects of our community have been common and long-standing vehicles through which we reflect on, critique, and laugh about ourselves and our society.

Most significantly, the spiritual worldview of our community frames, and assists in weathering, the human limitations and flaws that we Aurovilians routinely face in ourselves and others in the course of community life. These are understood to be symptomatic of the overarching stage of the spiritual consciousness in which humanity is presently caught, but importantly, it is also understood that this spiritual consciousness is in a process of evolution, and that we can choose – and if we have joined Auroville, it is presumed have chosen – to actively participate in.

## The Spiritually Prefigurative Nature of the "Utopian" Project of Auroville

In my work I further the collective theorization of utopian practice outlined above by qualifying it as prefigurative, and in the Auroville context specifically, as spiritually prefigurative, given that the practice of

---

2   This is particularly prevalent in communities with hierarchical and charismatic leadership, for example, Rajneeshpuram. See Latkin.

prefiguration is one in which a collective emulates in the present the attitudes and ways of organizing it envisions for the future (see Maeckelbergh,
"Doing"). The term "prefigurative" was coined in 1970 by the cultural anthropologist Margaret Mead, an early endorser of the Auroville project
(Mead, *Letter*) to herald the advent of a newly future-oriented "prefigurative culture" (Mead, "Prefigurative" 204). In the last decade, the concept
of prefiguration has been developed to theorize the alterglobalization
movement[3], by contemporary activist-anthropologists who observe that
"the people who make up the alterglobalisation movement [...] are intentionally prefigurative of the 'other world(s)' they would like to see," using
organizational means which reflect their desired ideals (Maeckelbergh,
*The Will* 4). While these scholars do not explicitly conceptualize prefigurative practice as utopian, it is central to how I understand utopian practice in the Auroville context. This is based on the shared principle that
"the struggle and the goal, the real and the ideal, become one in the present," despite, within, and transformative of the limitations of the latter
(Maeckelbergh, "Doing" 4).

     While scholarship on prefiguration remains focused on analyzing
social movements, today the term encapsulates alternative associations
from cooperatives to political mobilizations, and has recently been used to
describe intentional communities, given that they are a radical, embodied
exercise in redefining society according to alternative values, of the present
and for the future (see Monticelli; Farias). I see Auroville as belonging to
and standing out from all of these attempts in that is an *integral* exercise in
prefiguration, in both the dictionary and the spiritualized, Aurobindonian
use of the term. While most intentional communities focus on – even
though they may not be restricted to – a particular aspect of collective
living (e.g., ecovillages on environmentally sustainable lifestyles), and social
or political movements typically engage with specific causes and demands,
Auroville seeks to engage with all aspects of life in prefiguring society *as
a whole*, and to do so spiritually, following Sri Aurobindo's iconic phrase
"All life is yoga" (8). Under this aspirational aegis, a multiplicity of pursuits
are undertaken, from art to engineering, as well as the development of

3    Notably Marianne Maeckelbergh and David Graeber.

innovative and alternative communal practices, for example, of governance, economics, and education. While these are today institutionalized to a certain extent, reformulation is common given the community's overarching experimental and evolutionary ethos and praxis.

This flexible and open-ended political practice, which Sargisson argues is central to transgressive utopianism, is inscribed in Auroville's founding political philosophy concept and ideal – and designed to serve a spiritually prefigurative process of evolution. In 1972, just a few years after Auroville was established, someone asked its spiritually visionary founder, The Mother, "What political organisation do you want for Auroville?" and she responded, "a divine anarchy" (*Complete Works* 219). She never defined a system of governance for the community, for she anticipated that this would constrain its capacity to develop itself in accordance with the progressive spiritualization of life, which its members were to consciously participate in hastening. The kind of society that would emerge from this process could not be abstractly envisioned, it was to be elaborated in practice. It is this concretely utopian, embodied, and anticipatory articulation with a spiritualized evolution that leads me to further theorize Auroville as spiritually prefigurative. Importantly, the community's subjective self-understanding is a key basis for this; The *Auroville Charter* states that it will be the site of "spiritual and material researches," of an "unending education" and "constant progress," in service of a "divine consciousness."

## Spiritually Prefigurative Utopian Practice(s) in Auroville

Today, Auroville is a township located a few kilometers from the Indian coastal town of Puducherry, on a plateau ecologically restored and afforested by the community in its pioneering years. Its infrastructure includes residential settlements, schools and libraries, sports facilities, health and healing arts centers, multimedia performance venues and exhibition spaces, community canteens, restaurants and cafés, as well as small- to medium-scale (predominantly) crafts industries, institutes for scientific and educational research, a Town Hall and Visitors Centre, and at the center of the community, the Matrimandir, a space for spiritual concentration. This "City" area is surrounded by a "Green Belt" of farms, forest, ecological centers, and botanical gardens. Auroville's town plan projects a city of 50,000 permanent residents, occupying a circular area of about twenty square kilometers, and the community currently owns approximately 80 percent of its designated "City" area and 40 percent of its designated "Green Belt," its land holdings interspersed with farmland owned by local Tamils ("Land for Auroville" online).

In what ways is Auroville a spiritually prefigurative polity? The community has a wide range of activities – commercial and social enterprises, alternative schooling and environmental restoration, a vibrant artistic and cultural life – that would not typically be considered spiritual. Indeed the practice of Integral Yoga is to cultivate not only "spiritual consciousness within but also spiritual life without," by engaging in pursuits of worldly life with an applied spirituality, and thereby participating in transforming these (qtd. in Mukherjee 9).[4] In the following paragraphs I will highlight how three aspects of community life – education, work, and art – are spiritually prefigurative in nature.

Education in any society is a key site of deliberate social reproduction, and alternative pedagogies have been an important feature of many intentional communities; both Auroville and Findhorn are notable educational centers. Auroville has several primary and secondary schools, funded in part by the Indian Ministry of Human Resources Development, which engage and experiment with the pedagogical philosophy of "Integral Education" based on Integral Yoga and initially developed at the Sri Aurobindo Ashram (see Tanmaya). The premise of Integral Education is to foster a spiritually conscious, well-rounded, and self-directed development of the student; the objective is to form individuals who are aware of both the inner and outer dimensions and potentialities of education, and of the significance of pursuing such personal development throughout their lives.

---

4    It is important here to note that there are no prescribed spiritual practices or protocols in Auroville; Integral Yoga is a fundamentally anarchist spirituality in that it recognizes and affirms that each individual has a unique spiritual path, and is sovereign in its discovery and enactment.

This is relevant to realizing the societal ideal of Auroville as a place "of an unending education, constant progress, and a youth that never ages," as well as that of a society that builds on "all discoveries from without and from within" to prefigure a spiritualized future (*Auroville Charter*). While Auroville has developed original pedagogical practices adopted internationally (cf. *Awareness*), education has been a source of considerable contention within the community due to the perpetuation of mainstream educational practices within some of its schools, such as, for example, preparing students for Indian and international examinations in order to enable them to easily integrate into higher education institutions.

Work in Auroville is another significant site for spiritual development, central to community life given the founding statement that "Auroville is for those who want to do the yoga of work" (*Complete Works* 222). This meant that work was to be undertaken as a yogic practice through which individuals would progress spiritually, while also participating in a transformation of the world, by infusing consciousness into their fields of engagement. According to recent research, the ideals and understandings of spiritualized work are actively practiced by Aurovilians (see Pommerening; Seidlitz). While the flexible nature of work in the community – the ability to change professions, for instance, is both easy and commonplace – is celebrated for offering individuals opportunities to pursue their interests, there are also issues with people who lack competence for their chosen work persevering in it. The fact that this provides them with an opportunity for self-development is valued by other members of the community, however, the social and economic cost to the collective of their occupying positions they do not adequately fill is also a source of dissatisfaction. Despite this, such situations are often not addressed due to a community culture of reticence to overruling individual members.

Outside of the realm of work – and within it for some – creative pursuits are among the most popular self-development activities. Art has long played a central role in the utopian imaginary because it offers a space in which to challenge present conventions, and envision and embody alternatives. In Auroville, much artistic practice and performance is inspired by the body of literature on Integral Yoga and by the community's ideals. For the township's 50th anniversary in 2018, Aurovilian artists created multimedia works based on chapters of a key spiritual text, *On the way to Supermanhood*, and a theater group adapted chapters of the same volume for stage performance. The community's ideal of "unity in diversity" was symbolized and explored in a multidisciplinary community performance, "Soul Encounters for the Auroville Soul," which fused dance forms from various cultures, and culminated in a hatha yoga sequence that represented the epitome of spiritualized physical embodiment. These two recent works are representative of a rich and commonplace legacy of artistic practice in Auroville, the arts thus constituting a significant realm of exploration in spiritual utopianism.

As evidenced by these three pursuits, embodying consciousness is essential in defining them as spiritually prefigurative. It is also central to the understanding of what it means to become Aurovilian, for "Aurovilian" is not only perceived as a "community member," but as an ideal, embodied (id) entity, that many consider themselves to be only working toward – and that can thus itself be considered spiritually prefigurative and utopian in nature.

## Spiritual Embodiment and the Politics of Transformation

In *Utopian Bodies and the Politics of Transgression*, Sargisson argues that alternative lifestyle practices in intentional communities are "politicized partly because of their context: the fact that they occur in a consciously created and alternative space [...] and also by the consciousness of the actions themselves" (65). If the aspiration of Aurovilians, as a polity, is an embodied, individual, and collective evolution of spiritual consciousness in everyday life, then any activity – a physical discipline, artistic production, or political forum – in which Aurovilians intentionally engage with this process is politically significant in the Auroville context. While Sargisson observes and asserts that transgressive utopianism challenges paradigms and thus creates new conceptual and political spaces in which new ways of thinking and doing are possible, we should consider the transformational[5] potential of spiritually prefigurative utopianism, and of new ways of being, for political practice.

Political scientist and somatic (conscious movement) facilitator Anita Chari has highlighted in her work the importance of considering how embodied spiritual practices (such as tai chi or hatha yoga) develop relational capacities, for she argues this may give rise to "new political potentials" (236). I know that if people have had the experience of individual and shared conscious states, this will act as an embodied reference to strive for in collective contexts, including political and decisional forums,[6] because I have personally experienced it as a member of the Auroville community. I have shared conscious collective relational states with others in Auroville, most significantly in one of our spiritually prefigurative integral educational programs and personal development practices, "Awareness Through the Body," ("ATB") and drawn from such experiences in participating in community decision-making forums.

For example, I have used ATB techniques of withdrawing my attention from identification with emotional reactions or mental fixations on a particular issue, and actively centering it within myself, so that I could access a more grounded, harmonious, receptive, and expanded state of presence and awareness. This enabled me to re-connect, in a more holistic way, to the objectives of the process at hand, as well as to the others in the room – for which I was additionally informed by non-verbal experiences of connectedness fostered in collective activities of ATB.

Wilson has argued for the recognition of the capacity for similar practices to trigger a more conscious engagement, and both Anita Chari and James K. Rowe specifically highlight the inclusion of spiritual practices such as meditation and yoga in Occupy Wall Street – which, regrettably, does not figure in prefigurative literature centered on it, and other comparable social movements. Significantly, Rowe notes that "Embodied practices such as singing and dancing, along with spiritual forms such as prayer and ceremony, have been central to most successful social movements," and

---

5    The term has also recently come into use by activist organizations working at the
     intersection between subjective and social change. See Rowe.
6    An extrapolation others have made as well, see Litfin.

that spiritual practices are increasingly and instrumentally being used in many organizational contexts (208).

The literature on prefiguration is largely focused on alternative organizational and decision-making practices, and in light of this, I examine a practice in Auroville that is prefigurative of a spiritualized decision-making forum, and also exemplifies the transferability of conscious embodiment into political practice. Furthermore, it has a counterpart in social movement forums, such as Occupy Wall Street and the Global Justice Movement, which gave rise to the theorization of prefiguration; "Silent Presence-Keeping" in Auroville is comparable to their "vibes-watchers" role, albeit addressing a spiritual dimension.

"Vibes-watchers" are members of the facilitation team whose role it is to help address unproductive and inequitable process dynamics in assemblies – for example, noting that people are getting tired and frustrated and suggesting a break, pointing out that there has been an unpleasant shift in the tone of the conversation, or highlighting gender or race biases in the involvement of participants (see Graeber, *Democracy Project*). Rather than calling out participants on unhealthy dynamics, "Silent Presence-Keepers" act as embodied anchors and reminders of the spiritualization Aurovilians aspire to.

They sit in Auroville's collective decision-making forums, embodying silence. Silence not as in the absence of sound, but as a spiritual practice of quieting the activity of the individual ego – thoughts, emotional reactions, and impulses – in order to connect with and become a channel and anchor for a higher consciousness.[7] This is fundamental to the understanding of what an Aurovilian is called to do, in order to be a conscious citizen in the Auroville context, as is described below by a fellow Aurovilian:

> One feels at times, that a decision could be reached more effectively by simply [...] and in the most profound sense of the word, merge in Silence. Often we are pressed to acknowledge that as Aurovilians we are asked to purge ourselves of our limitations, purifying our intentions, becoming transparent and profoundly reflective [...] this places demands upon the very integrity of what it means to be an Aurovilian. (Roy)

7    For an analysis of the role and practice of silence in Auroville, including "Silent Presence-Keeping," see Vidal.

However, it bears noting that within Auroville, there also exists significant doubt, criticism, and even objection to explicitly spiritual practices being inserted into community decision-making processes. One "Working Group" (a small team of Aurovilians tasked with the administration of a specific area of community life) stated that while they could see a personal value for the individual practicing Silent Presence-Keeping among them, they did not experience a tangible contribution for the group deriving from his presence, and even felt uncomfortable by the attendance of someone who they perceived as entirely disengaged from their process. In a larger forum, the "Selection Process" for such "Working Groups," some felt that activities designed to facilitate connection with Auroville's founding spirituality – based on quotations from the founder, for instance – were not relevant to the task at hand, and even imposed an explicit way of relating to this spiritual legacy that went against the individually defined exploration it upholds.

## Conclusion: The Transformational Potential and "By-Products" of Spiritually Prefigurative Utopian Practice

> If Utopia is understood as the expression of the desire for a better way of being, then it is perhaps a (sometimes) secularized version of the spiritual quest to understand who we are, why we are here and how we connect with each other. (Levitas, *Utopia as Method* 11–12)

Given that the lifestyle practices of utopian communities are politicized, Sargisson remarks that their members are to be reconceived as "active citizens," instead of "dropouts" (74). One of the biggest criticisms of intentional communities is that they draw energy and activism away from working for social change in mainstream society, that they are insular and escapist projects. Yet they have made little known but significant contributions to the broader societies in which they are embedded, as harbingers of forward-looking practices born from and reflective of progressive values, later to be adopted into the mainstream.

New Harmony, the historical intentional community founded by Robert Owen in Indiana in 1814, is recognized as a pioneer of free public education and free public libraries open to men and women, which since have become US institutions (Schehr 28). Over the last fifty years, Auroville has been a focal point for pioneering innovative forms of collective and economic organization, renewable technologies, sustainable architecture, educational practices, and social enterprise, with award-winning local, re-gional, national, and international reach and impact: the Auroville Earth Institute holds the UNESCO Chair of Earthern Architecture, researching and educating people worldwide in earthern building technologies; Tamil Nadu state textbooks have recently incorporated educational content on waste management from the Auroville social enterprise Wasteless, reaching millions of local children (see "Awards").

I have heard several fellow Aurovilians describe these as simply "by-products" of the underlying spiritual mission of the community,[8] and it is fascinating for me to observe that a spiritually inspired society gives rise to progressive practices (a correlation which of course cannot be indiscrim-inately generalized). The transgressive application of spirituality, in (re) shaping public life, is especially interesting to consider given that a preva-lent criticism of spiritual practice is that it renders individuals apolitical; although of relevance to note is that academic work endorsing this critique is based on Buddhist-based practices, such as mindfulness, which empha-size detachment from worldly life (Chari 227; see Žižek). By contrast, the spiritual worldview of Integral Yoga is one that sees the world as a realm to be divinized through intentional engagement, and is key to giving rise in Auroville to spiritually informed action across realms, including in the community's political life.

Additionally, the underlying spirituality of the Auroville community helps its members in weathering what Sargisson observes are the "frus-trating" (2) challenges of transgressive utopian practice, corroborating similar observations made by other academics, notably that spiritual prac-tices assist in "fighting burnout, political cynicism, and hopelessness," in social movements (Wilson 185). To be constantly faced by individual and

8    Most recently at "The Bridge," Auroville's fiftieth anniversary conference.

collective limitations in the face of high ideals is no easy undertaking, as Sargent rightly observes, "ultimately utopianism is the transformation of everyday life. And intentional communities are particularly radical in that their members are willing to experiment with the transformation of their own lives. And all members of intentional communities must deal with this transformation every day" (49).

This challenging process provokes considerable self-criticism within intentional communities, however Sargisson also highlights that members "see themselves as playing a transformative role" (29); view their communities as spaces in which change is possible and can at the very least be explored, and that this has local influence and potentially wider impact. While some utopian communities, such as Auroville, act as centers of incubation of progressive, alternative practices that are transformative within and beyond their contexts, it is the socialization of their culture of transgressive utopianism, one that empowers members to actively (re) shape their worlds, that is at the heart of their transformational political potential. A key insight from the Auroville experience is that a spiritual and experimental exercise of prefigurative utopianism has proven conducive to fostering this.

# Bibliography

"Awards." *Auroville*. Online. <https://www.auroville.org/contents/8884>. Accessed 20 March 2019.

*Awareness Through the Body*. Online. <www.awarenessthroughthebody.com>. Accessed 7 April 2019.

Bloch, Ernst. *The Principle of Hope*. Trans. Neville Plaice, Stephen Plaice and Paul Knight, vol. 1, Cambridge: MIT Press, 1996.

Bouvard, Marguerite. *The Intentional Community Movement: Building a New Moral World*. Port Washington, New York: Kennikat, 1975.

Brown, Susan Love, ed. *Intentional Community: An Anthropological Perspective*. Albany: State University of New York Press, 2002.

Chari, Anita. "The Political Potential of Mindful Embodiment." *New Political Science* 38.2 (2016): 226–240. <https://doi.org/10.1080/07393148.2016.1153192>.

Clarence-Smith, Suryamayi. *Auroville: A Practical Experiment in Utopian Society.* 2015. University of California, Berkeley, BA Thesis.

*Collected Works of The Mother.* Vol. 13. Pondicherry: Sri Aurobindo Ashram Publications Department, 2003.

Cooper, Davina. *Everyday Utopias: The Conceptual Life of Promising Spaces.* Durham, NC and London: Duke University Press, 2014.

Dalal, A.S., ed. *Psychic Being: Soul – Its Nature, Mission and Evolution.* Pondicherry: Sri Aurobindo Ashram Publications Department, 1994.

Dinerstein, Ana Cecilia. "Concrete Utopia: (Re)producing Life in, against and beyond the Open Veins of Capital." *Public Seminar,* 7 December 2017. Online. <http://www.publicseminar.org/2017/12/concrete-utopia/>. Accessed 20 March 2019.

———. *The Politics of Autonomy in Latin America: The Art of Organising Hope.* Basingstoke: Palgrave McMillan, 2015.

Dinerstein, Ana Cecilia and Séverine Deneulin. "Hope Movements: Naming Mobilization in a Post-development World." *Development and Change* 43.2 (2012): 585–602. <https://doi:10.1111/j.1467-7660.2012.01765.x>.

Farias, Carine. "That's What Friends Are for: Hospitality and Affective Bonds Fostering Collective Empowerment in an Intentional Community." *Organization Studies* (2017): 1–19. <https://doi.org/10.1177/0170840616670437>.

Fossella, Tina and John Welwood. "Human Nature, Buddha Nature: On Spiritual Bypassing, Relationship, and the Dharma." *Tricycle: The Buddhist Review* 20.2 (2011): n. p.

Graeber, David. *Direct Action: An Ethnography.* Edinburgh: AK Press, 2010.

———. *The Democracy Project: A History, A Crisis, A Movement.* London: Allen Lane, 2013.

Kanter, Rosabeth Moss. *Commitment and Community: Communes and Utopias in Sociological Perspective.* Cambridge, MA: Harvard University Press, 1972.

Kateb, George *Utopia and Its Enemies.* New York: Free Press of Glencoe, 1963.

Latkin, Carl. "From Device to Vice: Social Control and Intergroup Conflict at Rajneeshpuram." *Sociological Analysis* 52.4 (1991): 363–377. <http://doi:10.2307/3710852>.

"Land for Auroville Unified." *Auroville.* Online. <https://www.auroville.org/contents/2902>. Accessed 29 April 2019.

Levitas, Ruth. *The Concept of Utopia.* Oxford: Peter Lang, 2011.

———. *Utopia as Method: The Imaginary Reconstitution of Society.* London: Palgrave Macmillan, 2013.

Litfin, Karen T. *Ecovillages: Lessons for Sustainable Community.* Cambridge: Polity, 2013.

——. "The Contemplative Pause: Insights for Teaching Politics in Turbulent Times." *Journal of Political Science Education*, 2018. <https://doi.org/10.1080 /15512169.2018.1512869>.

Maeckelbergh, Marianne. "Doing is Believing: Prefiguration as Strategic Practice in the Alterglobalisation Movement." *Social Movement Studies* 10.1 (2011): 1–20. <http://doi:10.1080/14742837.2011.545223>.

——. *The Will of the Many: How the Alterglobalisation Movement is Changing the Face of Democracy*. London: Pluto, 2009.

Mannheim, Karl. *Ideology and Utopia: An Introduction to the Sociology of Knowledge*. Trans. Bryan S. Turner. London: Routledge, 1991.

Mead, Margaret. "Prefigurative Cultures and Unknown Children." In *Youth: Divergent Perspectives*, ed. Peter K. Manning. New York: John Wiley and Sons, 1973. 193–206.

——. Letter to Whom It May Concern. October 30, 1973. Auroville Archives.

Meier, Janne. "Being Aurovilian: Constructions of Self, Spirituality and India in an International Community." *J@rgonia* 4.10 (2006). Online. <http://research. jyu.fi/jargonia/artikkelit/jargonia10.pdf>. Accessed 7 April 2019.

Metcalf, William James. *From Utopian Dreaming to Communal Reality: Cooperative Lifestyles in Australia*. Sydney: University of NSW Press, 1995.

——. *Shared Visions, Shared Lives: Communal Living around the Globe*. Findhorn, Forres: Findhorn Press, 1996.

Monticelli, Lara. "Embodying Alternatives to Capitalism in the 21st Century." *TripleC: Communication, Capitalism & Critique* 16.2 (2018): 501–517. <https:// doi.org/10.31269/triplec.v16i2.1032>

*Mother on Auroville – References in Mother's Agenda*. Pondicherry: Sri Aurobindo Ashram Publications, 1977.

Moylan, Tom. *Demand the Impossible: Science Fiction and the Utopian Imagination*. London: Methuen, 1986.

Mukherjee, Jugal Kishore. *Sri Aurobindo Ashram: Its Role, Responsibility, and Future Destiny: An Insider's Personal View*. Pondicherry: Sri Aurobindo International Centre of Education, 1997.

Pitzer, Donald E., ed. *America's Communal Utopias*. Chapel Hill: University of North Carolina Press, 1997.

Pommerening, Matthias. *Soul of Sustainability? Inner Dimensions of Work for a Sustainable Society. An Auroville Case Study*. 2017. Medical School Berlin, MSc. thesis.

Reinhalter, Jaya Priya. *Intentional Communities: Place-Based Articulations of Social Critique*. 2014. Hawaii Manoa, MA thesis.

Rowe, James K. "Micropolitics and Collective Liberation: Mind/Body Practice and Left Social Movements." *New Political Science* 38.2 (2016): 206–225. <https://doi.org/10.1080/07393148.2016.1153191>

Roy. "The Passage: On Decision-making in Auroville." Online. <https://www.auroville.org/contents/859>. Accessed 20 March 2019.

Sargent, Lyman Tower. *Utopianism: A Very Short Introduction.* Oxford: Oxford University Press, 2010.

Sargisson, Lucy. *Utopian Bodies and the Politics of Transgression.* London: Routledge, 2000.

Sargisson, Lucy and Lyman Tower Sargent. *Living in Utopia: New Zealand's Intentional Communities.* Aldershot: Ashgate, 2004.

Satprem. *On the Way to Supermanhood.* New York: Institute for Evolutionary Research, 1985.

Schehr, Robert C. *Dynamic Utopia: Establishing Intentional Communities as a New Social Movement.* Westport, CT: Bergin & Garvey, 1997.

Seidlitz, Larry. *Integral Yoga at Work.* Pondicherry: Indian Psychology Institute, 2016.

Shenker, Barry. *Intentional Communities: Ideology and Alienation in Communal Societies.* London: Routledge & Kegan Paul, 1986.

Sri Aurobindo. *The Synthesis of Yoga.* Pondicherry: Sri Aurobindo Ashram Publication Department, 1999.

Tanmaya, ed. "Sri Aurobindo and The Mother on Education: A New Education for a New Consciousness." Pondicherry: Sri Aurobindo Ashram, 2014.

The Mother. *The Auroville Charter.* Pondicherry: Sri Aurobindo Ashram, 1968.

——. *To Be a True Aurovilian.* Pondicherry: Sri Aurobindo Ashram, 1971.

——. *A Dream.* Pondicherry: Sri Aurobindo Ashram, 1954.

"The Mother on Auroville." *Auroville.* Online. <http://archive.auroville.org/vision/maonav_selected.htm>. Accessed 14 March 2019.

Vidal, Maël. *Manifesting the Invisible.* 2018. École des Hautes Études en Sciences Sociales, MA Thesis.

Wilson, Jeff. *Mindful America: The Mutual Transformation of Buddhist Meditation and American Culture.* Oxford: Oxford University Press, 2014.

Žižek, Slavoj. "From Western Marxism to Western Buddhism." *Cabinet* 2 (2001). Online. <http://www.cabinetmagazine.org/issues/2/western.php>. Accessed 14 March 2019.

Film and Television

SIMON SPIEGEL

# The Utopia of the Holy Land: The Zionist Propaganda Film *Land of Promise* as Utopian Text[1]

## Introduction

When it comes to the relationship between utopias and film, most researchers focus solely on fiction films. The conclusion they reach in the process is always more or less the same: as a form that needs conflict, clearly defined characters, and a dramatic arc, fiction films are highly unsuitable for positive utopias. With very few exceptions, research has therefore only looked at dystopian films that contain all the elements of a proper movie. But, when it comes to positive utopias, film seems to be barren ground.

As I have argued elsewhere (Spiegel, "Some Thoughts"; *Bilder*), this line of reasoning is problematic because it completely ignores the vast field of nonfiction film. This is quite unfortunate since documentary, and especially propaganda films, are in many ways closer to positive utopias than any fiction film. In this chapter, I am analyzing the Zionist propaganda film *Land of Promise/L'Chayim Hadashim* by Juda Leman (PS 1935), a film that, as I will show, can be read as a utopia in the Morean tradition, fitting this model much closer than any fiction film. Before tackling *Land of Promise*, however, I will first discuss the relationship between Zionism and utopianism in general.

---

1  This article is based on a chapter in *Bilder einer besseren Welt*, my study of utopias in nonfiction film.

## Zionism as Utopia

Can Zionism be called a utopia or a utopian project? At least for
Theodor Herzl, the father of modern Zionism, the answer seems clear.
In *Der Judenstaat* [*The Jewish State*], the founding document of modern
Zionism published in 1896, he counters, on the very first page, the possible accusation that the "restoration of the Jewish State" is a utopia. It is
not uncommon for propagators of bold political plans to distance themselves from utopias, which often carry the notion of either mere literary
play or, even worse, fanciful nonsense. To illustrate why *The Jewish State*
does not belong to the genre, Herzl compares his work to a contemporary
utopia – *Freiland* [*Freeland*], by his almost namesake, Theodor Hertzka,
first published in 1890. *Freiland*, which for a brief period was hugely successful and lead to Hertzka's nickname, "Austrian Bellamy," describes a
settler community in the territory of today's Kenya. Despite its popular
success, which even resulted in a failed attempt to implement Hertzka's
ideas, Herzl is by no means convinced of the former's approach.[2]

Herzl's main criticism, similar to the objections raised by Karl Marx
and Friedrich Engels, concerns one of the core features of classic utopias –
the detailed description of the "numerous cogged wheels fitting into each
other" (*Jewish State* 70). According to Herzl, the "complicated piece of
mechanism" (*Jewish State* 70) sketched out by Hertzka is worthless without
an "existent propelling force" that can set the whole machinery in motion.
Herzl, on the other hand, is confident to have found this force – it is "The
misery of the Jews" (*Jewish State* 70).

If we compare Herzl's booklet with other utopian texts, it does indeed
lack some of the genre's typical characteristics: it does not feature a fictional frame and also does without a detailed description of the alternative. Other staples of the genre, like the form of government, the judicial
system, education, and welfare, are touched on only briefly and in very
general terms. Herzl is not interested in portraying the future Jewish state;

---

2    There is not very much literature on Hertzka; among the exceptions are Jackson,
     Bach, Leucht 187–209.

rather, he concentrates on a point that most utopias leave out – the path to make it a reality.

Despite these differences, and although Herzl openly rejects the denominator "utopia" for his tractate, a closer look reveals that he is nevertheless firmly rooted in the utopian tradition. This becomes obvious in his novel, *Altneuland* [*Oldnewland*], published six years later, that is a proper utopia with all the familiar trappings of the genre. Here, Herzl does exactly what he strictly opposed in *The Jewish State*: he describes a Jewish commonwealth in Palestine with all the "artistically elaborated descriptions" (*Jewish State* 71) which he deemed counterproductive only a few years earlier.

Herzl's firm rejection of the term "utopia" certainly has strategic reasons. The author wants his idea to appear as a solid and well-reasoned proposal and not a fantastic dream. In *Altneuland*, all these objections seem to have vanished. However, even *The Jewish State* itself is not as far removed from the utopian tradition, as Herzl wants his readers to believe. While it is true that it is meant as a political program and not as a thought experiment – in contrast to most classic utopias – it is also, like all utopias, a reaction to glaring social problems.

Herzl's contradictory stance toward utopia mirrors his treatment in different fields of research. In utopian studies, he is conspicuously absent.[3] This is quite surprising, for if we consider his writings to be utopian, the state of Israel would be one of the very few realized, large-scale, utopias. Still, most reference works do not recognize Herzl as a rare example of a successful utopian writer but treat him only marginally (if at all). It might be that the rather non-utopian situation in the Middle East prevents scholars from calling Israel a utopia. Interestingly, these reservations do not seem to exist in communal studies, which have dealt extensively with the kibbutz movement (see below).

In Zionist studies, on the other hand, Herzl's pre-Zionist literary work has been largely neglected. It almost seems as if the journalist and author of light comedies is considered a dingy character who has to be separated from the visionary statesman he later became. One result of these limited

---

3    Among the few authors which treat Herzl from the point of view of utopian studies
     are Mumford, Heil, and Schoeps.

views on Herzl is that his literary oeuvre, and *Altneuland* in particular, has received very little attention.

Only in recent years has research begun to take Herzl seriously as an author and utopian writer. This re-appraisal has led to the insight that the rupture between Herzl, the writer, and Herzl, the Zionist, is not as dramatic as described in the past. For Herzl, his literary and political engagements were intimately intertwined, and he treated his Zionist activism, to some degree, as a quasi-literary project. From this point of view, *Altneuland* is not simply a fictional rehash of his political goals, but rather the moment where his original aspirations gain their proper form.[4]

This conclusion might seem a bit hyperbolic, but for my purpose, it is not essential whether or not Herzl saw himself primarily as a writer or as a political activist. What is much more important is that a text that is heavily influenced by the utopian tradition serves as the basis of modern Zionism.

In this regard, Herzl is only the best-known exponent of a larger trend. While genuine Jewish utopias were basically non-existent for a long period, the late nineteenth century saw, as a result of the emancipation of the Jews in Western Europe, a considerable amount of texts that dealt with a future Jewish State in Palestine. Most of these works did not gain wide traction, but Herzl has demonstrably read some of them.[5]

The various Jewish utopias differ significantly when it comes to how the Jewish state should be organized – for example, whether it should be a democratic republic or a monarchy. But they also share several fundamental traits. Most importantly, they all want to solve the same problem: "to save the Jews from persecution, discrimination, and humiliation" (Eliav-Feldon 91). In addition, they all deal with the same territory. For more than 2000 years, Eretz Israel was an otherworldly no-place for the Jews, but in the Zionist utopias, this transcendent idea becomes a real place that can be located on a map. Religious promise and political action fuse in a way that differs strongly from the classic utopia.

---

4   See on this the important study by Peck.
5   The most comprehensive study on Jewish utopias, *Ha-Mahar shel ha-Etmol*, by Rachel Elboim-Dror, is only available in Hebrew. For more on Jewish utopias, see also Eliav-Feldon, and Stolow 57–58.

Utopias based on religious concepts, but nevertheless built in the here and now, are by no means a new phenomenon. Examples can be found in eighteenth- and nineteenth-century Christian sects like the Mormons, the Shakers, the Amish, or the Hutterites. What distinguishes most Zionist utopias from these movements is their desire to build a modern state based on secular principles. Herzl himself is a case in point. As an assimilated Jew who celebrated Christmas and did not have his son circumcised, he was not interested in a theocracy. Still, Herzl – and with him the vast majority of Zionist writers – is heavily making use of religious terms and constantly alludes to the Bible. The main goal of this rhetoric is not a religious one though, but a mobilization of his fellow Jews (Eliav-Feldon 93).

In Zionist utopias, the utopian people are not an undefined mass, but a very specific socio-economic group – mainly the Jews of Eastern Europe. Like the barren desert of Palestine, which will be turned again into the land of milk and honey, they have to be transformed – from pale weaklings into *Muskeljuden* ("muscular Jews").[6] The (originally anti-Semitic) stereotype of the Jew who is unfit for life, but can be toughened by working the soil, is present in many Zionist utopian texts. As in most utopias, the new state depends on the creation of a New Man, and vice versa.

## Land of Promise

The idea to use film as means of communication arose very early in the Zionist movement, and Herzl himself was supportive of using the new medium to pique the interest of potential Zionists. The first attempt at the turn of the century, however, failed due to technical problems (Halachmi). It then took more than a decade to produce the first films documenting the Jewish settlement in Palestine. Many more followed in

6    The term "Muskeljude" was coined by the physician, Max Nordau, who was an important fellow combatant of Herzl. Nordau was a strong supporter of physical training for Jews. His appeal led to the founding of many Jewish sports clubs (Rüthers).

the 1920s and 1930s.[7] Given the close relationship between Zionism and
the utopian tradition, it comes as no surprise that many of these films
feature utopian elements. Ariel L. Feldestein deems *Life of the Jews of
Palestine* (D: Noah Sokolovsky, PS/RU 1913) the first attempt "to document on film the redemption of the Jewish people returning to their
homeland" (8). The film shows not only how the Jewish immigrants turn
the desert into arable land, but also emphasizes the difference between
"old Jews" born in the diaspora and the "new Jews" of Palestine. The latter
are examples of the utopian New Man – physically superior and united
by a common future: "while the Jewish communities across the Diaspora
were linked by the common past, the Jewish-Zionist community in Eretz
Israel has a shared future, a common effort to build a new unified Jewish
society under the wings of Zionism" (Feldestein 9). *Life of the Jews of
Palestine* employs various tropes that were firmly established in Zionist
discourse by that time, and which can also be found in later films. From
the point of view of film theory, it also illustrates how documentary and
propaganda film are closely related.

We often think of documentary and propaganda films as antithet-
ical – while the former shows us the world "as it is," the latter gives a wrong
impression and wants to manipulate its audience. In reality, the two fields
do, at least, partly overlap. How much they do depends mainly on how
narrowly we define propaganda. If we understand propaganda broadly, as
any kind of political communication, the resulting group is much bigger
compared to thinking of propaganda solely as a means to fight an external
enemy (Ellsworth; Neale). Film scholar Carl Plantinga argues that every
nonfictional movie, at least implicitly, takes a position toward the things
it shows, which already indicates a discursive and rhetorical closeness to
propaganda (99).

However we see the relation between documentary and propaganda
films, there is no doubt that *Life of the Jews of Palestine* is made with the
intention to present the achievements of the Zionists in a favorable light
and to move its audience. At the same time, it is also meant to document

---

7    On Zionist films in general and "Israeli cinema" before the founding of the state,
     see Tryster, *Israel*; and Feldestein.

what is happening in Palestine. The presentation may be biased, and negative aspects are probably left out. Still, its basic aim is to show the viewer what, and how, the Jewish settlers are doing.

Among the numerous Zionist films produced, *Land of Promise*, which I will focus on, is considered to be the most successful. It is, without any doubt, the most ambitious and expensive. With a running time of fifty-seven minutes, it was also the first sound film produced in Palestine.[8]

The peculiar fusion between biblical promise and political project, between reference to the past and orientation toward the future, which can be found in many Zionist utopias, is already apparent in the film's title sequence. To the sound of fanfare, a first title card appears that imitates the look of a stone inscription. After the film title and the name of the production company, a longer text appears – still "carved in stone" but with a more neutral font – which thanks everyone involved in the production. This is followed by a card announcing the cast – not less than "THE JEWISH PEOPLE REBUILDING PALESTINE."

So far, the design of the title sequence seems more apt for an historical drama than for a documentary. This is also true for the next part, which has a distinctly different look. The following roll title is set in a Gothic script and accompanied by choral singing:

> This is a drama of a people which is changing the Land of Promise into the land of fulfillment.
>
> It is a record of the struggles and triumphs of the hundreds of thousands of Jews who are lifting Palestine back into the ranks of the great civilized countries, preparing a Homeland for hundreds of thousands of other Jews now homeless throughout the world and thereby restoring the scattered Jewish Nation to a life of freedom and creativity.

---

8    Not to be confused with *Land of Promise/Banim Bonim* (D: Yaacov Ben-Dov, PS 1924). *Land of Promise* was released in several languages; today, only the German version, which was the first one released, and an English version, which had the widest circulation, are preserved (Tryster, *Land of Promise* 188). My analysis is based on the English version restored by the Steven Spielberg Jewish Film Archive and available on YouTube (<https://youtu.be/QDoD6W2z01s>).

This opening already includes many of the tropes that, according to Eliav-Feldon, characterize Zionist utopias in general; there is a clear reference to a long-gone past, or rather two different pasts. The stone inscriptions obviously refer to the ancient world of the Romans and therefore to an era of cultural and political blooming. The Gothic script, on the other hand, evokes, in a more diffuse way, a sense of religious tradition. Oddly enough, the font does not imitate the look of the Hebrew alphabet. Quite the contrary, Gothic letters are normally associated with medieval Christian texts. The film is not interested in such typographic subtleties though. The main point is clearly to give the text a religious flair.

The voice-over commentary, which can be heard after the roll title, strikes a similar note: "This is the land which God promised to Abraham. Once, while the Jews lived in this land, it was the center of a great civilization. When the Jews were driven out, the land gradually declined, primitive life returned." The images that are presented with this commentary show how desolate and backward the Holy Land has become in the interim. We see Arabs grazing their goats on stony slopes, goading donkeys, and sieving and threshing grain by hand. These images of the lives of the desert people are followed by shots of Jerusalem – and again, fanfares can be heard. Here, among the high stone walls, the people are better dressed, but the main impression is still one of a medieval city. This is quickly confirmed by the voice-over: "It remained unchanged throughout the centuries. The streets and bazaars within the old city are the same today as they were in the middle ages."

In Jerusalem, the focus shifts to the Jewish population. The commentary does not forget to stress that the city is a "sanctuary for three great religions," and we do see the Dome of the Rock, churches, a Christian cleric playing the organ, as well as the Via Dolorosa. Despite the demonstrated tolerance for other beliefs, there is little doubt about who has a rightful claim to this place: "But older than these by far are the memories which bind the Jewish people to Palestine, the birthplace of their religion and their nationhood." Accordingly, we see orthodox Jews, the grave of Rachel in Bethlehem, and men praying at the Wailing Wall. The film's point is the rightfulness of the Jewish claim on Palestine (Feldestein 167).

The scenes in the desert and in Jerusalem are mere prologue, though. After twelve minutes, the film turns to its proper subject. Images of the stormy sea are followed by dancing pioneers onboard a ship – Jewish immigrants on their way to Palestine. The remaining 45 minutes are solely dedicated to these pioneers and their deeds. We see strong men and women, marching in lockstep, building roads and irrigation systems under the burning sun and farming the land with modern machinery. The contrast to the opening of the film is palpable: while the Arabs toiled with medieval equipment on the seemingly barren ground, the Zionists use their know-how to turn Israel again into a prospering garden.

After agriculture, the film turns to the breeding of sheep, cattle, poultry, and even beekeeping – Palestine is indeed once again the land of milk and honey. A sequence in a kibbutz follows, in which the residents have their meal in a big communal dining room. The tools and buildings of the pioneers are state of the art, but now the film switches to Tel Aviv, which is presented as a vibrant metropolis comparable to Western cities.

After this, modern factories are shown, among them a chemical plant at the Dead Sea, and the editorial office and printing press of a newspaper. A headline written in Hebrew leads to the Levant Fair, an international trade fair held in Tel Aviv in the 1930s. Again, progress and international flair are emphasized. The flags of many countries fly on the roof of the main building while elegantly dressed visitors exit from buses and stroll through the pavilions where modern products are on display.

Religion, which is directly referenced in the opening, occurs rarely later on. One of the few moments where the specifically Jewish character of life in Palestine is mentioned comes after the fair sequence: the people of Tel Aviv prepare for Sabbat. As the commentary explains, the working week here lasts from Sunday morning to Friday noon. On Saturday, the holy Sabbat, all shops are closed. However, this is only a brief insertion, which is immediately followed by images of the busy city life; people spending time at the beach and enjoying sidewalk cafés and dance halls.

As a contrast to the old city of Jerusalem seen at the beginning, the film now moves to the "New Jerusalem" – bright, modern buildings such as a hospital and the Hebrew University. Before a crowded audience – among them David Ben Gurion and the British High Commissioner in Palestine,

Arthur Wauchope – a Hebrew version of Joseph Haydn's oratorio, *The Creation*, is performed in an open-air auditorium. Further stations in the film are the library of the Hebrew University, the Daniel Sieff Research Institute in Rehovot, and the Technical School in Haifa. A longer sequence, at a public meeting where a young worker gives a rousing speech, is followed by the last segment – harvesting and preparations for the holiday of Shavuot, which lead to a big parade. Repetitions of various shots seen earlier, which are superimposed over the pages of a Hebrew Bible, form an epilogue of sorts.

Although we learn little about its political and societal organization, the Palestine of *Land of Promise* is in many ways a utopia *in progress*. Several tropes that have their origin in the utopian tradition are visible throughout the film and are also mentioned by Feldestein in his study: the Jewish settlers are, with a few exceptions, *Muskeljuden*, strong and handsome New Men. There is no discernible difference between individual and community; everybody is working together for a common goal. This sense of unity is additionally stressed by the score, which acts as a bridge between different characters. In the kibbutz sequence, a kind of musical relay is performed in which each verse of a song is sung by someone else; from a woman peeling potatoes to a man shaving to another woman hanging up the laundry, and finally to an agricultural worker milking a cow. The pioneers sing and work in sync, "as if they are one body, a united force" (Feldestein 167).

The overall appearance of *Land of Promise* is quite typical for propaganda films of the period. Similar images of agricultural machines, marching workers, and low-angle shots of muscular pioneers can also be found in Soviet and National Socialist productions. But especially in comparison to the latter, *Land of Promise* is forcefully modern and completely lacks the eschatological dimension of National Socialism.[9] While Zionism makes use of religious rhetoric, the return to the Promised Land is a decidedly

9    Critics of utopia often treat National Socialism as a paradigmatic example of the
     inherent danger of any utopian project. While some typical aspects of utopianism,
     like the creation of a New Man and viz. a new society, can be found in National
     Socialism, it is not a coherent design of a state. There is no text in which Hitler pre-
     sents his idea of Germany after the *Endsieg*. In many ways, National Socialism is not
     a unified ideology but a hodgepodge of modernist and archaic convictions that are

secular project, not a messianic one, and Palestine is presented as a progressive and forward-looking country – in agriculture, factories, science,
leisure, or politics.

The kibbutz is a utopian project within Zionism. The kibbutzim, which
first arose in the 1910s as part of socialist Zionism, and then became more
widely recognized, possess many utopian features. Like in More's *Utopia*,
owning private property is largely suspended, and inside the kibbutz, money
is abandoned. Housing, clothing, and food are provided; land and means
of production are common property and are managed collectively. Tasks
like education, cooking, and eating, or making the laundry, are centrally
organized (Zilbersheid 421). While there are differing opinions whether
Zionism can be called a utopian movement, the kibbutzim are regularly
discussed in the context of utopian intentional communities; Melford
E. Spiro even calls them the "largest utopian movement in history" (557).

A long sequence is dedicated to this particular utopia, and the film
seems to assume that its audience has already heard of the "famous" kibbutzim. Their importance – not only for the Jewish settlers, but also for
the whole world – is especially stressed:

> Famous above all are the cooperative colonies of Palestine, where a national idealism
> is linked with a social idealism. And the work of every man and woman is directed
> to a social and not a personal goal. Out of these cooperative colonies will come
> undoubtedly new forms of human organization valuable to Jewish homeland and
> instructive to the rest of the world.

Despite the serious demeanor of the voice-over commentary, other aspects
stand out in the images we see. The sequence begins with boys and girls
exercising together. After the sound of a gong, everyone rushes into the
communal room for lunch. Common meals are a trope of utopian literature. In More's *Utopia*, children silently serve the adults and eat only what
they are handed from the table, but in *Land of Promise*, laughing children are feasting – a girl even feeds her teddy bear. The already mentioned

---

at odds with each other. From this point of view, it comes as no surprise that there
is no "NS utopia" (cf. Hermand 17–35, Kershaw, Schölderle 423f.).

musical relay ends the sequence. Life in the kibbutz does not seem to be regulated and marked by deprivations, but rather, a joyous enterprise.

The kibbutz is utopia realized, but it is not the only form of living available in Palestine. In *Land of Promise*, there is no contradiction or even friction between the socialist society of the kibbutz and the sophisticated life in the metropolis of Tel Aviv. Tensions simply do not exist, neither between Jews and Arabs nor inside the Jewish community: "In fact, there are no conflicts in it at all. *Land of Promise* presents the positive side of life in Eretz Israel and plays down the sacrifice underlying it, without which it would have been impossible to create life in the new land" (Feldestein 181–182).

Utopias are never confined only to the better society; they always talk about the ills that they are meant to cure. But *Land of Promise* dedicates remarkably little time to the plight of the Jews. There are no images of starving Jews in ghettos, and pogroms are never mentioned explicitly. Only toward the end of the early scene aboard the ship is the misery of European Jewry briefly mentioned. We see immigrants queuing in front of tables where functionaries distribute them into different groups. The commentary describes the scene as follows:

> Pioneers and refugees from countries of the oppression where Jews are free to be anything but Jews. Young and old, they are going now to a land which accepts them as its own and not merely as strangers to be tolerated. Yesterday, prisoners of the ghetto, prisoners of their own false hopes. Tomorrow, they will march to their work in the Jewish settlements.

The film which premiered the same year the Nuremberg Laws were enacted does not dwell on the past, which, for the Jews of the diaspora – and therefore for the intended audience – is actually the present, but immediately heads toward the future. The pioneers who only yesterday were living in ghettos will very soon be building streets, carving stone, and digging fountains in Jewish settlements "to restore to Palestine's soil its long-neglected fruitfulness."

Already Herzl spends very little time in describing the plight of the Jews. He knew that his readers were acutely aware of what he was speaking about. Forty years later, the situation of the Jews had even worsened in many places. The viewers of *Land of Promise* did not need a lesson about the sorry state of the Jews. It is quite likely that the filmmakers very deliberately left out depressing scenes and instead focused on the achievements of the Jewish settlers.

Although the problem to which the Zionist utopia reacts is deemphasized, the film still opposes a negative state of affairs with a utopian alternative. But the role of the precarious present that must be overcome is delegated to uncared-for Palestine. A central phrase, which the commentary repeatedly uses, is the "long-neglected fruitfulness" (Tryster, *Land of Promise* 201). From the film's point of view, the problem Zionism must fix is not just the misery of the Jews, but also the centuries of neglect that Palestine had to suffer.

The eviction of the Jews marked the beginning of the decline of the Holy Land, and now, with their return, it is blossoming again. The Zionist utopia is not just about building a new state, but also about making good on the biblical promise, about the return to gone glory. This rhetorical trope, already present in the writings of Herzl and his predecessors, can also be found in many Zionist films. Nicholas Baer's description of *Theodor Herzl, der Bannerträger des jüdischen Volkes* (D: Otto Kreisler, AT 1921), which was produced fifteen years earlier, proves to be equally apt for *Land of Promise*: "juxtaposing two millennia of lachrymose Exile against joyous periods of Jewish nationhood (both in antiquity and in an imminent, redemptive future in Zion)" (240). Glorious past and miserable present are interwoven with regard to a newly splendid future; the deeply rooted Jewish longing for biblical Zion is transformed into a political project.

In the film, this leads to simultaneous time layers. While the geographic location of the Zionist utopia is clearly defined, it is temporally placed in a no-time – or at least in a present that is, at the same time, past as well as future. The backward country of the Arabs, the past that must be overcome, is equally part of contemporary Palestine as the dawning utopian future of the Zionists. Propaganda films often depict the desired future – the victorious election, the destruction of the enemy, the successful conclusion of a modernization campaign – as if it was already happening. The better future made possible by the regime is not far away, but not yet a reality; it only takes one last effort to make it happen. This can also be observed in *Land of Promise*. Although the commentary stresses the opposition between dark past and glorious future, the Jewish utopia in Palestine is treated as if it was already established. By documenting the present, *Land of Promise* does not show how the future could or should look, but rather tries to convince the viewer that better times are already here.

The multiple time layers do not run in parallel, but are mostly separate. The past is almost exclusively shown in the prologue. Here, *Land of Promise* presents backward Palestine, which is then put into contrast with the emerging Jewish state. Interestingly enough, it is not only the Arabs that stand for backwardness, but also the Jews praying at the Wailing Wall. Though the film is never explicitly anti-religious, it is nonetheless striking that Orthodox Judaism is only visible in a few shots of mostly old men. On the subject of the Jews who lived in Palestine before the advent of the Zionist, the commentary says the following: "Most of them had come in their old age from distant countries to die in Palestine and be buried in its sacred soil." These old Jews, for whom the Holy Land is not much more than a graveyard, belong, like the Arabs, to a past that must be overcome. Youthful pioneers who reawaken the almost dead land now take their place.

In addition, the comparison of splendid past, primitive present, and glorious future serves to justify the colonization of the already inhabited land. The Arab population is not presented as hostile or aggressive, but rather is treated with benevolent condescension. These are friendly people, but they are obviously unable to manage the great Jewish heritage in an adequate way. This is a sufficient justification for the Zionist project.

The question of whether Zionism was, right from the start, a colonial project that sought to cast out the Arab population – by violent means, if necessary – has been discussed extensively. From today's point of view, it is certainly striking how little time Herzl spends on the role of the Arab population in the Jewish state. The mere idea that the Arabs could oppose the Jewish settlement is never even considered. Quite to the contrary, the text constantly emphasizes how much the Arab population will profit from the achievements of the Jewish settlers and will therefore welcome them.

Whether this is a sign of Herzl's own racism, his naiveté, or a combination of both, is hard to decide. Whatever it was, in the mid-1930s, when

*Land of Promise* was released, naiveté was no longer a proper excuse. At that time, the conflict between Arabs and Jews was plain to see. There had been numerous violent riots, and in 1936, a year after the film's premiere, the Arab Revolt in Palestine began, which in 1939 lead to a drastic reduction of Jewish immigration to Palestine.

Against this backdrop, it is not surprising that the British board of censors came to the conclusion that the mixture of condescension and disregard, which *Land of Promise* displays toward the Arabs, was not appropriate and therefore demanded the removal of all the scenes in the prologue that show Arab daily life from the Hebrew version shown in Palestine (Tryster, *Land of Promise* 207).

The Zionist organizations that distributed the film did not have such qualms. *Land of Promise* was shown with great success all over the world and served as an excellent source of propaganda and mobilization:

> Wherever it was seen, regardless of whether the actual exhibition of the film showed a profit in book-keeping terms, contributions to Zionist bodies rose sharply, in some cases by hundreds of per cent, a rise attributed by the officials involved in the fund-raising directly to the film. (Tryster, *Land of Promise* 207)

## Conclusion

*Land of Promise* shares many traits with classic literary utopias. One of its distinctive features is that its utopia is presented as already existing. The Jewish state is characterized by its actual presence, its *utopian realism*. Although *Land of Promise* opposes old and new Palestine, it is not so much a utopia of time as of place. The better future is already here – just somewhere else. This rhetorical structure is probably quite common for a certain type of propaganda; to work as a tool for mobilization, the promised better times must not appear to be completely out of reach, but rather, must be presented as almost palpable.

# Bibliography

Bach, Ulrich E. "Seeking Emptiness: Theodor Hertzka's Colonial Utopia *Freiland* (1890)." *Utopian Studies* 22.1 (2011): 74–90. doi: 10.1353/utp.2011.0003.

Baer, Nicholas. "The Rebirth of a Nation: Cinema, Herzlian Zionism, and Emotion in Jewish History." *Leo Baeck Institute Year Book* 59.1 (2014): 233–248. doi: 10.1093/leobaeck/ybu011.

Eliav-Feldon, Miriam. " 'If You Will It, It Is No Fairy Tale': The First Jewish Utopias." *The Jewish Journal of Sociology* 25.2 (1983): 85–103.

Elboim-Dror, Rachel. *Ha-Mahar shel ha-Etmol*. Jerusalem: Yad Izhak Ben-Zvi, 1993.

Ellsworth, Elizabeth. "I Pledge Allegiance: The Politics of Reading and Using Educational Films." *Curriculum Inquiry* 21.1 (1991): 41–64.

Feldestein, Ariel L. *Cinema and Zionism. The Development of a Nation Through Film*. London: Vallentine Mitchell, 2012.

Halachmi, Joseph. "Abraham Neufeld and the Beginnings of the Zionist Film." *Film History* 10.1 (1998): 90–97.

Heil, Hans-Jürgen. *Von der zionistischen Utopie zum Staate Israel: ein Staatsentwurf und seine Verwirklichung. Eine Untersuchung zum Verhältnis von Utopie und Realität*. Unpublished PhD thesis. Würzburg: Julius-Maximilians-Universität Würzburg, 1972.

Hertzka, Theodor. *Freiland. Ein sociales Zukunftsbild*. Leipzig: Duncker & Humblot, 1890.

Herzl, Theodor. *Altneuland. Old-new Land*. Haifa: Haifa Publication, 1960.

——. *The Jewish State*. New York: Dover Publications, 1988.

Hermand, Jost. *Der alte Traum vom neuen Reich: Völkische Utopien und Nationalsozialismus*. Frankfurt am Main: Athenäum, 1988.

Jackson, Paul. "*Freiland*: Theodor Hertzka's Liberal-Socialist Utopia." *German Life and Letters* 33.4 (1980): 269–275.

Kershaw, Ian. "Adolf Hitler und die Realisierung der nationalsozialistischen Rassenutopie." *Utopie und die politische Herrschaft im Europa der Zwischenkriegszeit*. Ed. Wolfgang Hardtwig. München: R. Oldenbourg Verlag, 2003, 133–144.

*Land of Promise/Banim Bonim*. Directed by Yaacov Ben-Dov, PS 1924.

*Land of Promise/L'Chayim Hadashim*. Directed by Juda Leman, PS 1935.

Leucht, Robert. *Dynamiken politischer Imagination. Die deutschsprachige Utopie von Stifter bis Döblin in ihren internationalen Kontexten, 1848–1930*. Berlin/Boston, MA: De Gruyter, 2016. doi: 10.1515/9783110434910.

*Life of the Jews of Palestine*. Directed by Noah Sokolovsky, PS/RU 1913.

Mumford, Lewis. "Herzl's Utopia." *Menorah Journal* 9 (1923): 155–195.

Neale, Steve. "Propaganda." *Screen* 18.3 (1977): 9–40.

Peck, Clemens. *Im Labor der Utopie. Theodor Herzl und das Altneuland-Projekt.* Berlin: Jüdischer Verlag im Suhrkamp Verlag, 2012.

Plantinga, Carl R. *Rhetoric and Representation in Nonfiction Film.* Cambridge: Cambridge University Press, 1997.

Rüthers, Monica. "Von der Ausgrenzung zum Nationalstolz. 'Weibische' Juden und 'Muskeljuden.'" *Der Traum von Israel. Die Ursprünge des modernen Zionismus.* Ed. Heiko Haumann. Weinheim: Beltz Athenäum, 1998, 319–329.

Schölderle, Thomas. *Utopia und Utopie. Thomas Morus, die Geschichte der Utopie und die Kontroverse um ihren Begriff.* Baden-Baden: Nomos, 2011.

Schoeps, Julius. "Wenn ihr wollt, ist es kein Märchen: Theodor Herzls Staatsutopie und die Vision des Judenstaates in seinem Roman *Altneuland.*" *Von kommenden Zeiten: Geschichtsprophetien im 19. und 20. Jahrhundert.* Ed. Joachim H. Knoll and Julius H. Schoeps. Stuttgart: Burg Verlag, 1984, 107–121.

Spiegel, Simon. *Bilder einer besseren Welt. Die Utopie im nichtfiktionalen Film.* Schüren: Marburg, 2019. doi: 10.23799/9783741000829.

——. "Some Thoughts on the Utopian Film." *Science Fiction Film & Television* 10.1 (2017): 53–79. doi:10.3828/sfftv.2017.3.

Spiro, Melford E. "Utopia and Its Discontents: The Kibbutz and Its Historical Vicissitudes." *American Anthropologist* 106.3 (2004): 556–568. doi: 10.1525/aa.2004.106.3.556.

Stolow, Jeremy. "Utopia and Geopolitics in Theodor Herzl's *Altneuland.*" *Utopian Studies* 8.1 (1997): 55–76.

*Theodor Herzl, der Bannerträger des jüdischen Volkes.* Directed by Otto Kreisler. AT 1921

Tryster, Hillel. *Israel before Israel. Silent Cinema in the Holy Land.* London: British Film Institute, 1996.

——. "*The Land of Promise* (1935): A Case Study in Zionist Film Propaganda." *Historical Journal of Film, Radio and Television* 15.2 (1995): 187–217. doi: 10.1080/01439689500260131.

Zilbersheid, Uri. "The Israeli Kibbutz: From Utopia to Dystopia." *Critique* 35.3 (2007): 413–434. doi: 10.1080/03017600701676845.

LAURA WINTER

# "Trial and Error" – Mediating Estrangement in the Quest for Utopia in *The Walking Dead* (2010–Present)

## Seeking the Utopian Impulse in the Post-Apocalyptic Landscape

Whether in novel, film or television series, the figure of the zombie is more popular than ever. Aditya Chakrabortty, for instance, argues that we even live in the *age of the zombie*: "Britain in 2018 is stalked by zombie ideas, zombie politicians, zombie institutions – stripped of credibility and authority, yet somehow still presiding over our lives" (online). The idea of the zombie permeates various socio-cultural reflections. In recent decades, the zombie metaphor is often evoked in regard to the pathologies of late capitalism because the causes for zombification have changed, as Céline Keller demonstrates in her audio-visual exploration of the utopian potential of zombiism: "what before could have only been summoned by magic, is now caused by something real" (online). Irrespective of its cause, the metaphorical potential of the zombie allows to depict the socio-cultural mood, society's fears and anxieties: the mindless consumer, the anonymous mass, the impossible body.

It is with little surprise, then, that *The Walking Dead* has been celebrated as one of the most successful television series in history (cf. BBC News; Stolworthy, "*The Walking Dead* Remains"). The AMC channel has recently greenlit an upcoming *third* series in "the expanding universe of *The Walking Dead*" (AMC Networks). Ever since the pilot episode in 2010, the audience has been involved in the struggle of the fictional core group of survivors to manage life in a world inhabited by the "walking dead" after the outbreak of a virus. Soon it becomes clear that the title of the series does not only refer to the zombies but even more so to the *survivors* of the apocalypse. Adhering to its generic expectations, the series features spectacular slaughtering scenes and succeeds in depicting a post-apocalyptic nightmare, in which life is brutish and short. But as the series matures over the seasons, it seems to offer valuable insights *beyond* the spectacle of eliminating the anonymous mass of the monstrous Other. Tammy Garland and colleagues propose that the comic book series by Robert Kirkman, upon which the television series is based, "represents one of the deepest and most complex treatments of post-apocalyptic survival" (62). Consequentially, the narrative complexity of *The Walking Dead* emerges as a fruitful ground for various critical analyses (see, e.g., Canavan; Garland et al.; Raymen; or Sugg).

*The Walking Dead* progressively turns from a zombie-centered narrative into a narrative about community building and the pursuit of collective, sustainable utopian practices. The core group's vision of the "new world" becomes concrete when the war with the "Saviors," a group led by the main antagonist Negan (Jeffrey Dean Morgan), is finally ended toward the end of Season 8. Uniting the forces of survivors who share the same vision, the core group aims to rebuild a viable society from scratch and proactively build the future instead of simply struggling to survive. The problem of "the walkers" (i.e., the zombies) – though they continue to remain the ultimate threat – slowly ceases to be the focus of the series. Surprisingly, the term zombie is not mentioned once in eight seasons. For the core group of survivors, the term "walkers" has emerged to be the most common reference to the zombies. There are at least thirteen different terms for the undead in the series, such as biters, cold bodies, creepers, or dead ones (see Tung). This is surprising for a series about zombies, but apparently this linguistic restriction was the intention of the creator: Kirkman wanted to create a universe in which zombie fiction did not exist (see Stolworthy, "*The Walking Dead*"). This narrative decision increases the level of estrangement for the characters as they are not able to draw on survival knowledge gained through fiction: the walkers are a hitherto unknown and extraneous antagonistic force which must thus be categorized by the characters from scratch. Unlike zombie fiction depicted in closed formats such as films, the seriality of *The Walking Dead* enables the viewer insights into long-term developments *years into* the post-apocalypse. An isolated focus merely on the zombie figure in *The Walking Dead* would thus mask out latent but important utopian aspects within the series, such as the striving for a better world despite a world made up of zombie ideas and "zombie categories" (Beck 203).

Beyond fictional and theoretical treatments of the concept of utopia, utopianism can also take shape as "lived experiments" in various forms (Sargisson, *Fool's* 15). Lucy Sargisson's empirical studies of "concrete utopias" in the form of intentional communities are an important contribution to the utopian discourse in the twenty-first century. In her article "Strange Places: Estrangement, Utopianism, and Intentional Communities," Sargisson illuminates the paradoxical relationship between estrangement and utopianism by drawing from her observations from a collaborative fieldwork project within over fifty intentional communities in Britain and New Zealand (cf. 394). Interestingly, Sargisson has observed that intentional communities require a certain estrangement for their utopian practices: "Just as utopian fiction requires some level of estrangement for critical distance or cognition, so intentional communities require it to pursue their collective projects" ("Strange" 407). Estrangement emerges as an ambiguous concept which intentional communities struggle with but also rely on. In this context, estrangement may describe the affective distance found in formerly close relationships as well as the physical separation from external surroundings. Too much of it, however, can be dangerous: "Too much physical estrangement can mean that life in an intentional community is materially unsustainable. And too much affective estrangement can contribute to corrupt internal power relations, collective alienation, and a slide from eutopic intent to dystopic outcome" (Sargisson, "Strange" 402).

Sargisson's empirical research on intentional communities provides a tool to extract the utopian impulse from a *post-apocalyptic* narrative such as *The Walking Dead*. The goal of this chapter is to draw attention to the zombie and the rival survivors as a source of estrangement and subsequently flesh out how the ambiguous nature of estrangement and its paradoxical relationship with community can also be discovered in the fictional microcosm of *The Walking Dead*. In this brutish post-apocalyptic landscape of

North America, community building is crucial. Survival is the ultimate drive for the formation of groups, as Katherine Sugg aptly notes: "The tasks of forming human groups into functioning defensive communities – and living rather than the dying – compel a recourse to 'premodern' ways of life and skills that include scavenging, living off the land, and defending oneself against aggressors, both the hordes of the undead and other humans" (800).

The world full of walkers has become an estranged one to the characters: a formerly familiar-turned-hostile space which continuously challenges the survival of the core group, led by protagonist Rick Grimes (Andrew Lincoln).[1] But this estranged world also facilitates the efforts of community building in the long-run. Over the course of the seasons, the unintentional survivor group made up mostly of strangers evolves bottom-up into a strong community – "eutopic in intent" – with a clear collective endeavor: to create a good life in a world that demands constant alertness and restless mobility (Sargisson, "Strange" 393). Their quest for a sustainable utopia, however, is (necessarily) dramatically complicated and depicted as a process marked by continuous trial and error.

## Double Estrangement: Nature/Walkers and Rival Survivors

The struggle of the group is amplified by having to negotiate double estrangement. First, they must learn to adapt to a world suddenly turned hostile, as formerly peaceful natural landscapes are soon infiltrated by the walkers. Second, the survivor group must seek affective estrangement from scavenging rival survivors who depend on the same limited resources left over from the "old" world.

---

1    Garland et al. argue that in the comic books "the real enemy is patriarchy, not the monsters" (65). To a larger extent, the same is true for the television adaptation. Although the creators succeed in providing a more nuanced picture by including female leaders in the later seasons, the problems of patriarchal power structures seem to persist.

With regard to the utopian visions of intentional communities, Sargisson observed that many were "anti-materialist and often involved a life 'closer to nature,' one with a deeper spiritual connection to place" ("Strange" 402). Because cities are overrun by the walkers, the characters in *The Walking Dead* are forced to abandon highly populated areas and find shelter in small towns and the woods, which are assumed to be at least somewhat less frequented by the walkers. In the viewer's reality, living "off the grid" has by now turned into an attractive option for people who want to turn away from materialist society. In *The Walking Dead*, this lifestyle is no longer a deliberate choice but a challenge which needs to be mastered quickly in order to ensure survival. In the first season, Rick Grimes reunites with his family and a small group of other survivors just outside of the now zombie-infested city of Atlanta before they realize that even the outskirts are no longer safe (S1:E4, "Vatos"). The world of the characters is radically different from the pre-apocalypse world and they must (re)learn to manage life without electricity, without permanent access to food and shelter.[2]

The walkers intensify the already estranged space of nature. The wandering corpses lurk everywhere; they are decoyed by light and sound and do not shun any obstacle to reach their objective: to consume flesh. The walkers "do not form a community, much less a society; there is no code of ethics, there is no progress, no change, no redemption" (Heinze and Petzold 58). They are "all body" and depicted as the most instinctual and regressive being. While *one* character can easily handle *one* walker, a walker *herd* must be strategically dealt with and requires seamless verbal and physical coordination of a group. Nevertheless, although single walkers might be technically easier to deal with, the characters are emotionally strained when confronted with a loved one-turned zombie. In the pilot episode "Days Gone Bye," the character Morgan (Lennie James), for example, is incapable of pulling the trigger on his "turned" wife due to his emotional attachment. The unresponsive behavior and the dull eyes estrange the once

---

2   By depicting characters washing their clothes in the river (e.g., S1:E3, "Tell It to The Frogs"), strolling through the woods, and seeking shelter in remote huts, the series provides a stark contrast to most lifestyles in the twenty-first century. At the same time, this may hint at the viewer's desire for a simpler lifestyle in an accelerated and tech-saturated world.

dear person. In this way, the walkers intensify the level of estrangement for the characters also on a very personal level. As Sargisson argues regarding "estranged" relationships:

> In colloquial terms, "estranged" relationships evoke a sense of loss and deterioration. The estranged partner, child, or parent – once familiar and trusted – is now distant, removed, and remote. Each has become "a stranger" to us. Similarly, the stranger, conceptually cast as Other, is the unknown and feared outsider who belongs outside the boundaries of the familiar: "our" community, country, place, or culture. Estrangement may be necessary, then, but it is extremely uncomfortable to endure. It is necessary for group survival, but life in a perpetually estranged space can be difficult. ("Strange" 401)

Another example of dealing with this paradox appears in Season 3, when the Governor clearly struggles with the estranged relationship with his "turned" daughter Penny; he keeps her restrained and "alive" in his closet (S3:E5, "Say the Word"). The walkers, thus, are not (only) the anonymous anti-subject; some of them still resemble the shell of what was once filled with life. Nevertheless, even "turned" loved ones must be kept separated from the group to minimize the risk of attacks. The affective estrangement from the walkers, especially those once held dear, is difficult to endure but facilitates the retreat into groups among the living where continuous mutual support is the last resort for hope.

The second source of estrangement stems from the hostility of and deliberate separation from rival survivors. In this world, "inter-human conflict" arises from scarce resources and the fight for survival causes even relationships with other human beings to become estranged (Raymen 6). Throughout their journey, the core group repeatedly faces various antagonistic groups, such as the Woodbury community led by the authoritarian Governor (Season 3), the cannibals at Terminus (Season 4), and finally the ruthless Saviors in Season 6. All of the groups differ in their approach to make sense of the world, but each one of them has the same goal: survival. Due to the identification with the core group from the very first episode, the viewer is bound to sympathize with them and initially see other survivors as morally inferior. *All* survivor groups, however, follow their instinct of self-interest. Even this post-apocalyptic landscape, in which the social and economic order has come to an end, is still marked by "intense competitiveness and ruthless individualism" (Raymen 7).[3] The core group, too, kill if they have to: "Both protagonists and antagonists frequently transcend ethical and moral norms through killing, looting and invading other groups' communities and compounds, all in the name of 'keeping their people safe'" (Raymen 11). Rival survivors, in particular, seem to be driven by what Zygmunt Bauman refers to as the logic of the "hunting utopia": they no longer believe in sustainable solutions benefiting the collective, they live driven solely by self-interest (see Jacobsen 229). In never giving up hope and always holding on to their vision to create a better world throughout the seasons, however, the core group differs from other survivor groups. By following the protagonists from the beginning, the audience is thus bound to believe that they are the ones "eutopic in intent" (Sargisson, "Strange" 393).

In short, the core group of survivors in *The Walking Dead* must negotiate double estrangement. On the one hand, the omnipresence of walkers forces the group to live a life "off the grid," on the other hand, the rivalry among survivors necessitates affective distance even from other human beings. These conditions lead to a permanent state of exception and a perpetually estranged space for the characters: "The various characters and groups live under constant precarious conditions, with the perpetual threat of displacement by forces external to their control" (Raymen 7).

## Maintaining and Mediating Estrangement in a Perpetually Estranged Space

In the comic books, Garland et al. observe that "[a]long with survival, one of the primary concerns throughout *The Walking Dead* is the drive on the part of men and women to be coupled" (75). Though cultivating

---

3     In a way, then, even though "it is easier to imagine the end of the world than the end of capitalism" (Jameson 199), this perpetually estranged space still echoes conditions of the neoliberalist logic and "capitalist realism" (see Fisher).

romantic subplots keeps up necessary tension for the audience in the television series adaptation as well, the notion of the core group becoming a strong unit is no less important. Members of the core group soon realize that life under extreme conditions as such can only be sustainably dealt with as a community, as character Eugene (Josh McDermitt) admits: "I know empirically and definitely I cannot survive on my own" (S5:E5, "Self Help"). Eugene, though highly intelligent, is one of many characters who depends on others leading the way. Leaders play an important role for group coherence in *The Walking Dead*. Time and again, the series depicts how "[d]eliberate manipulation by leaders and/or collective shifts to extremity can very quickly spin a group into darkly dystopic reality" (Sargisson, "Strange" 417). The antagonistic communities of Woodbury and the Sanctuary are a case in point. Rick as the leader of the core group, too, undergoes several transformations throughout the seasons. In the episode "Beside the Dying Fire" in Season 2, he claims that "this is not a democracy anymore" only to realize one season later that "[w]e're the reason we're still here, not me" (S3:E15, "The Sorrowful Life"). This realization slowly trickles down to the members of the group: Glenn (Steven Yeun) is sure "[w]e can make it together. But we can *only* make it together" (S5:E10, "Them"; emphasis added). The utopian impulse in *The Walking Dead* stems from Rick's group's continuous evolvement into a strong community to create the "new world" *despite* having to negotiate double estrangement. They do not follow the credo of the antagonistic Governor of Woodbury, who is convinced that "In this life now, you kill or you die. Or you die and you kill" (S3:E16, "Welcome to the Tombs").

*The Walking Dead* gradually transforms into a narrative about community, resilience, and adaptation to a totally estranged place. Each group in the fictional world differs in their approach on how to deal with this environment. Building a community based on unshattered hope, strong ethics, and a sustainable vision is depicted as crucial for long-term survival. Estrangement, albeit difficult to deal with, facilitates "critical distance and group coherence" and leads the characters to realize that they need a collective ethos to ensure a sustainable future for the group members (Sargisson, "Strange" 393). Sargisson argues that intentional communities "are strange places, full of dreams, hopes, and disappointments as groups of individuals work collectively to realise a better life. In order to pursue their vision of the good life, these groups require space (in which to experiment), individual security, and group coherence. Estrangement can facilitate these" ("Strange" 396).

In addition to the collective ethos, it is a safe place which helps the community to grow stronger when living in a perpetually estranged space. The constant fear of attacks by rivals or walkers leads the community to seek deliberate spatial isolation in various locations. On their journey, Rick and his group continually try to find a place where they can settle down. The Center for Disease Control (Season 1), Hershel's farm (Season 2), the prison (Season 3) or Terminus (Season 4) – all remain but temporary shelters for the growing community. Until they take over the walled-off community Alexandria in Season 5, "[c]haracters on the show have lived at dozens of potentially permanent and sustainable settlements which the characters are eventually forced to vacate as they are destroyed, overrun by 'walkers' or ruined by other rival groups" (Raymen 7). Even though the group needs a safe place to engage in utopian practices, residing in a particular place for too long might turn out to be dangerous, as Carol (Melissa McBride) warns: "If we get comfortable here, we let our guard down, this place is gonna make us weak" (S5:E12, "Remember"). Nevertheless, leader Rick Grimes is convinced that they can eventually find a place to permanently settle down. Having finally found a safe haven in Alexandria, the core group of survivors necessarily becomes increasingly cautious about opening their gates to strangers.

Though the community's resiliency increases over the seasons, they remain vulnerable to unforeseen threats lurking beyond the wall. Negative experiences with strangers in the past uphold the affective estrangement toward future encounters with other survivors. Taking a look at real-life intentional communities, Sargisson observed that "[e]ntrance and exit rules play an important role in maintaining group coherence and stability" ("Strange" 408). Having learned from their mistakes, Rick and his group scrutinize potential new members of the group by asking the same three questions: "How many walkers have you killed – how many people have you killed – why?" This is the moral coda of the "boundary mechanisms" the group has developed over the years (Sargisson, "Strange" 408). Through these questions, the core group aims to receive further insights into the way potential new members deal with and make sense of the hostile world. It is not the answers per se, but rather the reaction toward these asked questions that help the group decide to open the gates or not. Rick as leader of the group often appeals to the human core within all survivors, when he states, for instance:

> Now you put down your weapons, walk through those gates you're one of us. We let go of all of it, and nobody dies. Everyone who's alive right now. Everyone who's made it this far. We've all done the worst kind of things just to stay alive. But we can still come back. We're not too far gone. We get to come back. I know we all can change. (S4:E8, "Too Far Gone")

Rick is aware that most of the survivors had to commit atrocities in order to survive. The individual past of a potential newcomer in the group is thus not an exclusion criterion. Becoming naïve, however, can have severe consequences. The acceptance of new members is most critical in times when the group is facing extreme conditions beyond their control. Mirroring Sargisson's findings within intentional communities, hastily accepted new members "in the middle of a crisis" often endanger the collective spirit and even the existence of the survivor group in *The Walking Dead* ("Strange" 400).

The external world remains a dangerous place and due to the walkers, an estranged place. Rick Grimes knows that "the dead and the living" beyond the walls will try to get in (S5:E16, "Conquer"). Alexandria provides a place with walls high enough to be safe from the walkers, and the gates ensure the maintenance of clear enter-and-exit rules, a deliberate "physical estrangement" needed to explore and focus on utopian practices (Sargisson, "Strange" 397). Physical estrangement is difficult, however, because this isolation further "generates mutual ignorance and suspicion" toward those on the other side of the wall (Sargisson, "Strange" 403). Raymen argues aptly that the retreat into a walled-off community "cultivates and intensifies a broader fear and stance of aggressiveness not only towards the 'walkers' but towards other survivors as well, who are cast as 'outsiders,' viewed not as people but as abstract threats and invaders seeking to aggressively plunder resources and disrupt the protagonists' way of life"

(6). This isolation, the deliberate spatial estrangement in a "perpetually estranged space," is crucial for the community's survival but hampers the realization of the community's vision beyond their own walls. The insulation scales down the cognitive map of striving toward a sustainable utopia and the physical isolation bears the danger of limited resources. The establishment of several communities in different locations, through which exchange of resources can take place, becomes a vital strategy to create a sustainable life for future generations.

With the victory over the Saviors at the end of Season 8, the community finally seems to be able to settle down in Alexandria, from where sustainable utopian practices can be further explored: this is achieved by both maintaining estrangement through physical separation from the strong external Other (i.e., the "walkers") and by mediating their affective estrangement toward other survivors. Clear boundary mechanisms and controlled interactions minimize the exposure to risks. After the main antagonist Negan is defeated, Rick and his group "open the gate" for the remaining Saviors even though they have been living under Negan's ruthless and authoritarian rule. The affective estrangement is thus mediated by promoting "a distanced and mutual respect for the Other" (Sargisson, "Strange" 410). In the final episode of Season 8, Rick is aware that humanity needs to finally unite against the strong external Other. Pointing at a walker herd, he states:

> Negan's alive, but his way of doing things is over. Anyone who can't live with that will pay the price, I promise you that. Any person here who would live in peace and fairness, who would find common ground – this world is yours, by right. We are life. That's death! And it's coming for us, unless we stand together. So go home. Then the work begins. The new world begins. All this ... all this is just what was. There's gotta be something after. (S8:E16, "Wrath")

With an outbreak of the virus on a global scale, it is clear that the survivor group is incapable of creating a world entirely devoid of danger and fear. *The Walking Dead* survivor group has no other choice but to employ an incremental approach to utopia; they know that they are unable to create a perfectly safe world, but they continuously strive for a *better* one within their scope of agency. Nevertheless, the characters have learned how to deal with walkers more effectively due to the experience collected over the years. With the careful vetting and acceptance of new members, the community even grows in size and the estranged and hostile place beyond the walls can be tackled jointly. Allowing the boundaries of the safe haven to become porous to a certain level, the focus on negotiating the strong external Other is revitalized among the community, which once again facilitates "critical distance and group coherence" and strengthens the collective vision to create a better life on common ground (Sargisson, "Strange" 393).

In the later seasons, the series increasingly focuses on the evolvement of the joint survivor communities (Alexandria, the Sanctuary, Hilltop, the Kingdom) in their attempt to re-establish a societal order. The established communities, closed and open at once, represent what Sargisson refers to as "[u]topias in process: spaces in which the good life is explored and pursued" ("Strange" 393). Though each gate remains highly supervised and strong enter-and-exit rules exist, alliances are formed among the communities who share the same vision, and interactions take place that benefit the greater good. Counsels are appointed, a bridge is built, agricultural practices are enforced, and the audience witnesses the concrete result of a vision that was never given up by the core survivor group, even in the most challenging times.[4]

## Conclusions

Unlike blockbuster post-apocalyptic fiction, *The Walking Dead* offers an extensive fictional microcosm for utopian inquiries in the twenty-first century due to its narrative complexity emerging from seriality. As was shown, *The Walking Dead* is more than a story about zombies. It is a story about the magnitude of social cohesion and the evolvement of

---

4    Season 9 features lighter episodes, foreshadowing a bright future for the characters. This tentative peace, however, is soon threatened by a new antagonistic group, the Whisperers, as well as from within, as certain leadership styles are questioned, and resources continue to remain scarce.

communities in a perpetually estranged space. Lucy Sargisson's findings about intentional communities and their paradoxical relationship with estrangement provide a tool to extract the utopian impulse (even) from a post-apocalyptic narrative.

The goal of this chapter was not to interpret the figure of the zombie – because by now it seems as though the zombie metaphor can "mean virtually anything" (Helmore online). Rather it intended to draw attention to the post-apocalyptic landscape as a source of estrangement and subsequently to the emerging values displayed by the fictional community, values and principles that are increasingly buried nowadays: helpful hands, hope, and a collective vision. In this way, the series has the potential to trigger the viewer emotionally, especially since the sense of community and real face-to-face interaction is on decline in today's tech-saturated environment. The utopian impulse in *The Walking Dead* universe stems from the promotion of the key values uniting a community despite extreme levels of estrangement. Not least, and eclipsing the commercial aspect, *The Walking Dead* unites thousands of people not only in front of the television screen on Sunday nights but also at the annual "Walker Stalker" conventions all over the world. The wide resonance of *The Walking Dead* promises its relevance as a fictional microcosm not only for the study of the contemporary dominant mood in society but also for gaining insights into utopian discourse in the twenty-first century. Estrangement, be it technically through the zombie figure for the audience, or implicitly on a narrative level for the characters, is fundamental to utopianism. What *The Walking Dead* shows us, then, is that even in a world full of zombie ideas, it is possible to build a better world from within.

# Bibliography

AMC Networks. "AMC Greenlights Third Series in *The Walking Dead* Universe." *Press Release*, 8 April 2019. Online. <https://www.amc.com/shows/the-walking-dead/talk/2019/04/amc-announces-new-series-in-the-walking-dead-universe-to-premiere-in-2020>. Accessed 10 April 2019.

BBC News. "Walking Dead breaks US cable TV record." 14 October 2014. Online. <http://www.bbc.com/news/entertainment-arts-29611037>. Accessed 3 January 2016.

Beck, Ulrich and Elisabeth Beck-Gernsheim. *Individualization: Institutionalized Individualism and its Social and Political Consequences*. Trans. Patrick Camiller. London: SAGE, 2001.

Canavan, Gerry. "'We Are the Walking Dead': Race, Time, and Survival in Zombie Narrative." *Extrapolation* 51.3 (2010): 431–453.

Chakrabortty, Aditya. "Britain Is Being Stalked by a Zombie Elite." *The Guardian*, 17 January 2018. Online. <https://www.theguardian.com/commentisfree/2018/jan/17/britain-zombie-elite-politicians-economy>. Accessed 12 October 2018.

Fisher, Mark. *Capitalist Realism: Is There No Alternative?* Winchester: Zero Books, 2009.

Garland, Tammy S., Nickie Phillips and Scott Vollum. "Gender Politics and *The Walking Dead*: Gendered Violence and the Reestablishment of Patriarchy." *Feminist Criminology* 13.1 (2016): 59–86.

Heinze, Rüdiger and Jochen Petzold. "No More Room in Hell: Utopian Moments in the Dystopia of *28 Days Later*." *Zeitschrift für Anglistik und Amerikanistik – A Quarterly of Language, Literature and Culture* 55.1 (2007): 53–68.

Helmore, Edward. "The Brits Who Took the Slow Road to Success – by Killing the Zombie Hordes." *The Guardian*, 23 October 2016. Online. <https://www.theguardian.com/tv-and-radio/2016/oct/22/the-walking-dead-andrew-lincoln-slow-road-us-success>. Accessed 14 October 2018.

Jacobsen, Michael H. "Solid Modernity, Liquid Utopia – Liquid Modernity, Solid Utopia: Ubiquitous Utopianism as a Trademark of the Work of Zygmunt Bauman." *The Contemporary Bauman*. Ed. Anthony Elliott. New York: Routledge, 2007. 217–240.

Jameson, Fredric. *Archaeologies of the Future: The Desire Called Utopia and Other Science Fictions*. London: Verso, 2005.

Keller, Céline. "When the Undead Dream of Living – The Utopian Potential of Zombiism." *Krustelkram* 2018. Online. <https://www.krustelkram.com/utopian-dreaming/2018/7/17/when-the-undead-dream-of-living-the-utopian-potential-of-zombiism>. Accessed 11 November 2018.

Kirkman, Robert. *The Walking Dead*. Berkeley, CA: Image Comics, 2003 – present.

Raymen, Thomas. "Living in the End Times Through Popular Culture: An Ultra-Realist Analysis of *The Walking Dead* as Popular Criminology." *Crime, Media, Culture* 14.3 (2017): 1–19.

Sargisson, Lucy. *Fool's Gold? Utopianism in the Twenty-First Century*. Basingstoke: Palgrave Macmillan, 2012.

———. "Strange Places: Estrangement, Utopianism, and Intentional Communities." *Utopian Studies* 18.3 (2007): 393–424.

Stolworthy, Jacob. "*The Walking Dead* Remains One of Cable TV's Highest-Viewed US Dramas after 8 Seasons." *The Guardian*, 28 February 2018. Online. <https://www.independent.co.uk/arts-entertainment/tv/news/the-walking-dead-season-8-viewing-figures-episode-8-honor-carl-dies-rick-andrew-lincoln-amc-a8232396.html>. Accessed 5 April 2019.

———. "*The Walking Dead* Season 7: This Is Why the Word 'Zombie' Is Never Used." *The Independent*, 7 December 2016. Online. <https://www.independent.co.uk/arts-entertainment/tv/news/the-walking-dead-season-7-theres-a-reason-why-the-word-zombie-is-a-big-no-no-a7461246.html>. Accessed 5 January 2019.

Sugg, Katherine. "*The Walking Dead*: Late Liberalism and Masculine Subjection in Apocalypse Fictions." *Journal of American Studies* 49.4 (2015): 793–811.

*The Walking Dead*. Dir. Frank Darabont et al. AMC Studios, 2010 – present. TV/DVD.

—— Season 1, Episode 1 "Days Gone Bye."

—— Season 1, Episode 3 "Tell It to the Frogs."

—— Season 1, Episode 4 "Vatos."

—— Season 2, Episode 13 "Beside the Dying Fire."

—— Season 3, Episode 5 "Say the Word."

—— Season 3, Episode 15 "The Sorrowful Life."

—— Season 3, Episode 16 "Welcome to the Tombs."

—— Season 4, Episode 8 "Too Far Gone."

—— Season 5, Episode 5 "Self Help."

—— Season 5 Episode 10 "Them."

—— Season 5, Episode 12 "Remember."

—— Season 5, Episode 16 "Conquer."

—— Season 8, Episode 16 "Wrath."

Tung, Angela. "13 Ways of Saying 'Zombie' on *The Walking Dead*." *Mental Floss*, 30 March 2015. Online. <http://mentalfloss.com/article/62572/13-ways-saying-zombie-walking-dead>. Accessed 5 January 2019.

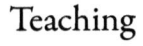

Teaching

IBTISAM AHMED, DAVID M. BELL, ELENA COLOMBO, AND
ROBYN MUIR

# Utopia, Pedagogy, and Care: A Conversation

## Introduction

The following is an edited transcript of a conversation among three of
Lucy Sargisson's current PhD students (Ibtisam Ahmed, Elena Colombo,
and Robyn Muir) and one former PhD student (David M. Bell). With the
exception of Elena, all of us were also taught by Lucy as undergraduates.
In discussing our pedagogical experiences with Lucy, we realized that we
had all been profoundly affected not just by her expertise in and enthusiasm for feminist utopian social theory, but by her astounding capacity
for care. The conversation thus gave us the chance to explore not only
how Lucy's work has shaped our own work in the field of utopian studies
(Ibtisam, Elena, and David) and feminist cultural studies (Robyn), but
to acknowledge the manner in which this care has mediated our pedagogical relationships with her. In the spirit of a utopianism that undoes
and remakes the world, we also interrogate the relationships between
Lucy's utopian theory, her pedagogy, and her care, critically situating
them in relation to an academic milieu that is all too frequently uncaring,
and profoundly dystopian.

> DAVID: I first encountered Lucy when an undergraduate studying
> Politics at the University of Nottingham, where I was taught by
> her on a number of modules, most notably Feminist Political
> Theory and Political Utopianism. Unlike much of what I encoun-
> tered on my degree, these didn't take the post-political terrain of
> technocratic governance as a given, but encouraged students to

challenge and unpick assumptions, returning the world once again to possibility.

IBTISAM: I also first met Lucy through Political Utopianism. What drew me to the class was its description in the module handbook, which stated that it dealt with human hope and the imagination; and sought to develop an understanding of utopianism through both real world and fictional examples. That set it aside from many other modules, which drew quite a stark dividing line between fiction and reality. Prior to then I'd never really considered utopianism beyond its mainstream understanding.

Her teaching was unique: you really felt as if you were on an equal footing with her. The hierarchies usually present between expert and newcomer just weren't there. Of course, we knew she had expertise, that was very clear, but she knew that this came from a particular position of privilege, and right from the very first seminar, she welcomed new perspectives. As a person of color, I felt I could bring something different to the module, and Lucy validated and encouraged that.

She also supervised my undergraduate dissertation and ultimately helped me develop my PhD proposal along similar lines. She remembered me despite my move to a different university in the interim, and promptly responded with both care and interest; and that has remained a constant: she cares about me as a scholar and a person. That, I think, ties into the ethics of care which comes across in her utopianism. She lives what she teaches.

ROBYN: I like to see my meeting with Lucy as fate. When I knew I was going to Nottingham to study Politics I did a bit of research about the department, and came across a series of YouTube videos they had produced called "Politics in 60 Seconds," in which an academic outlined a particular political concept within a minute. Lucy had one on utopia (Sargisson "Utopia"). I instinctively clicked on it and was enthralled. Academic ideas and concepts could seem inaccessible when you're that age, but she made it vital and accessible. I had heard of utopia, but I didn't truly understand what it meant. Lucy's sixty seconds of shared knowledge intrigued me. Then, in

the first week of my undergraduate degree I was assigned my personal tutor, and it was Lucy.

DAVID: It wasn't just *what* Lucy taught that's stayed with me, but *how*
she taught. She had this astonishing ability to dig into students'
firmly held positions such that they started to reflect on how those
positions (1) are actually political; (2) are attachments to power,
rather than free-floating "opinions"; and (3) are open to contestation. And I include myself in this: many times, she would ask a
question that excavated this whole substrate of ideological attachment that I had no idea was there.

That can be quite harrowing: people are attached to these views because they are attached to the material power structures from which they
derive. But Lucy always did this with an astonishing care which mitigated
against the kind of defensiveness I've so often experienced when trying
to challenge views in this way. That care is, of course, both an ability and
a privilege, as well as a form of labor, and I often think about how Lucy
used it pedagogically.[1]

ROBYN: Lucy was also a seminar tutor for my first-year political
theory modules, where she really challenged students to think
critically. At one point I became frustrated with an essay question, until I spoke to her. The advice she gave me changed the way
I thought, and still think, about approaching questions today: she
suggested that I argue against the essay question itself and draw out
my criticism that way. Her advice opened up my critical thinking
and gave me the confidence to write about my ideas.

In the second year of my degree, I had gone to see Disney's *Frozen*
(2013) at the cinema. I kept thinking about how both of the female

---

1 In referring to care as a "privilege," I am highlighting the politics of whose care is
recognized as care: those whose care manifests, or is interpreted as, anger, for example, may not be able to use their care pedagogically in the same way that Lucy
did. And anger is, of course, a phenomenon mediated through relationships to
power (such that women of color, e.g., are more likely to be read as "angry").

protagonists were so different from the previous princesses Disney had produced. I started to think carefully about how the image of women had changed throughout the production of the princess films, and although I had already had an idea for my final year dissertation in mind, I kept coming back to the princesses. A lot of people questioned it, its validity, reliability, and whether it was political at all. I found myself seeking Lucy for advice, and I left her office feeling confident about my proposal after discussing my ideas. Even after I handed in my dissertation and applied for my postgraduate degree, I knew that it was Lucy that I wanted to work with. To this day as my supervisor, her enthusiasm for my research has remained. Of course, as I am continually developing as a researcher, she challenges me to think critically about what I am doing and how I am doing it. She has helped me become a critical, reflexive interdisciplinary scholar who seeks to politicize what others perceive as trivial matters. Initially my confidence in my knowledge and skills would falter, but Lucy would always remind me that my work is valuable, even in the most subtle of ways. Those continual affirmations are so important, particularly in the face of imposter syndrome. There's an interesting recent essay on imposter syndrome as "public feeling" by Maddie Breeze (2019), who argues that it's not a matter of individual self-esteem, it is tied in to recreating racist, sexist, classist, and ableist hierarchies within higher education, and society more broadly. It's not just affirmation, though: Lucy just seems to know you better than you know yourself. She can see what it is that you need before you know that you need something, but rather than tell you she guides you in the right direction so you can find it yourself. She nourishes you and supports you on that journey: her care is astonishing.

ELENA: My first contact with Lucy was in 2015. This was after I obtained my Master's degree in Contemporary English Literature from the University of Milan, with a thesis on the utopian aspect of Octavia E. Butler's work. I had always been interested in utopian literature, and I wanted to take the opportunity of the thesis to expand my knowledge of it. My supervisor, an expert on science fiction, could not give me much guidance on utopian theory, and the lack of resources available for reference in my university made the whole task quite challenging. In addition, my – admittedly – naïve reliance on mainly literary sources limited my work – not that I could have known that at the time. However, those months spent researching were the most rewarding in my university career, and I finally graduated with honors.

Afterward, I toyed for some time with the idea of doing a PhD. With vague hope, I put together a proposal and sent it out to a number of utopian studies scholars I knew of. Among them was Ruth Levitas, who advised me to reach out to Lucy, knowing that her research interests came really close to mine: environmentalism, literature, intentional communities, and utopianism. I avidly read *Fool's Gold* (2012), all the time wondering why I had never read her work before and wishing I had written it myself.

I didn't hear back from Lucy for a long time, but I still remember finding her response in my mailbox on December 23rd – a proper Christmas present, to my mind. She was enthusiastic about my proposal, and so incredibly kind. Obviously, there was a catch: if I wanted her to be my supervisor, I would have to move from Literature to Politics, a prospect simultaneously thrilling and terrifying. It was only Lucy's constant reassurance, both during the application and in the early stages of my PhD that kept me grounded and gave me the security to continue. Doing interdisciplinary research is not easy, especially when you have to try to carve your own space in a department you are completely unfamiliar with. In addition to that, I was also moving from Italian to British academia – not an easy task. It was a real challenge, and it was Lucy's support and faith in me that made me brave enough to face it.

ROBYN: She reads people and situations so well: she knows when and how to provide support and when to probe. There is such experience and wisdom behind her care, which comes across in both her supervision and her academic work.

DAVID: I want to reflect critically on this care in the context of a higher education system that is so often uncaring and, in fact, actively damaging, and which relies on gendered divisions of labor to mitigate that damage (Hawkins). Because let's be clear: that care is labor. We've all said how much it has helped us, and while some of that operates on the terrain of emotional well-being, it can't be separated from whatever academic capital it has helped us accrue. And, of course, that labor enormously benefits the department and the university too. It is difficult to untangle the potential utopian use value of that care from its exchange value within an academic economy that pretends it is founded on the former but is in fact reproduced by the latter. Lucy's affective capacity – her ability to be caring and centering – makes clear the truth of Marxist-feminism's claim that there is no (academic) production without reproduction; or, to put it another way, that reproductive labor is, in fact, productive (Mies).

So we can't simply celebrate care in an uncaring system. Rather, I'd advocate bringing Lucy's care into combination with her insistence on utopianism to think through whether it might have a sort of utopian surplus. Could it have a use value that exceeds the circulation of exchange value within higher education? One that estranges us from the everyday operations of that circulation? That educates our desire about how things might be otherwise? And one that actually instantiates that otherwise?

IBTISAM: I think this is crucial. Lucy shows us that education can be done differently. I really value how she undercuts competitiveness in higher education, which normally interpolates us as entrepreneurial subjects trained to compete from the earliest career stages. In fact, I've had to compete with you, Elena, for funding, though I think we both got it in the end! Lucy does this in a way that neither undermines our (self-)worth as scholars nor simply trains us for a career in higher education as a space of competition (Brandist).

ELENA: I agree, the fact that we were able to support each other, despite the competition (something that happened again between Robyn and myself afterward), was crucial at that time; and it is easy to see, in hindsight, how Lucy's example influenced our attitude. It is a mixture of professionalism and care that stands out in the world of academia. It is a quality, however, that is often undervalued and taken for granted, especially when coming from a woman.

ROBYN: The idea that women should be caring and nurturing is something that I've thought about a lot. The concept of care is gendered, with women often being constructed as "nurturers" and caring responsibilities being naturally allocated to them within family structures (Poole & Isaacs 529–530; Tong 163). I want to be clear here when I say that care and caring is not a bad thing, and it is certainly not a bad thing to do if you are a woman. The issue is that care is consistently being associated with women and is being undervalued. Providing care, whether it is physical or emotional, is labor.

DAVID: We need to think about a care that doesn't just reproduce this world but unmakes it. Thinking about Lucy's care alongside her work on utopia – and thinking of them as equally important (not something current academic economies do!) – might allow us to arrive at a utopian orientation toward what care *could* do, what it sometimes does in the cramped spaces of possibility the world provides us, and how Lucy has shaped us and our worlds.[2]

IBTISAM: Lucy's work has shaped my knowledge on the subject of utopia to an extraordinary extent, and I've always been drawn to her insistence that we critically engage with situations and come up with solutions. Her work gives us the tools to recognize that many things can be utopian, but that not everything is utopian: "critical engagement" is crucial. A desire to change the world isn't enough, and utopias don't happen just because those in power say they have. There needs to be a collective, democratic intent to interrogate and change. We can see this with decolonization and its conflation with independence. It's not enough to say that Bangladesh,

---

2　For a utopian reading of the Marxist-feminist project of demanding wages for unpaid gendered labor (often criticized for being reformist), see Weeks. On the problems with care and the potential for a utopian care that undoes the world, see Lewis.

my country, is decolonized because it's independent, as many do (see Rizvi; Bergman): there needs to be that critical engagement with the realities of independence. Lucy's work on utopianism has helped me to insist on these factors and to understand decolonization as a utopian process, and it made me actively look for like-minded scholars, such as Ashis Nandy[3] and Kolar Aparna.[4]

ELENA: Lucy's tri-fold definition of utopianism as requiring a dissatisfaction with and criticism of the present, an engagement in contemporary debates, and the desiring and imagining of alternatives has been crucial for my research and my general approach to utopian studies (Sargisson, *Fool's* 9). It is a definition that opens a whole range of cultural, literary, and political phenomena to utopianism (and vice versa). On a personal level, it allows me to justify my position as an academic in the field of politics. When I first approached utopias, it was from the perspective of a literature student: in order to identify the genre, I learned to focus on convention, structures, and themes. This, however, was problematic for me, as I felt it wasn't the right way to go: something was missing. Lucy's definition was like a missing piece in a jigsaw puzzle; it helped me in clarifying my understanding of the phenomenon of utopianism in general and the classification of the various literary genres as utopian expressions. It also enabled me to focus more on the content of utopian cultural phenomena. As Lucy writes in *Contemporary Feminist Utopianism*, "the study of utopianism is an inexhaustible and fascinating process but requires a broad-ranging background and can lead to the 'Jack of all trades' syndrome. This tension is explored by the new utopianism, the radicalness of

3 Especially in his chapter "Towards a Third World Utopia" (20–55), where he discusses the need to understand utopianism, and, indeed, political theory, as not being inherently Eurocentric – a concept I had not seen really interrogated at British universities until I was encouraged to do so in Lucy's classroom vis-a-vis wider utopian studies scholarship.

4 The need to challenge structural barriers to knowledge is particularly highlighted in the chapter co-written with Olivier Kramsch, "Asylum University: Re-situating Knowledge-exchange along Cross-border Positionalities" (93–107).

which I have suggested is its self-conscious and resourceful transgression of boundaries. [...] [C]onceptualization is privileged over concept" (227).

IBTISAM: I've found Lucy's work really productive for allowing me to theorize competing utopianisms too. It's enabled me to understand colonialism as a (sometimes self-consciously) utopian formation: a desire to create perfect societies in what were seen as "empty" or "chaotic" regions of the world and I cannot think of a better way to examine the "civilising mission" at the heart of the analyses of Catherine Hall (12) and the "reasons of Empire" described by Eric Hobsbawm (328). Lucy's work really drilled home that oppressive systems of governance (such as fascism) often come from a specific vision of utopian thought. If I had approached my research without this consideration, I would have been quick to judge colonialism as oppressive without any nuance toward its intent, and any form of anti-colonialism to be formulaic and united in its utopianism. Her books and supervision have led me to the nuances within this debate. As a result, it lets me engage with scholarship that defends colonialism (such as Niall Ferguson's *Empire*) and challenge it with greater conviction. More importantly, it enables me to understand that not all forms of decolonization come from an equal power dynamic, nor are they intrinsically compatible. For example, in my research on the British Raj, I explored competing forms of religious emancipation and reform, like the Deobandi Movement (primarily Muslim) and the Self-Respect Movement (primarily Hindu). They tackled context-specific issues and represented two opposing liberation models (Deobandi focusing on purely Muslim solidarity and Self-Respect actively breaking down Hindu isolationism). With the renewed perspective Lucy gave me, I have come to understand these two strands of decolonization as equally legitimate but clearly distinct forms of utopian thinking and utopian action – because I no longer focus on an idea of perfectionism but on responding to material concerns.

DAVID: I've taken an enormous amount from Lucy's political insistence that we cannot abstract our utopianism from our understandings of the world, nor can we project it onto a world free from power. Her work makes clear the politics of her methodological insistence on utopianism requiring a critical engagement with the world as it is. It tells us that the way we understand the world informs how we act in or seek to transform it (and that this can be productive), and that those understandings are bound up with structures and operations of power and resistance. Such understandings are common sense for many on the left today – certainly in the wake of standpoint theory – but I think they're too often ignored, overlooked or rejected within utopian studies. This tends to the too easy celebration of visions of something else simply because they're (supposedly) utopian; or positions an understanding of our differing material relationships to power as somehow undercutting the solidarity needed to create utopia (Levitas, "We Argue" 259–260; Coleman).

IBTISAM: Key for me was the rejection of binaries that's so central to Lucy's work. Through this I first encountered the idea that dystopia isn't simply the opposite of utopia but that they contain one another (Sargisson, *Fool's* 8–10). That was extremely useful in helping me frame my current research: the subjective nature of colonial authorities thinking particular arrangements are utopian, while those colonized very much disagreed. And furthermore, understanding the differences between how competing forms of decolonization appealed to different community groups.

ELENA: That idea of rejection of binaries, which leads to the inevitable interplay between utopia and dystopia, is also central to my research, as well as the skepticism toward utopianisms oriented to perfection. In attempting to deepen the understanding of contemporary critical dystopias, I found myself going back to the beginnings to trace the evolution of the literary genre, in parallel with the growing debate on the definition of utopia and utopianism. The moment of transition from utopianism as creation of blueprints to expression of "social dreaming," of hope and desire for something better (as discussed by Bloch; Suvin; Levitas, *Concept*; Sargent; Moylan and Baccolini; Moylan) marks the shift, in literature, to the hybrid forms of critical utopias and dystopias. These new forms offer a more accurate reflection of the complexity of the present in their more nuanced, ambiguous approaches – thus spurring my interest in their inner workings. As the interaction between the "two spirits" of utopia, criticism and hope, evolves in the political theory side of the scholarship, it is also reflected in the growth of the new literary genres – not only in themes and ideas, but in the structures, as well (Elliott 20). This parallelism between the political side and the more formally literary side of the scholarship has allowed me to cross comfortably the lines between literature and politics, and to be where I am now.

DAVID: Yes, though that requires thinking beyond subjective assessments. Or at least, beyond the common sense understanding of the term, which relies on a liberal understanding of the subject as operating (ideally) autonomously from regimes and flows of power. Rather, the position of the subject who makes those claims is bound up by very material (and often violent) relationships, as in the case of colonialism. Although I'm using quite a different language from Lucy here, I think this comes across strongly in *Contemporary Feminist Utopianism*.

Lucy's insistence that there are forms of utopianism that might operate against each other has been important for me to. So in *Contemporary Feminist Utopianism* she outlines a patriarchal utopianism that "marks a desired end to history, terminates progress, and presents the final result of politics"; and a "difficult and slippery" feminist utopianism that transgresses finitude, keeping the future radically open as a space of possibility (226, 230). While I came to the study of utopianism with a preference for the latter, that preference was largely existential and, in fact, quite masculine: change for its own sake. What Lucy's work makes clear is that this second utopianism is in fact not driven simply by a compulsion for change, but is by those who find the present arrangements of power intolerable; something I've tried to develop through my reading of Sara Ahmed's "affect alien" as a potentially utopian figure (Ahmed passim; Bell 148–155).

I have also drawn from the idea that utopia and dystopia are strangely, ambiguously imbricated forms, but to this I have added anti-utopianism and post-utopia. I can trace the genesis of this analysis, which I develop in *Rethinking Utopia* (Bell 21–25), to Lucy's claim in *Contemporary Feminist Utopianism* that a utopianism oriented to perfection "symbolizes death: the death of movement, the death of progress and process, development and change; the death, in other words, of politics" (37). What leapt out at me here was that this was profoundly anti-utopian: there is "no need for utopianism in [this kind of] utopia" (Bell 66). And when this is applied to neoliberalism's claim to have resulted in "the end of history," this becomes post-utopian too (see Fukuyama).

ROBYN: Lucy's methodological and disciplinary pluralism, and the privileging of conceptualization over concept, has been really important for me too, though I don't work in the field of utopian studies. Lucy's work has helped me understand the political elements of everyday culture, particularly in fiction. It has enabled me to engage phenomena that aren't the subject of "capital P" Politics and think about how they might be otherwise. For me, we must always examine forms of oppression from the grassroots in order to truly understand the origins of discrimination. In order to understand how and why women are oppressed, we need to critically explore spaces that begin during our development as individuals. So, I feel confident that in engaging with representations of femininity in the figure of the Disney Princesses, I'm doing political work that matters. The utopian orientation of Lucy's work, meanwhile, has helped me escape an overly empirical mode of working: it's not simply about identifying the truth, but creating "a new conceptual space" for other ways of being and living (*Fool's* 91). One of those things for many children is Disney films. But looking beyond this, many other areas of childhood that are considered trivial must also be explored to understand how discrimination forms. Space, within this context, is both conceptual and geographical. Your understanding of yourself and others is to an extent bound by your environment; however, when images of men and women are created through film, that space also becomes conceptual. The interdisciplinarity that seems so natural in her work is really important too: it's not just that a wide range of phenomena are political, it's that other disciplines have much to offer the study of politics.

IBTISAM: This loops back to some of what we were saying about Lucy's pedagogy. In her undergraduate module, we were encouraged to apply utopian analysis to a range of cultural phenomena in addition to classic works of utopian fiction. And the essay question was open: we were to write about some phenomena through a lens of utopia. The responses ended up examining superheroes, museums, dubstep music, and video games, among others. Utopianism doesn't just have three faces anymore (Sargent); it has a thousand! And a thousand more! And may they keep blooming.

Lucy also doesn't gatekeep how we use her work. In fact, she always encourages us to extend and challenge her work: that's perhaps when she gets most excited in a supervision meeting, in fact. I remember her actively telling me to disagree with her and there have been several times where that helped me defend my thinking – particularly in my belief that utopias *can* occur as a series of moments rather than exclusively as one definitive act of change.

DAVID: Yes, and I wanted to talk about where I disagree with some of what Lucy's written too. While I am very much on the side of a utopianism that is open-ended, I want to hold on to the notion of utopia as a place. This, for me, is what gives utopianism its specificity, and differentiates it from radical politics more broadly: the fact that it is oriented to the reproduction of place either imagined or real (and that's not a binary). I only realized this after being dissatisfied with the quite profound "topophobia" that I found in *Contemporary Feminist Utopianism*. The chapter "Utopia as No Place," in particular, positions place on the side of closure, stasis, and the death of politics; and utopia as necessarily "no place" because to be a place would be to succumb to finality (Sargisson 98–132).

Only "conceptual space" of the kind that Robyn mentioned earlier is permitted (Sargisson, *Contemporary* 121). Frustrated by this, I read more about different understandings of place, encountering Indigenous understandings of place as a way to name "the relationship of things to each other" (Deloria & Wildcat 22–23); and the work of geographers such as Doreen Massey, who sees place as a relational form marked and (re)produced by operations of power (Massey). So that frustration was productive: through it I came to an understanding of place as necessarily open to political, and thus utopian, remaking; and to utopianism as a particularly geographic form.

A frustration I find less productive is the reading of Angela Carter's *The Passion of New Eve* (1977) in *Contemporary Feminist Utopianism* (202–203). Lucy Nicholas has outlined resonances between Lucy's deconstructivist, anti-essentialist utopianism and queer theory's rejections of the gender binary, and that's a reading I broadly share. But the invocation of *The Passion of New Eve* as a work of feminist utopianism works against it. While the novel certainly tries to undo the gender binary, its use of the character Tristessa to suggest that trans people *uphold* the gender binary by performing a parody of femininity is a decidedly transphobic position. The possibilities to understand trans identities and experiences were, of course, less widespread in the mid-1990s, so I do not say this to condemn but rather to underline the importance of process, change, and continued critical evaluation not just in utopianism, but in utopian studies too (see Binnie). To quote *Fool's Gold*, "we need [...] to have shifting working definitions of ourselves that are always contextualized and open to challenges from within and mindful of the dangers of speaking for others: identity politics is about something that both *must and cannot* be named" (96, italics in original).

ROBYN: I think for me, as someone who is not situated within utopian studies, nor am I someone that directly engages with utopian thinking, it is Lucy's pedagogy and scholarship that I have been able to learn and grow from. I have been taught and supervised by Lucy since 2012, and she has had a huge impact on my own teaching. During my undergraduate degree, her continual practice of not only teaching us content, but actually teaching us to engage with and challenge that content was crucial for my learning and understanding. As someone who now teaches undergraduate students, I have ensured that I continue Lucy's pedagogy as part of my own teaching.

I have also learnt so much from Lucy as a scholar, despite our difference in topics! The confidence that she has helped me to develop is immeasurable, and I think that shows through the methods and theories I have chosen to use within my own work, despite not all of them being commonly used by political scholars. And I think this goes back to the idea of conceptual space we were discussing earlier, not only has Lucy's research and scholarship encouraged us to create and develop new conceptual spaces, it is also her pedagogy and care that have contributed to developing an environment where we feel we can create those spaces.

ELENA: I think, Robyn, that what you just described is quite utopian in itself. As a Graduate Teaching Assistant in Politics, like yourself, I know the trial that is creating a space for the students where they could feel safe enough to express their opinions, but also never stagnant, always challenged to relate those theories with the reality of contemporaneity, to engage critically with the works they are studying. It is in that challenge of criticism and engagement that our work as teachers, I believe, takes a utopian nuance. It is not only the creation of that space utopian in itself, but it is also in the critical, but constructive attitude we encourage in the students. Utopias, in Lucy's words, "seek to change the world" (*Fool's* 8) and hopefully, maybe in even some small way, our students will go and do exactly that.

## Conclusion

*Contemporary Feminist Utopianism* has a rather reluctant conclusion, suspicious of a concept that "terminates a discussion and presents the final result or decision, judgment of which has been reached (ideally) by reasoning" (226). Like a looping record we, too, reject conclusion. This conversation has not been a Socratic exercise in reason aimed at finding a universal truth, but rather a four-way interrogation of how Lucy's work – and we mean work in every sense of the term – has impacted on us. This conversation, like Lucy's work, and like the utopianism she develops and advocates, is not one of finitude and closure, but is an interrogation of the spaces that she has opened up for others to remake. Like Lucy, we must keep being difficult, and keep being slippery.

## Bibliography

Abensour, Miguel. "Persistent Utopia." *Constellations: An International Journal of Critical and Democratic Theory* 15.3 (2008): 406–421.

Ahmed, Sara. *The Promise of Happiness*. Durham, NC: Duke University Press, 2010.

Aparna, Kolar and Kramsch, Olivier. "Asylum University: Re-situating Knowledge-exchange along Cross-border Positionalities." *Decolonising the University*. Ed. Gurinder Bhambra et al. London: Pluto, 2018. 93–107.

Bell, David M. *Rethinking Utopia. Place, Power, Affect*. New York: Routledge. 2017.

Bergman, David. "The Politics of Bangladesh's Genocide Debate." *The New York Times*, 5 April 2016. Online. <https://www.nytimes.com/2016/04/06/opinion/the-politics-of-bangladeshs-genocide-debate.html>. Accessed April 2019.

Berlant, Lauren. *Cruel Optimism*. Durham, NC: Duke University Press, 2011.

Bloch, Ernst. *The Principle of Hope*, Vol. 1. Trans. N. Plaice, S. Plaice & P. Knight. London: Wiley-Blackwell, 1986.

Binnie, Imogen. "Interview with the Ghost of Angela Carter." *Pretty Queer Magazine* 2011. Online. <http://prettyqueer.tumblr.com/post/11325371307/interview-with-the-ghost-of-angela-carter>. Accessed April 2019.

Bogue, Ronald. "Deleuze and Guattari and the Future of Politics: Science Fiction, Protocols and the People to Come." *Deleuze and Guattari Studies* 5 (Suppl) (2011): 77–97.

Brandist, Craig. "The Perestroika of Academic Labour: The Neoliberal Transformation of Higher Education and the Resurrection of the 'Command Economy.'" *Ephemera: Theory & Politics in Organization* 17.3 (2017): 583–608.

Breeze, Maddie. "Imposter Syndrome as a Public Feeling." *The Sociological Review*, 11 March 2019. Online. <https://www.thesociologicalreview.com/imposter-syndrome-as-a-public-feeling/>. Accessed June 2019.

Carter, Angela. *The Passion of New Eve*. London: Victor Gollancz, 1977.

Coleman, Nathaniel. "No Solidarity: The Fall of Public (Wo)Man; 'Identity Politics' and the End of Utopia?" Paper presented at "Solidarity and Utopia." 18th Conference of the Utopian Studies Society. European Solidarity Centre, Gdańsk, July 2017.

Deloria, Vine Jr., and Daniel Wildcat. *Power and Place: Indian Education in America*. Golden, CO: Fulcrum Resources, 2001.

Elliott, Robert C. *The Shape of Utopia: Studies in a Literary Genre*. Chicago: University of Chicago Press, 1970.

Ferguson, Niall. *Empire: How Britain Made the Modern World*. London: Penguin, 2018.

Fukuyama, Francis. *The End of History and the Last Man*. New York: Free Press, 1992.

Hall, Catherine. *Civilising Subjects: Metropole and Colony in the English Imagination 1830–1867*. Chicago: University of Chicago Press, 2002.

Hawkins, Harriet. "On Mentoring – Reflections on Academic Caring as a Feminist Practice." *Gender and Feminist Geographies Research Group*, 12 February 2018. Online. <http://www.gfgrg.org/on-mentoring-reflections-on-academic-caring-as-a-feminist-practice-by-harriet-hawkins/>. Accessed April 2019.

Hobsbawm, Eric. *The Age of Empire: 1875–1914*. London: Weidenfeld & Nicolson, 1987.

Levitas, Ruth. *The Concept of Utopia*. Syracuse, NY: Syracuse University Press, 1990.

——. *Utopia as Method: The Imaginary Reconstitution of Society*. Basingstoke: Palgrave Macmillan, 2013.

——. "We Argue How Else?" Tom Moylan. *Demand the Impossible: Science Fiction and the Utopian Imagination*, 2nd edn. Ed. Raffaella Baccolini. Oxford: Peter Lang, 2014. 257–262.

Lewis, Sophie. *Full Surrogacy Now: Feminism Against Family*. London: Verso, 2019.

Massey, Doreen. *Space, Place, and Gender*. Minneapolis: University of Minnesota Press, 1994.

Mies, Maria. *Patriarchy and Accumulation on a World Scale: Women in the International Division of Labour*. London: Zed Books, 1986.

Moylan, Tom. *Demand the Impossible: Science Fiction and the Utopian Imagination*, 2nd edn. Ed. Raffaella Baccolini. Oxford: Peter Lang, 2014.

Moylan, Tom and Raffaella Baccolini, eds. *Utopia Method Vision: The Use Value of Social Dreaming*. Oxford: Peter Lang, 2011.

Nandy, Ashis. *Traditions, Tyranny, and Utopias: Essays in the Politics of Awareness*. Oxford: Oxford University Press, 1987.

Nicholas, Lucy. "A Radical Queer Utopian Future: A Reciprocal Relation Beyond Sexual Difference." *Thirdspace: A Journal of Feminist Theory and Culture* 8.2 (2009): n.p.

Poole, Marilyn and Dallas Isaacs. "Caring: A Gendered Concept." *Women's Studies International Forum* 20.4 (1997): 529–536.

Rizvi, Gowher. "Transcript: Gowher Rizvi on the State of Politics in Bangladesh." *Al Jazeera*, 20 March 2019. Online. <https://www.aljazeera.com/pro-grammes/headtohead/2019/03/transcript-gowher-rizvi-state-politics-bangladesh-190319085444403.html>. Accessed April 2019.

Sargent, Lyman Tower. "The Three Faces of Utopianism Revisited." *Utopian Studies* 5.1 (1994): 1–37.

Sargisson, Lucy. *Contemporary Feminist Utopianism*. London: Routledge, 1996.

——. *Fool's Gold? Utopianism in the Twenty-First Century*. London: Palgrave Macmillan, 2012.

——. "Utopia – Dr. Lucy Sargisson." *YouTube*, uploaded by *60secondspolitics*, 30 March 2010. Online. <https://www.youtube.com/watch?v=INtkOFMoYgc&t=15s>. Accessed June 2019.

Suvin, Darko. "Defining the Literary Genre of Utopia: Some Historical Semantics, Some Genealogy, a Proposal and a Plea." *Studies in the Literary Imagination* 6.2 (1973): 121–145.

Tong, Rosemarie. *Feminist Thought. A More Comprehensive Introduction*. Boulder, CO: Westview, 2009.

Tormey, Simon, and Jules Townshend. *Key Thinkers from Critical Theory to Post-Marxism*. Vol. 13. Thousand Oaks, CA: Sage, 2006.

Weeks, Kathi. *The Problem with Work: Feminism, Marxism, Antiwork Politics, and Postwork Imaginaries*. Durham, NC: Duke University Press, 2011.

RHIANNON FIRTH

# Gratitude for a Utopian Friendship

I heard about this Festschrift after the conversation with Lucy Sargisson's other PhD students had already taken place, but I did not want to miss the chance of contributing to this volume. I am very thankful to Lyman Tower Sargent for inviting me to submit this stand-alone contribution after having read the beautiful conversation piece on "Utopia, Pedagogy and Care" by Ibtisam Ahmed, David M. Bell, Elena Colombo, and Robyn Muir. Similarly to their contribution, I hope to reflect on some of the ways in which Lucy's work (again, in every sense of the term) has affected me. I found this piece rather difficult to write because I consider my relationship with Lucy not simply as that of an erstwhile student to their supervisor, but as a lifelong friendship, and friendships are personal, and hard to write about. Nonetheless I view this as a wonderful opportunity to reflect and to express gratitude for the ways in which Lucy's mentorship, support, and guidance have moved my life. Lucy's political project has been about breaking down the boundaries between the public and the private, and I have often felt inspired by the deep integrity between Lucy's academic project and her lived life.

My path to meeting Lucy began in 2003, after I had completed a degree in Combined Studies at the University of Leicester. It was a broad-based degree in which I selected to focus on Politics, English, and Economic and Social History. Despite obtaining a First, and having a real passion for environmental politics, I did not initially consider pursuing an academic path, and attempted to enter the job market in Leicester where I had also grown up. After a year of dismal jobs, the dole, and struggling to find fulfilling ways to spend my time, I decided to look at ways to do something more stimulating. One of my undergraduate lecturers had previously tried to encourage me to undertake postgraduate study, so I got back in touch to discuss my options. He suggested I apply for ESRC 1 + 3 funding to do a Master and a PhD, and he recommended Lucy as someone at Nottingham who he thought would make a great supervisor and would support my interests.

When I first approached Lucy, I had very little confidence and did not really think I belonged in academia. Robyn in the contribution mentioned "imposter syndrome" and this is certainly something I can relate to, even now, but especially then. I had some rather vague and underdeveloped ideas about wanting to study alternative lifestyles as political forms, having spent several years hanging out in the rave and traveler scene in Leicestershire, and wanted to link this somehow to my interests in environmentalism and feminism. Lucy suggested I read her book *Utopian Bodies and the Politics of Transgression*, and a few other sources on lived utopias while she worked with me to develop my proposal. Since I was no longer registered at any university, Lucy secured my access to the library at Nottingham, and I remember vividly my excitement in travelling up to Nottingham University to use the library having booked a week's leave from work. I was aware how competitive the funding was and never really thought I would be successful, but reading Lucy's work on intentional communities (*Utopian Bodies*) reignited my passion for study and her support with my proposal helped to build my confidence. I was successful in securing the funding, which ultimately changed the course of my life, as I am almost certain I would not have undertaken postgraduate studies at that point without the funding and Lucy's encouragement.

I moved to Nottingham and began my studies in 2004. I visited my first intentional communities during my Master's fieldwork at Lucy's encouragement, and throughout the MA year and my PhD I visited eleven different intentional communities, ecovillages, and autonomous social centers around the UK. I was very anxious at every stage of this process. I was nervous to send emails in case I received no reply, I was scared of travelling alone to meet strangers, I was scared they would laugh at my interview questions, I was worried that the data I collected would not be good enough and my thesis would fall on its face, and I faced some intensely chaotic personal crises that really threw me back and held up my work. Lucy was there every step of the way with encouragement, support, and genuine concern and interest. Lucy's support not only changed my life academically, but also, despite my initial hesitancy, led me to fall in love with the intentional communities movement and autonomous social centers, and to visit and support these spaces whenever the opportunity arises.

I would like to echo David's point about Lucy practicing a form of care with a utopian excess that estranges us from the everyday circulation of exchange value, and also Ibtisam's point about Lucy's outlook challenging the taken-for-granted competitiveness of higher education. Lucy's work and crucially her distinction between totalizing and transgressive utopias (*Contemporary passim*, but particularly 63–97) has been central to my own work on anarchist utopias (cf. Firth) and on feminist consciousness raising (cf. Firth and Robinson). This distinction has enabled me to conceptualize the exteriority of anti-authoritarian desire in relation to structures of domination, whilst acknowledging that these co-exist in hybrid forms. Whilst, following Lucy, I find it useful to problematize simple binaries, this particular distinction is less a definitional boundary than an attitude and a praxis toward difference and multiplicity: does one desire to control and suppress it, to direct everything toward sameness and identity, or does one desire to nourish difference and enable it to flourish? Reading the prior piece by the conversation participants, considered alongside my own trajectory, has made me realize quite how wonderfully varied her supervisees' research has been over the years, and the role that Lucy has played in tending and caring for this multiplicity of ideas, and enabling her supervisees and students to flourish in many different directions.

One thing that really sticks in my mind is Lucy's gentle rebelliousness and transgressions, and her quietly witty anti-authoritarianism. During supervisions, she had a habit of making me laugh when I was taking my work, or myself, too seriously. I remember her poking gentle fun at the work of hard-going theorists like Max Stirner and Gilles Deleuze and Félix Guattari after I had spent long hours trying to get to grips with what they were saying. She reminded me that no matter how difficult or authoritative a voice may seem, it is not beyond critique or humor. I also remember an intensely anxious episode before giving one of my first conference papers. I had done lots of fieldwork, had tons of data, but had not yet formed a coherent argument. Lucy's advice was to "just show them lots of pictures and tell stories about your fieldwork. You've got some great pictures and stories, everyone is tired at the end of the day in these conferences and they'll appreciate the break." At the time, I was in awe of the alienating formality of academic conferences. Lucy's advice seemed invigoratingly irreverent and unpretentious, yet practical, and it was good advice. Academics often pay scant attention to our own embodiment and too frequently pour immense energy into hiding our vulnerabilities from one another. I have given my own supervisees the same advice under similar circumstances, but more than this I think that Lucy's advice was emblematic of a broader attitude that expressing one's own vulnerabilities openly and honestly is a powerful act of rebellion in a hostile and competitive academic environment.

Marie Louise Berneri contrasts utopias based on plans of societies functioning mechanically, where humans are turned into "Taylorised robots, subordinated by the machines they serve," with those utopias that have been "the living dreams of poets" (309, 317). Not only does Lucy live, write, and reproduce in her work, friendship and care, the latter utopia – but I also remember her having written some pretty awesome poetry, and making beautiful ceramic pots too. She would be the last in the line to become a Taylorized academic robot. The biggest influence that Lucy has had in my life is through her practical advice and lived example of how to survive as a sensitive, creative, and humble yet uncompromisingly honest and radical person in a competitive and sometimes hostile academic environment. She will always be an inspiration to me.

# Bibliography

Berneri, Marie Louise. *Journey through Utopia*. Oakland, CA: PM Press, 2019 [1950].
Firth, Rhiannon. *Utopian Politics: Citizenship and Practice*. London: Routledge, 2012.
Firth, Rhiannon and Andrew Robinson. "For a Revival of Feminist Consciousness-Raising: Horizontal transformation of epistemologies and transgression of neoliberal TimeSpace." *Gender and Education* 28.3 (2016): 343–358.
Sargisson, Lucy. *Contemporary Feminist Utopianism*. London: Routledge, 1996.
———. *Utopian Bodies and the Politics of Transgression*. London: Routledge, 2000.

Responses

DAVINA COOPER

# Afterword

This richly varied and interesting collection exemplifies the inspiration and guidance, which Lucy Sargisson has long provided to many, as a scholar, teacher, colleague, and friend. Sargisson was my entry point into utopian studies. Her conceptual work in utopian political theory and feminism, alongside her original empirical research on intentional communities (detailed in the chapter by Baccolini and Sargent), stimulated and shaped my early interest in utopia as a set of ideas and literatures, and remains one of my primary go-to sources in thinking about what the utopian means, is, and does. In this short afterword, I want to reflect on the utopian, as read through the contributions of this book – contributions, in turn, shaped by Sargisson's scholarship. Specifically, I want to consider what utopian studies brings to the wider, if sometimes too compartmentalized, field of radical scholarship. In what follows, I focus on attachment, care, and movement – three themes to emerge in this collection.

As utopian studies grows into a well-established field, its relationship to other literatures becomes more pressing. This collection explores the disciplinary influences of history, literary analysis, social theory, politics, postcolonialism, and environmental and women's studies, among others, on utopian scholarship. It also demonstrates the ongoing conversations between utopia and other radical organizing frames, including prefiguration, anarchism, environmentalism, and feminism. Sargisson's work has long been important in bridging and connecting these different fields (see also Gordon; Levitas; Pötz). Yet, for me, this collection also signifies the value in further exploring the distinctive contribution that utopian studies makes, and could make, to radical scholarship more generally. Do its terms, for instance, perform the same critical-hopeful function as prefiguration and the radical imagination? Do references to anarchist spaces, intentional communities, and everyday utopias identify common phenomena; or are there productive differences in how these terms are or might be used?

Utopia and its field of study can be distinguished from other related fields in several ways. They can be distinguished by traditions and history, including the genealogies surrounding utopia's eponymous text. They can be distinguished by utopia's complex, sometimes fraught, relationship to an imaginary ideal – an ideal that utopian studies currently disavows in favor of quotidian, fragmented enactments – even as, in veering away from an ideal rather than towards it, utopias and utopian studies are defined and shaped by their (post-perfect) relationship to this normative ideal. Utopian studies can also be distinguished by its concepts and concerns. One feature distinguishing the utopian from other radical approaches is its distinctive relationship to the dystopian, a relationship which – while one of contrast – is also, importantly, one of co-constitution, anticipation, and entanglement, as hopes and warnings mingle. Utopian studies has a special relationship to those devastating possibilities that, assigned to a dystopian future, appear as present-day tendencies or fears as Almudena Machado-Jiménez and Dunja M. Mohr (this volume) explore. And we can distinguish utopian studies by the distinctive methods developing in its field, such as Ruth Levitas's groundbreaking work on the imaginary reconstitution of society as a way of forging and thinking towards better futures.

Posing the question of distinctness doesn't mean arguing for utopian studies' exceptionalism. Nor does it imply that there is a single right meaning or contribution that can be tied to either the utopian or related and contiguous ideas. Terms of radical refashioning are used in varied and overlapping ways, and there seems little obvious value in selectively pinning them down or fighting over their conceptual borders and turf. I raise the issue of utopia's place within a wider field here, in light of Sargisson's work and the discussions in this collection, because it seems important to have different radical literatures speak to (and develop through) one another, to benefit collectively from the diverse foci, concepts, and traditions they collectively express. As others have argued, there is an urgent need for a rich post-critical lexicon, one fed by conversations at the interstices of utopian studies, transformative politics, the radical imaginary, and prefiguration – literatures in turn fed by socialist, anarchist, postcolonial, feminist, queer, ecological, and other politics.

One coupling that arises in this volume, and which demonstrates the value of putting utopia into relationship with other radical terms, involves prefiguration. Prefiguration and utopia can be, and often are, used in overlapping or convergent ways: as accounts of concrete, partial, grounded, and everyday utopias coincide with accounts of prefigurative spaces as sites of progressive and radical innovation. But prefiguration and utopia can pull in different directions. Utopia may foreground images and narrations of what could be, while prefiguration attends to practical enactments. Participants engaged in radical innovation may also prefer one or other term. Some intentional communities prefer the designation of utopia to that of prefiguration on the grounds the latter suggests the rehearsal of a future-real. Others object to being described as utopia because it seems to suggest fixity, perfection, and fantasy. Drawing from the different ideas, practices, and histories that the two concepts carry supports a rich and multilayered conversation, where different dimensions of a hopeful politics – including of time, affect, strategy, imagining, and materiality – can be discussed.

One aspect of this conversation is how to account for the complex character of what *is*, when aspects of it diverge from conventional notions of what present practice entails. Prefiguration offers ways of thinking about the "as if," in contexts where participants act as if the conditions authorizing and legitimating their actions were already in place. For instance, we might think of practitioners of local currencies acting as if they have the right and capacity to create money, including forms of money that operate on counterhegemonic terms when it comes to what money is and does. Yet, in tandem with difficulties of operationalization, challenges over the authority to create new kinds of money beg questions about whether these new forms – where money is, for instance, a non-accumulable, non-exploitative record of past interactions and facilitator of new ones – can be (and have been) realized. We might therefore approach disputed monies, like other prefigurative practices, as existing instead in the realm of the fictive/real – neither realized nor unrealized exclusively, but simultaneously both.

Utopian studies also contributes to accounts of the equivocal or paradoxical character of what *is*, when it acquires a form and meaning that sits uncomfortably with mainstream norms. In her writing, Sargisson often returns to utopia's etymology as the no place/good place (e.g., Sargisson, *Fool's* 7), a duality that captures a quality integral to utopia even when utopias emerge as on-the-ground practices. Reading social innovations as utopias suggests a form of presence: yet one whose existence within prevailing grids of intelligibility and power is also cast in doubt. Grounded, minor, and everyday utopias may seem real, even nearby, places but their characterization as utopian expresses an elusive, dreamlike quality, a ghostly anticipation of what could be (see also Thaler). While taking place, and often taking place very successfully, they remain simultaneously unbelievable such that a person on hearing about a place for the first time might incredulously ask, can such a thing really exist?

The paradoxical relationship of present/absent also shapes, and emerges in, utopia's relationship to its context and neighbors. Interdependence is an important theme in many fictional and practiced utopias, but an ambivalent relationship between intentional communities and their neighbors also emerges. We witness this in Lucy Sargisson's work with Lyman Tower Sargent (2017) on intentional communities in New Zealand – a research project discussed by several contributors to this book. In his contribution, David M. Bell explores the importance of placeness to the utopian. We might think of placeness as drawing attention to relations of contiguity and neighboring in terms of the encounters and narratives that shape, abut, and overflow a space. Fictional utopias adopt diverse approaches to their wider geopolitical (and temporal) context. Sometimes the relationship of utopia to other places emerges (into visibility); sometimes it does not. But fictional utopias' creation, albeit unevenly, of a more fully imagined world – or planetary system – of which the utopian society is but one part contrasts with typical imaginaries of practically enacted utopias, which often suggest something far more siloed. Democratic schools, intentional communities, and food utopias, for example, may be part of wider radical networks; they are also far from unaffected by or disconnected from government policy and wider social and cultural life. Yet, too often, they appear as solitary peaks of inventive practice, with no visible relationship to (or ontological equivalence within) the wider sector they imaginatively and critically reenact, as it goes about its daily practice beneath the clouds.

One challenge, then, within the utopian social imaginary, is how to think (and think about) relations of interdependence between utopian and other spaces, including mainstream ones. Another is to develop distinctive forms of place, insulated and protected from a hostile wider context. Fictional utopias provide rich images of these home-worlds. So too do practical experiments in living. In their chapters, Chris Coates and Suryamayi Clarence-Smith (this volume) discuss the various ways intentional communities claim and forge home. Indeed, as communities live their everyday practices in deliberately prefigurative ways, they reverse wider claims as to their fictionality. A skeptical mainstream may routinely dismiss utopian spaces and possibilities as wishful make-believe but, as Coates describes, intentional communities cast fictionality back on mainstream life, highlighting and unsettling its presumption that happiness and normality are to be found in privatized, nuclear, commodity-oriented households.

At the same time, as this book details, much utopian discussion focuses on the challenges that fictional and material communities face in building counterfactual home-spaces that are socially just, communal, environmentally sustainable, and democratic. These "critical utopias" challenge, adapt, and revitalize the utopian tradition by addressing the uncertainties, failings, and improvised strategies that sustaining dynamic and changing spaces produces (see also Moylan; Sargisson, *Fool's*; and Lohmann; Mohr, this volume). Creating new kinds of homes means creating new structures, rules, and ways of resolving conflict. It also means creating new kinds of comfort, pleasure, and belonging (see Tabone); and, as a utopian task, changing the conditions and forms that these feelings and sensations take: from new kinds of smells to new kinds of touch. If home is imagined and practiced in collectivized ways, this task is an ambitious one. For it is not simply the challenge of creating an innovative shared domestic space but of doing so in conditions where wider regulatory frameworks structure what is possible. This is something Heather Piper and Ian Stronach helpfully discuss, in their account of a democratic residential school negotiating wider intensified norms about adult-child touch.

Utopian scholarship often draws on the notion of *heimat*, as developed by Ernst Bloch, to address the challenge of changing humans' relationship to the world in which they dwell (Varsam, this volume; see also Moir).

The question of home-making is one that can be approached at different temporal-spatial scales (indeed, scalar movement and its combining is a hallmark of utopian thinking). But in considering the place of connection, familiarity, and belonging, I want to use a more vernacular term, namely of *heimishe* – a Yiddish word for hominess that signals (usually) small-scale, unpretentious comforts and familiarities. *Heimishe* gestures, in diasporic conditions, to a minor-stream coziness that is sometimes self-deprecating, and ironic, but not only, with its invocation of an imagined relation of connection in conditions of profound dis-ease. *Heimishe* spaces and people (including cinematic and other fictional characters) are familiar and un-threatening. They are the sites "where we could be" and "where we could be comfortable." We might read these as everyday defenses against social alienation. *Heimishe* expresses a migrant community's yearning to feel at home, manifested through simple places, figures, and artefacts, in conditions where at homeness remains fragile and elusive, and where a temporary in-placeness is imagined and claimed through acts of (hopeful) recognition. As such, *heimishe* constitutes a "making do" in (and of) the present rather than a future possibility that is strived for. Yet, can this claimed hominess be in any way utopian? The utopian has an ambivalent relationship to familiarity and home, as its critical turn to estrangement demonstrates (Sargisson, "Strange"; Winter, this volume). But does this drive to make the familiar unfamiliar presuppose a hegemonic relationship to what *is*? For, arguably, it is when mainstream life "fits," even for those disadvantaged and exploited by its conditions, that utopia's estranging function becomes most necessary – denaturalizing taken-for-granted practices, such as pri-vate property, war, competition, and hierarchy, to demonstrate that their existence is not inevitable. For constituencies whose relationship to soci-ality is already uncomfortable or estranged, other processes, as Mohr also discusses, may prove more pressing (see also Tabone).

Might we then think of developing a *heimishe* relationship to the world in general – remaking a terrain too often experienced as hostile and alienating? This could mean creating spaces of comfort, ease, and homi-ness in conditions of renewed (or different) attention to the earth, life, and beyond-the-world processes. Yet, as this collection explores, creating new forms of belonging and attachment risk being at the expense of, and create the conditions for, others' dis-ease and dis-attachment. Striving for familiarity, as a general assumed good, can also over-privilege safety, secure the illusion of its presence, and generate disdain or discomfort toward whatever gets read as unknown. Home becomes homeland and hominess assumes a nationalist form.

The alignment of homeland and nation is explored by Simon Spiegel (this volume) in relation to Zionism, and its historical relationship to Israel as a controversial utopian project (see also Herman). One challenge, then, is whether states can become homey in other ways. Can imagining their hominess *or acting as if it were already there* undercut or refuse conventional state-based claims to sovereignty, exceptionality, grandeur, and aspired-to leadership? Can it replace these norms with others oriented to a comfortable, enabling, unremarkable welfare that supports bodies (Cooper, "Feeling")?

Relations of care and cultivation emerge in this collection as important practices. Even workspaces, such as the university, can on occasion prove welcoming and home-like (in a broad expansive sense) through the actions and labor of their members (see Ahmed, Bell, Colombo, and Muir; and Firth, this volume). Care and tending – of both self and others – have a positive valence. An essential part of a good, thriving academic culture as this collection attests, care is one which people take up to different degrees and in different ways. Yet, at the level of institutional policy and action, shaping and guiding life has also incited critique from different left quarters. Gardens, for instance, may nourish, and gardening may build ecological responsibility, attentiveness, and literacy (see also Reis, this volume). But gardening can also feed a nationalist rhetoric of political justification (Spiegel, this volume). Cultivating and tending to the social can create overly managed and disciplined worlds, where wildness is disavowed, and certain life-forms supported at the expense of others (see also Bauman; Comaroff and Comaroff; Mottier). Some of the tensions in the metaphor of gardening appear in this collection. A parallel set of difficulties arise in relation to ideas of responsibility (see also Varsam, this volume). When public or collective bodies assume responsibility for people's well-being and social conditions, including at a distance, this can seem progressive and empowering, but it can also be objectifying and disempowering as

Pat Noxolo, Parvati Raghuram, and Clare Madge draw on postcolonial studies to explore.

Care ethics, radical forms of responsibility, and use of gardening metaphors have been widely discussed in postcolonial, feminist, and anarchist work. Does utopian thinking bring something distinctive to this conversation? One place this might be found is in the relationship between what is imagined (or designed) and what takes place – where what takes place is not set apart from what is imagined but remains always mediated by it. The utopian provides a register for exploring modes of imagined and practiced care that take shape against and apart from mainstream conventional practices in ways that are neither perfect nor static. Instead, they may prove innovative and adventurous as they incline toward new hopeful ideas about what care could become – from the care developed in intentional communities to ecological practices of responsibility to the carefulness shown in crafting inventive, deemed-to-be-valuable, but nevertheless risky spaces (and practices), such as feminist public sex sites. In an important sense, through the images created and the practices trialed, the utopian re-allocates attention – away from current practice and its limits, which too often absorb all the available oxygen. By paying detailed attention to the challenges of creating something innovative and sought-after, the utopian claims the right to distribute its own epistemic care in the face of a status quo that both assumes an entitlement to attention and to determining what should receive attention (even as it relies on and benefits from the everyday dis-attention which normalization carries).

Finally, let us briefly turn to the question of how attention shifts, and what flows from it, as people and societies travel – between the utopian and non-utopian (Lohmann, this volume). Visiting utopias is typically associated with fiction, and with authors, such as More, Morris, and Piercy. While contemporary utopian novels often adopt other forms, the arrival of a visitor who has come, often unexpectedly, from another place or time is a staple part of the utopian sensibility. This is a visitor overflowing with questions and doubts, confident in their skepticism, even as they soon start to grasp the riches, fulfilments, good sense, and pleasures that the new place has to offer. But as their attachment grows, and they begin to settle, the transient status of their presence becomes ever more marked.

The realization that their visit will soon end channels and intensifies, in many cases, a gnawing, sharply rendered desire to stay – to be part of the better world they have glimpsed and briefly inhabited. Utopias are, in many respects, melancholic places of temporary possibility, and this is true for the reader too. Their emergent desire for what could be, stimulated by the place they have vicariously entered, finds itself spinning in midair as they too are flung back out, and as utopia closes behind them.

Academics also travel to utopias and other intentional communities. Yet, unlike the momentum toward attachment of the initially skeptical, fictive traveler, academics often exhibit a reversed emotional arc as initial optimism and excitement become replaced by disappointment and growing cynicism. This trajectory was described to me by a fed-up participant whom I hoped to interview when I started studying Local Exchange and Trading Schemes (LETS) in 2001. His words stayed with me through my research into LETS and other everyday utopias (see Cooper, "Everyday"). Chris Coates's chapter (this volume), likewise, provides an important reminder of how the visiting academic may be viewed by the intentional communities they study. His chapter poses sharp questions about the possibility, indeed the necessity, of being a different kind of academic visitor.

Utopias involve travel and change through time and space. Can utopian thinking contribute something distinctive to our understandings of those socially encoded journeys undertaken by individuals, communities, and societies in the absence of a utopian destination? There is the utopian ethical traveler, who seeks to make a positive or at least neutral impact as they journey, refusing to harm or dump garbage (literal or figurative) in the places they have visited and passed through. A different perspective is provided by Sarah Keenan, who has written evocatively on the complex and dynamic idea of "taking space with you" ("Subversive" 8). Drawing on her work, we might think of the utopian traveler as the bearer of an evolving utopian space, which they carry with them – a space that is constituted by the ethics, commitments, relations, and processes that cohere into a utopian attitude. But what about the socially encoded travels of communities and societies, as well as of individuals (recognizing all three are processes in formation rather than fixed entities)? Here, utopias are neither just the visited and imagined places nor the relations that individual visitors bear with them as they travel, but a way of thinking about the evolving relationship of wider institutionalized society to manifested or enacted hopefulness – the social life that is desired, sought, struggled for and attempted.

In her discussion of a North London neighborhood, Kilburn, the geographer Doreen Massey writes, "Instead then, of thinking of places as areas with boundaries around, they can be imagined as articulated moments in networks of social relations and understandings, [...] where a large proportion of those relations, experiences and understandings are constructed on a far larger scale than what we happen to define for that moment as the place itself, whether that be a street, or a region or even a continent" (28). If places are continuously being remade by such wider social processes, we might ask: what then is the utopian place or, to put it another way, the places of utopia given the mobile, evolving, contradictory relations utopia sutures? Do we find utopia in the looking glass: the intangible, imaginary, unreachable vision damningly reflecting society back, from multiple places, *as it really is*? Is utopia part of the social magnetosphere, created by mainstream life, but necessarily apart from it; is it to be found in the episodic eruptions extruded by a society under pressure; or in the rich dynamic creations of dissatisfied collective existence? There is no single certain answer. We cannot know utopia's place, not least because the question itself depends on the conceptual line we draw between what is imagined and what is actualized – a relationship shaped by purpose and context. On the left, many interpret utopia's place negatively, as one of masking – deflecting attention or poorly compensating for the harms of capitalist society. Yet, within the contours of contemporary radical politics, a more positive place for the utopian – as a necessary aspect of any society, with ambitions for a hopeful future – continues to surface.

This collection demonstrates the importance of the utopian as a force that drives, stimulates, and dwells within different imaginative and practical projects. What it also demonstrates is the importance of utopias' conditions of creation and recreation. Many kinds of societies produce wishful visions of what could be. The difficulty lies in how to generate the conditions that enable utopian ideas and images to flourish – in terms of being communicated, enacted, experimented with, and argued over. Often the question of what is needed becomes a call-out for freedom of thought – albeit as something that requires support and not simply the absence of restraint. Yet, equally – if not more – important are the material conditions that allow ideas to be *practiced* – not as new orthodoxies or fixed claims to perfection but as provisional, plural, and dialogic collaborations that take shape as doings as well as imaginative speech. Lucy Sargisson's wonderfully rich and extensive body of work foregrounds the social, cultural, ecological, and emotional challenges of forging, as well as desiring and imagining, better ways of living. Through her writing, she powerfully demonstrates why creating the conditions for the utopian to assume a significant social place, in the governing, organizing, and experiencing of life, is neither a distraction nor a luxury but an urgent political task.

## Bibliography

Bauman, Zygmunt. *Modernity and Ambivalence*. Cambridge: Polity, 1991.
Comaroff, Jean and John L. Comaroff. "Naturing the Nation: Aliens, Apocalypse, and the Postcolonial State." *Social Identities* 7.2 (2001): 233–265.
Cooper, Davina. *Everyday Utopias: The Conceptual Life of Promising Spaces*. Durham, NC: Duke University Press, 2014.
——. *Feeling like a State: Desire, Denial, and the Recasting of Authority*. Durham, NC: Duke University Press, 2019.
Gordon, Uri. "Prefigurative Politics Between Ethical Practice and Absent Promise." *Political Studies* 66.2 (2018): 521–537.
Herman, Didi. "Christian Israel." *Reimagining the State: Theoretical Challenges and Transformative Possibilities*. Ed. Davina Cooper, Nikita Dhawan, and Janet Newman. Abingdon, Oxon: Routledge, 2020. 114–132.
Keenan, Sarah. *Subversive Property: Law and the Production of Spaces of Belonging*. New York: Routledge, 2014.
Levitas, Ruth. *Utopia as Method: The Imaginary Reconstitution of Society*. London: Palgrave Macmillan, 2013.
Massey, Doreen. "A Global Sense of Place." *Marxism Today* (June 1991): 24–29.
Moir, Cat. "Casting a Picture. Utopia, *Heimat* and the Materialist Concept of History." *Anthropology & Materialism. A Journal of Social Research* 3 (2016): 1–18.

Mottier, Véronique. "Eugenics, Politics, and the State: Social Democracy and the Swiss 'Gardening State.'" *Studies in History and Philosophy of Science, Part C: Studies in History and Philosophy of Biological and Biomedical Sciences* 39.2 (2008): 263–269.

Moylan, Tom. *Demand the Impossible: Science Fiction and the Utopian Imagination.* New York: Methuen, 1986.

Noxolo, Pat, Parvati Raghuram, and Clare Madge. "Unsettling Responsibility: Postcolonial Interventions." *Transactions of the Institute of British Geographers* 37.3 (2012): 418–429.

Piper, Heather and Ian Stronach. "Can Liberal Education Make a Comeback? The Case of 'Relational Touch' at Summerhill School." *American Educational Research Journal* 45.1 (March 2008): 6–37.

Pötz, Martin. "Utopian Imagination in Activism: Making the Case for Social Dreaming in Change from the Grassroots." *Interface: A Journal on Social Movements* 11.1 (2019): 123–146.

Raghuram, Parvati, Clare Madge, and Pat Noxolo. "Rethinking Responsibility and Care for a Postcolonial World." *Geoforum* 40.1 (2009): 5–13.

Sargisson, Lucy. *Fool's Gold? Utopianism in the Twenty-First Century.* London: Palgrave Macmillan, 2012.

——. "Strange Places: Estrangement, Utopianism, and Intentional Communities." *Utopian Studies* 18.3 (2007): 393–425.

Sargisson, Lucy and Lyman Tower Sargent. *Living in Utopia: New Zealand's Intentional Communities.* Abingdon, Oxon: Routledge, 2016.

Tabone, Mark A. "Dystopia, Utopia, and 'Home' in Toni Morrison's *Home.*" *Utopian Studies* 29.3 (2018): 291–308.

Thaler, Mathias. "Peace as a Minor, Grounded Utopia: On Prefigurative and Testimonial Pacifism." *Perspectives on Politics* 17.4 (2019): 1003–1018.

LUCY SARGISSON

# The Strangest Place: Thoughts on Being a Guest at Your Own Funeral, or "Regrets, I Have a Few"

*Imagine that you're sitting in the outer ring of a small theatre, set in the round. Light streams in through huge windows. A soft breeze plays around the room, bringing gentle scents of rose and geranium and salty fresh air. Whenever silence falls in the room, as it often does, gentle sounds of the sea can be heard from outside. Waves over pebbles. You're watching and listening. Awed. Every now and then, someone rises from their seat and walks down to the stage, where they say a few words – or a lot of words – before resuming their seat. Some of these people are close friends of yours. Some have been your mentors. Some are people you've met a few times. Some you haven't met before. And, because it's your funeral, everyone is saying something that relates, somehow, to you. Suddenly, everyone turns to face you and you're invited to respond. What would you say? This is surely the strangest place you've ever been.*

People who have met me will know that I am rarely lost for words. But I am now. Perhaps it's the symptoms of Multiple Sclerosis (I took early retirement in 2017 at the age of 53 because the M.S. with which I lived, worked, and struggled for sixteen years had deteriorated to the point at which I could not continue), but I really don't think so ... I think this is just an impossible task.

I want to thank everyone who has contributed to this volume, and yet, I find myself inadequate even to this. I am overwhelmed: flooded with respect, admiration, and gratitude. More than anything, I am aware of how little I know and how much more there is about which to think. When I retired, I gave away most of my books, but I kept my utopia/nism collection and, as I write, I can see on my shelves books by Raffaella Baccolini, David M. Bell, Chris Coates, Davina Cooper, Rhiannon Firth, Ruth Levitas, Dunja M. Mohr, Tom Moylan, and Lyman Tower Sargent. (Yes, my shelves are alphabetically arranged.) Lyman's open-access annotated bibliography of utopian literature is the top bookmark on my laptop (https://openpublishing.psu.edu/utopia). I need to revisit them all. And, reading the chapters in this volume, I'm aware of new cases of utopianism to think about – new to me, that is, such as Auroville Community (Suryamayi Clarence-Smith), Louise O'Neill's *Only Ever Yours* (Almudena Machado-Jiménez), J.M. Coetzee's *Life & Times of Michael K* (Maria Varsam), and I need to watch *The Walking Dead* (Laura Winter). I realize there are genres or expressions of buried utopianism to excavate (Zionist propaganda materials (Simon Spiegel). I'm reminded of old favorites to revisit: Joanna Russ and Marge Piercy (Sarah Lohmann). I've encountered fresh and exciting ideas to play with: I am intrigued by the thought of an ecological utopianism buried in ancient texts ( José Eduardo Reis). I love the idea of transgressive utopianism entangled in the Anthropocene (Dunja M. Mohr). I am pleased that people find a contribution in my work, that my ideas are being stretched, challenged, and played with. My work owes huge debts to others, not least Tom Moylan, Lyman Tower Sargent, and Ruth Levitas. It's great to have been part of a huge utopian conversation. It's good to feel part of it still, even if I no longer have very much to say.

## On Being (a) Utopian

I propose to address a theme that flows through this volume (Ruth Levitas, Chris Coates, Ibtisam Ahmed, Elena Colombo, Robyn Muir, Rhiannon Firth, and especially Tom Moylan). This is the idea, coined by Moylan, of being – or becoming (a) utopian. The remainder of my contribution focuses on that theme and I briefly consider just three aspects: first, being someone who studies utopianism; second, being someone who has a utopian sensibility; and finally, I reflect upon some of the ways in which I might have been a better utopian. Each of these three strands has a connecting thread, which I will endeavor to reveal. Methodologically, this should be taken as autoethnographic auto-critique. It is non-generalizable and non-replicable and is based on a single case study. My PhD students will note that it is, therefore, deeply unreliable.

Being (a) utopian scholar, or a scholar of utopia, has been difficult but I do not regret trying. Nor do I regret my skipping across disciplines, although this has made journal publication tricky. The topic itself is marginal, and the word "utopia" invites contempt. Students will say "that's utopian" when they mean "that's SO naïve." Colleagues (perhaps especially social scientists) will sneer, dismiss or, perhaps worse, indulge. For me, utopia has not been a hobby, it's been the only subject of my research. It's the core of my professional being. I do take a playful approach and that's because play is part of being utopian. But it's play with serious intent. So, when I was promoted to a Personal Chair and I was asked "Would you prefer the title Professor of Politics or Professor of Politics Theory?" I said, "Utopian Studies." Several weeks later I was informed that this was possible, but I was cautioned to reconsider. The title might devalue my professional standing. I have no wish to expose chips on my shoulder (I really don't have any) but it is true that being a utopian in the world of academia is kind of lonely.

Being (a) utopian person, or a person oriented toward a utopian sensibility, is easy on a good day. It's impossible on a bad day but I do not regret trying. As I read through the chapters that comprise this volume, a poem came to mind. It begins like this:

> It doesn't interest me
> what you do for a living.
> I want to know
> what you ache for
> and if you dare to dream
> of meeting your heart's longing.
> It doesn't interest me
> how old you are.
> I want to know
> if you will risk
> looking like a fool
> for love
> for your dream
> for the adventure of being alive.
> Oriah Mountain Dreamer, *The Invitation*.

I first encountered this prose poem during a visit to an intentional community, back in the late 1990s and, for me, it captures a utopian sensibility (Tom Moylan was right about many things in his beautiful essay "Becoming (a) Utopian," not least the observation that I was transformed by my encounters with the lived utopians who comprise intentional communities.) The poem speaks to – or perhaps I mean from – a place that we might call ontological, or Self/Other, or self-other, or selfother, or I-Thou (Levitas, this volume). I read it as an invitation to approach the world with an open heart – and to allow others to do likewise. Doing so invites – demands – requires us to set aside the safe and comforting barriers, myths, stories, and narratives in which habitually we cloak ourselves. It demands that we greet others openly, with authenticity. This may be deeply unwise, in the workplace, but on a good day, when I'm feeling strong, this is me. On a bad day I can't be around people at all because it requires energy. Ahmed, Bell, Colombo, and Muir note, in this volume, that "care is labor" and being utopian requires care.

Regrets ...

Something I admire about people who live in intentional communities is that they try to "walk their talk." Of course they don't succeed, all of the time, or every day. Prefigurative utopianism is a powerful idea and I embrace it intellectually, politically, and ontologically, but it's freakin' tough, as they say. Two things to note about intentional communities (tautologically but importantly) are that they are intentional and they are *communities*. This latter poses challenges: other people can be tricky and negative interpersonal dynamics and clashes over principle can be devastating. But intentional communities are collectives, and this is important. It's beyond important: it is crucial, and it brings me, in a roundabout way, to my first and biggest regret. I regret that I did not work, on a daily basis, embedded in a utopian collective. For example, there was a moment, in the early 2000s, in which I could have tried to establish a Centre of Utopian Studies at my home institution (the University of Nottingham). At that time and in that particular context, this idea struck me as empire-building and egoistic – and so I didn't. I regret this. It would have been worth ruffling a few feathers and worth risking the purity of my ego. The Utopian Studies Society *is* a community of scholars (Levitas, this volume) and its conferences were a powerful annual tonic, a touchstone of positivity and critical friendship. But M.S. made conferences so tough – exhausting beyond my powers of description. Something on my doorstep would have helped. I regret trying to be a utopian (scholar and person) without the daily support (and challenge) of community.

## ... I Have a Few ...

I have other regrets: I regret that my early writings weren't more accessible. Several contributors to this volume found something useful in *Contemporary Feminist Utopianism* and I am humbled by this but, as Tom Moylan notes, very few people read *Utopian Bodies and the Politics of Transgression*. I regret that this contribution about those admirable and difficult (indeed, admirably difficult) (see Coates, this volume) people in intentional communities came in a book that few of them could read. Trapped in the expectations of standards in academic writing, I obscured my work with complexity. I regret publishing books that cost so much. Trapped in the expectations of academic standards of publication, I went to respected publishers who, it turned out, charged incredible amounts for their books. My last book (my personal favorite, incidentally) *Fools Gold? Utopianism in the Twenty-First Century* went on sale at £60. I found this obscene. Finally, I regret that I became overwhelmed by M.S. just when things were becoming *really* interesting. Just when I'd developed the professional confidence to ignore the traps above (by writing with a light touch, publishing in "less esteemed" locations, and focusing more on producing useful outputs for community members/activists and less on furthering my own career) I became incapable of writing much at all. And, just when I'd reached the point in my intellectual trajectory (accurately, albeit generously traced by Tom Moylan in this volume) when things became most important, I ran out of steam. My work has moved from high theory through fiction and, via intentional communities, to various lived experiments. It had reached everyday life. My friend and patient collaborator Lyman Tower Sargent has been waiting for at least five years for me to help him to complete our book about Utopia in Everyday Life. I hope he will finish it, even if I can't. It's important.

The thread binding together this self-indulgent account of regrets is important enough to make me think that the indulgence may be appropriate. It is the importance of other people, connection, community, collaboration, support, challenge, critical friendship, critical mass (or indeed any mass). My first book was published in 1996. In 2001, or thereabouts, I developed Multiple Sclerosis. My struggles with this condition led me to forget to the most fundamental defining aspect of being utopian: it requires a collective. It requires collaboration. And, to have agency, it requires organization: "Thus, we must choose Utopia. We must choose the belief that the world can be radically improved; *we must dream socially*; and we must allow our social dreams to affect our lives" (Sargent, "Choosing" 306).

*Imagine that you work at a university in a Centre of Utopian Studies. Your peers and colleagues encourage you to produce sharply argued, clear and thoughtful outputs that satisfy the institutional requirements and offer something of value to the various actors and activists you have studied. You sit back at your desk, feeling the privilege of job satisfaction. This morning you'll be presenting your work at a staff seminar. The Centre has funded some activists to attend. You know the reception of your work will be robust, but you trust that it will be offered in a spirit of critical support. You're looking forward to it, very much. You smile as you think of the pictures and stories that'll be woven around your theory. This afternoon you'll be attending a colleague's funeral, but that's okay. She was ready to go. The sun is shining, and you know she'd appreciate that.*

# Lucy Sargisson's Publications

## Books

Sargisson, Lucy. *Fool's Gold? Utopianism in the Twenty-First Century*. London: Palgrave Macmillan, 2012.

Sargisson, Lucy and Lyman Tower Sargent. *Living in Utopia: New Zealand's Intentional Communities*. Aldershot: Ashgate, 2004. Extract published as "Lessons from New Zealand." *Diggers & Dreamers: The Guide to Communal Living 2008/2009*. Ed. Sarah Bunker, Chris Coates, and Jonathan How. London: Diggers and Dreamers Publications, 2007. 89–102.

Sargisson, Lucy. *Utopian Bodies and the Politics of Transgression*. London and New York: Routledge, 2000.

Sargisson, Lucy. *Contemporary Feminist Utopianism*. London: Routledge, 1996.

Sargisson, Lucy. *Contemporary Feminist Utopianism I: Form and Content*. Keele Research Paper, 11. Keele, England: Department of Politics, Keele University, 1995.

Sargisson, Lucy. *Contemporary Feminist Utopianism II: Function*. Keele Research Paper, 15. Keele, England: Department of Politics, Keele University, 1995.

## Articles

Sargisson, Lucy. "Swimming Against the Tide: Collaborative Housing and Practices of Sharing." *Sharing Economies in Times of Crisis*. Ed. Anthony Ince and Sarah Marie Hall. London: Routledge, 2018. 145–159.

Sargisson, Lucy and Lyman Tower Sargent. "Lived Utopianism: Everyday Life and Intentional Communities." *Communal Societies* 37.1 (2017): 1–23.

Sargent, Lyman Tower and Lucy Sargisson. "Sex in Utopia: Eutopian and Dystopian Sexual Relations." *Utopian Studies* 25.2 (2014): 299–320.

Sargisson, Lucy. "A Breath of Fresh Air." Tom Moylan. *Demand the Impossible: Science Fiction and the Utopian Imagination*. Ed. Raffaella Baccolini. Oxford: Peter Lang, 2014. 231.

Sargisson, Lucy. "Utopianism in the Architecture of New Urbanism and Cohousing." *Green Utopianism: Perspectives, Politics and Micro-Practices*. Ed. Karin Bradley and Johan Hedrén. London: Routledge, 2014. 226–242.

Sargisson, Lucy. "Dystopias Do Matter." *Dystopia(n) Matters: On the Page, on Screen, on Stage*. Ed. Fátima Vieira. Newcastle on Tyne: Cambridge Scholars Publishing, 2013. 40–41.

Sargisson, Lucy. "A Democracy of All Nature: Taking a Utopian Approach." *Politics* 33.2 (2013): 124–134.

Sargisson, Lucy. "Second-Wave Cohousing: A Modern Utopia?" *Utopian Studies* 23.1 (2012): 28–56.

Sargisson, Lucy. "Cohousing Evolution in Scandinavia and the USA." *Cohousing in Britain. A Diggers & Dreamers Review*. Ed. Sarah Bunker, Chris Coates, Martin Field, and Jonathan How. London: Diggers and Dreamers Publications, 2011. 23–42.

Sargisson, Lucy. "Friends Have All Things in Common: Utopian Property Relations." *British Journal of Politics and International Relations* 12.1 (2010): 22–36.

Sargisson, Lucy. "Sustainability and the Intentional Community: Green Intentional Communities." *The Transition to Sustainable Living and Practice*. Ed. Liam Leonard and John Barry. Bingley, England: Emerald Group Publishing. 2009. 171–192.

Sargisson, Lucy. "Reflections: Can Utopianism Exist Without Intent?" *Journal for Cultural Research* 13.1 (2009): 89–94.

Coates, Chris and Lucy Sargisson. "Do Intentional Communities Matter?" *Diggers & Dreamers: The Guide to Communal Living 2008/2009*. Ed. Sarah Bunker, Chris Coates, and Jonathan How. London: Diggers and Dreamers Publications, 2007. 103–111.

Sargisson, Lucy. "Religious Fundamentalism and Utopianism in the 21st Century." *Journal of Political Ideologies* 12.3 (2007): 269–287.

Sargisson, Lucy. "Strange Places: Estrangement, Utopianism, and Intentional Communities." *Utopian Studies* 18.3 (2007): 393–424.

Sargisson, Lucy. "Imperfect Utopias: Green Intentional Communities." *Advances in Ecopolitics* 1.1 (2007): 1–24.

Sargisson, Lucy. "The Curious Relationship Between Politics and Utopia." *Utopia Method Vision: The Use Value of Social Dreaming*. Ed. Tom Moylan and Raffaella Baccolini. Oxford: Peter Lang, 2007. 25–46.

Sargisson, Lucy. "Why Utopia Matters." *Utopia Matters: Politics and Theory. Politics, Literature and the Arts.* Ed. Fátima Vieira and Marinella Freitas. Oporto: Editora da Universidade do Porto, 2005. 51–53.

Sargisson, Lucy. "Justice Inside Utopia? The Case of Intentional Communities in New Zealand." *Contemporary Justice Review* 7.3 (2004): 321–333.

Levitas, Ruth and Lucy Sargisson. "Utopia in Dark Times: Optimism/Pessimism and Utopia/Dystopia." *Dark Horizons: Science Fiction and the Dystopian Imagination.* Ed. Raffaella Baccolini and Tom Moylan. London and New York: Routledge, 2003. 13–27.

Sargisson, Lucy. "Surviving Conflict: New Zealand's Intentional Communities." *New Zealand Sociology* 18.2 (2003): 225–250.

Sargisson, Lucy. "Politicising the Quotidian." *Environmental Politics* 10.2 (2001): 68–89.

Sargisson, Lucy. "What's Wrong with Ecofeminism?" *Environmental Politics* 10.1 (2001): 52–64.

Sargisson, Lucy. "Green Utopias of Self and Other." *Critical Review of International Social and Political Philosophy* 3.2/3 (2000): 140–156. Rpt. in *The Philosophy of Utopia.* Ed. Barbara Goodwin. London: Frank Cass, 2001. 140–156.

Sargisson, Lucy. "Why Feminism Needs Utopianism." *Diggers & Dreamers 2000– 2001.* Ed. Sarah Bunker, Chris Coates, David Hodgson, and Jonathan How. London: Diggers and Dreamers Publications, 1999. 51–57.

Sargisson, Lucy. "Contemporary Feminist Utopianism: The Equality/Difference Dilemma." *Contemporary Political Studies* – Political Studies Association of the United Kingdom 1 (1997): 272–282.

Sargisson, Lucy. "Contemporary Feminist Utopianism: Practising Utopia on Utopia." *Literature and the Political Imagination.* Ed. John Horton and Andrea T. Baumeister. London and New York: Routledge, 1996. 238–255.

# Editors

**Raffaella Baccolini** is Professor of British and American Literature and Gender Studies at the University of Bologna, Forlì Campus. She has published several articles on women's writing, dystopia and science fiction, trauma and memory, modernism, and Young Adult literature. She has edited several volumes, among which are *Dark Horizons: Science Fiction and the Dystopian Imagination* (with Tom Moylan, Routledge, 2003) and *Utopia, Method, Vision: The Use Value of Social Dreaming* (also with Tom Moylan, Peter Lang, 2007). She was the coordinator of the European project G-BOOK – Gender Identity: Child Readers and Library Collections. She is currently working on kindness, solidarity, and feminist education as utopian, political acts.

**Lyman Tower Sargent** is Professor Emeritus of Political Science at the University of Missouri-St. Louis, and he has been a Visiting Professor or fellowship holder at universities in England and New Zealand and a Visiting Member of the Institute for Advanced Study (Princeton). He was the founding Editor of *Utopian Studies* (1990–2004) and has published numerous books and articles, mostly in utopian studies. He is the recipient of the Distinguished Scholar Award of both the Society for Utopian Studies and the Communal Studies Association. The Society for Utopian Studies has named this award the Lyman Tower Sargent Distinguished Scholar Award.

# Contributors

IBTISAM AHMED is a doctoral research student at the School of Politics and IR, the University of Nottingham. His thesis, titled "The Decolonial Killjoy: The British Raj as a Space of Political Utopia," is supervised by Lucy Sargisson, and it aims to highlight the emancipatory potential of various anti-colonial utopias. He has been published in journals such as *Sociology Study* and *The Round Table*. He is co-editor with Elena Colombo and Robyn Muir of *The Politics of Culture* (2020), to which he contributed "The Queer Immigrant Body as a Space of Utopia: The Politics of *Young Avengers'* Wiccan and Hulkling." He is part of the directorial team for the London Science Fiction Research Community, with a special focus on the theme of "Activism and Resistance."

DAVID M. BELL is a writer living in Nottingham. He is interested in collective struggle and aesthetic practice within, against, and beyond this and any present. He was supervised by Lucy Sargisson for a PhD thinking utopianism through the work of Gilles Deleuze, which was awarded in 2013. He is the author of *Rethinking Utopia: Place, Power, Affect* (Routledge, 2017) as well as articles in journals including *Utopian Studies, Political Studies Review*, and the *International Journal of Social Research Methodology*. He is a member of the Out of the Woods writing collective, whose *Hope Against Hope: Writings on Ecological Crisis* was published by Common Notions in 2020.

SURYAMAYI CLARENCE-SMITH is a native member of "Auroville," the largest intentional community in the world. Her autoethnographic research examines and informs utopian and prefigurative practice, focusing on alternative modes of political and economic organization. She has a PhD in International Development from the University of Sussex (2019) and a BA in Interdisciplinary Studies from the University of California, Berkeley (2015).

CHRIS COATES is a former squatter, street performer, clown, father, carpenter, site and project manager, peace activist, self-builder, Engineer of the Imagination, and Green Party councilor. Lived, loved, and worked for twenty years at People in Common, a small living/working cooperative in Burnley that grew out of the radical underground of the 1970s before moving to Lancaster. Author of two books on the history of intentional communities in the UK, editor of Diggers & Dreamers, and a board member of the International Communal Studies Association. Chris is a former founder member of Lancaster Cohousing and still lives there with his partner.

ELENA COLOMBO is a doctoral researcher in the School of Politics and International Relations at the University of Nottingham, with Lucy Sargisson and Steven Fielding as supervisors. Her research focuses on the expressions of utopian hope within ecocritical dystopian novels. She is currently associated with the Centre for the Study of Social and Global Justice (CSSGJ) and the Nottingham Centre for Normative Political Theory (CONCEPT) at the School. She is co-editor with Ibtisam Ahmed and Robyn Muir of *The Politics of Culture: An Interdisciplinary Interrogation of Popular Culture* (2020), to which she contributed "Know Who You Are: *Moana* and Ecofeminism," with Robyn Muir.

DAVINA COOPER is a Research Professor at Dickson Poon School of Law, King's College London. Her interdisciplinary work addresses the challenges of developing new conceptual methodologies to support transformative politics, focusing on the state, gender, equality, prefiguration, and cultural conflict. Recent research includes an ESRC project on the Future of Legal Gender, 2018–2021. She is also the author of six books including *Feeling like a State: Desire, Denial, and the Recasting of Authority* (Duke, 2019) and *Everyday Utopias: The Conceptual Life of Promising Spaces* (Duke, 2014).

RHIANNON FIRTH is currently Senior Research Officer in Sociology at the University of Essex. She undertook her PhD supervised by Lucy Sargisson and Simon Tormey between 2004 and 2010 at the University of Nottingham. Her research interests include intentional communities, anarchist utopias, and autonomous social movements.

RUTH LEVITAS is Professor Emerita of Sociology at the University of Bristol. She was founding Chair of Utopian Studies Society Europe and is a former Chair and Vice-Chair of the William Morris Society. She is the Recipient of the Distinguished Scholar Award of the Society for Utopian Studies and the Sociological Review Award for Outstanding Scholarship. She has published numerous articles in Utopian Studies, as well as *The Concept of Utopia* (Philip Allan 1990, Peter Lang 2010, 2011) and *Utopia as Method* (Palgrave Macmillan 2013). She also writes on poverty, inequality, politics, and social policy.

SARAH LOHMANN received a PhD in English Literature at Durham University, where she is now working as an Honorary Associate in the Department of English Studies. Her thesis spanned utopian and science fiction studies, systems theory, and analytic philosophy, providing an interdisciplinary structural framework for the analysis of utopian literature in terms of dynamic chronotopes. In particular, she focused on interpreting twentieth-century feminist utopian novels through the lens of complexity theory. She is currently preparing her thesis for publication while conducting further research on utopian literature by women, systems theory, and the intersections of fiction and philosophy.

ALMUDENA MACHADO-JIMÉNEZ is a PhD candidate at the University of Jaén, where she works as a lecturer at the Department of English Philology. She has also been a visiting researcher at the SOAS University of London, and she is the vice-president of the Association of Young Researchers on English Studies (ASYRAS). Her current research centers on gender studies and dystopian fiction, particularly on the notions of rape culture, eating disorders, and compliant motherhood within contemporary patriarchal utopias.

DUNJA M. MOHR, University of Erfurt, Germany, works in Anglophone literary and cultural studies and has just completed a monograph on twentieth- and twenty-first-century *Frankenstein* media adaptations. She wrote the award-winning *Worlds Apart? Dualism and Transgression in Contemporary Female Dystopias* (2005), edited *Embracing the Other: Addressing Xenophobia in the New Literatures in English* (2008), and co-edited the *ZAA* special issue *9/11 as Catalyst* (2010) and *Radical Planes? 9/11 and Patterns of Continuity* (2016). For her current research project "Approximating the non-human," she received a DAAD research fellowship and taught as a visiting professor at the CCEAE/IRTG, Université de Montréal, Canada.

TOM MOYLAN is Professor Emeritus and member of the Ralahine Centre for Utopian Studies at the University of Limerick. He is the author of *Demand the Impossible: Science Fiction and the Utopian Imagination* (1986; 2014), *Scraps of the Untainted Sky: Science Fiction, Utopia, Dystopia* (2000), and *Becoming Utopian: The Culture and Politics of Radical Transformation* (2020).

ROBYN MUIR received her PhD from the School of Politics and International Relations in the University of Nottingham. Her research focuses on the images of femininity within the Disney Princess phenomenon, which is supervised by Lucy Sargisson. She is co-editor with Ibtisam Ahmed and Elena Colombo of *The Politics of Culture: An Interdisciplinary Interrogation of Popular Culture* (2020), to which she contributed "Know Who You Are: *Moana* and Ecofeminism," with Elena Colombo. She is currently co-editing a book on representations of evil women within literature, culture, and film. Her research interests include feminist methodology, representation of gender within popular culture and cultural phenomenon, and the politics of merchandising.

JOSÉ EDUARDO REIS is Associate Professor of literary studies at the University of Trás-os-Montes and Alto Douro (Portugal). He is a full researcher at the Institute of Comparative Literature of the Faculty of Letters of Oporto University. As a comparatist he has published regularly with a main focus on the topic of literary utopianism. He is a reviewer for American *Journal of Utopian Studies* and a member of the editorial board of the Portuguese and French academic journals *Letras Vivas*, *Nova Águia*, *Cultura entre Culturas*, *Atlante*.

LUCY SARGISSON was the world's first Professor of Utopian Studies. She worked at the Universities of Keele (1993–1996) and Nottingham (1996–2017), from where she took early retirement owing to the deterioration of the Multiple Sclerosis with which she has struggled since 2001. She is Professor Emeritus of the School of Politics and International Relations, University of Nottingham. She now lives in Cornwall, where she swims in cold water, tries to dance on numb feet, and where she will, perhaps, one day, finish that final book (on Utopia and Every Day Life).

SIMON SPIEGEL is a lecturer at the Department of Film Studies at the University of Zurich and Privatdozent at the University of Bayreuth. He is the author of *Bilder einer besseren Welt. Die Utopie im fiktionalen Film* (Schüren Verlag, 2019) and co-editor of *Utopia and Reality Documentary, Activism and Imagined Worlds* (University of Wales Press, 2020) as well as co-editor of the *Zeitschrift für Fantastikforschung*.

MARIA VARSAM obtained her BA in English Language and Philology from Aristotle University (Thessaloniki, Greece), and went on to obtain an MA in Women's Studies and English (Lancaster University) and an MPhil at the Centre for the Study of Literature and Theology (Glasgow University). She obtained her Doctoral degree from the University of Nottingham with a thesis on Anglophone dystopian literature. She has published papers in journals and essay collections in the areas of dystopian fiction, neo-slave narratives, and women's writing. She is interested in issues of gender, genre, sacrifice, and trauma.

LAURA WINTER is a PhD student at the Chair of English Literary and Cultural Studies at the University of Mannheim, Germany. Her research focuses on the relations between technology, culture, and the good life in contemporary dystopian and post-apocalyptic fiction. In her dissertation project, she specializes in the cultural and social impact of technology, investigating the depiction of twenty-first-century digital landscapes in

British and American television series such as *Black Mirror, Mr. Robot,* and *Westworld.* Her latest publication is "Tweet Others How You Wish to be Tweeted: Digital Technology and the Sense of Community in Charlie Brooker's *Black Mirror* (2011-)." *Community, Seriality and the State of the Nation: British and Irish Television Series in the 21st Century.* Ed. Caroline Lusin and Ralf Haekel (Narr Francke Attempto, 2019).

# Index

# Ralahine Utopian Studies

*Ralahine Utopian Studies* is the publishing project of the Ralahine Centre for Utopian Studies at the University of Limerick in association with the University of Bologna, the University of Cyprus, the University of Florida and the University of Maine.

The series publishes high-quality scholarship that addresses the theory and practice of utopianism (including Anglophone, continental European and indigenous and postcolonial traditions, and contemporary and historical periods). Publications (in English and other European languages) include original monographs and essay collections (including theoretical, textual and ethnographic/institutional research), English-language translations of utopian scholarship in other national languages, reissues of classic scholarly works that are out of print and annotated editions of original utopian literary and other texts (including translations).

While the series editors seek work that engages with the current scholarship and debates in the field of utopian studies, they will not privilege any particular critical or theoretical orientation. They welcome submissions by established or emerging scholars working within or outside the academy. Given the multilingual and interdisciplinary remit of the series, the editors especially welcome comparative studies in any disciplinary or transdisciplinary framework.

Those interested in contributing to the series are invited to submit a detailed project outline to one of the series editors listed below.

Email queries can also be sent to ireland@peterlang.com.

Series editors:
Raffaella Baccolini (University of Bologna)
Antonis Balasopoulos (University of Cyprus)
Joachim Fischer (University of Limerick)
Michael J. Griffin (University of Limerick)
Naomi Jacobs (University of Maine)
Michael G. Kelly (University of Limerick)
Tom Moylan (University of Limerick)
Phillip E. Wegner (University of Florida)

Ralahine Centre for Utopian Studies, University of Limerick
http://www3.ul.ie/ralahinecentre/